Sir Charles Bell

The Anatomy and Philosophy of Expression

As Connected with the Fine Arts

Sir Charles Bell

The Anatomy and Philosophy of Expression
As Connected with the Fine Arts

ISBN/EAN: 9783337069940

Printed in Europe, USA, Canada, Australia, Japan

Cover: Foto ©Thomas Meinert / pixelio.de

More available books at **www.hansebooks.com**

THE

ANATOMY AND PHILOSOPHY

OF

EXPRESSION

AS CONNECTED WITH THE FINE ARTS.

BY

(SIR) CHARLES BELL, K.H.

𝔉𝔦𝔣𝔱𝔥 𝔈𝔡𝔦𝔱𝔦𝔬𝔫.

LONDON:
HENRY G. BOHN, YORK STREET, COVENT GARDEN.
1865.

LONDON:
PRINTED BY R. CLAY, SON, AND TAYLOR,
BREAD STREET HILL.

PREFACE TO THE THIRD EDITION.

THESE Essays formed the earliest and the latest occu-
pation of the lamented author's leisure hours;—and they
now appear under the disadvantages which must attend
a posthumous publication.

It was the habit of the author, in his literary compositions, to sketch his first ideas as they arose ; and parts
of this work were found, evidently intended to be revised
and corrected. They are faithfully added to the text of
the last edition, where they bear upon the subject.

The following prefatory remarks are from the pen of the
late Professor Bell,* to whom, in the warmth of brotherly
affection, the second edition of the work had been inscribed.

_____

The Essays which are now presented to the public in
their enlarged form, were originally composed, as the author

* George Joseph Bell, Professor of the Law of Scotland in the University
of Edinburgh. He died September 23, 1843.

fondly said in his dedication, "when we studied together before the serious pursuits of life began;" but were not published till the year 1806, after the author had left Edinburgh and fixed his residence in London. A second edition appeared in 1824 ; but he resisted every call for a new impression, until he should have had an opportunity of verifying in Italy the principles of criticism in art, by the study of the works of the great masters in painting and sculpture.

With this view he visited the Continent in 1840 ; and on his return he recomposed the whole for a new edition, introducing occasional extracts from his journal, sometimes to enforce the texts and sometimes to show from what authority he drew his conclusions.

In a declining state of health he had taken advantage of a recess in his professorial duties in the University of Edinburgh to revisit his friends in England. He hoped in the leisure of the country to give this work a final revisal for the press ; but before he had fulfilled his wishes in this respect, his life was terminated by an access of his illness at Hallow Park, in Worcestershire, on the 29th of April, 1842.

In the speculations of which this work is the result, and in the interesting inquiries to which they led, Sir Charles

Bell was accustomed to seek relief from the wearing anxiety which, from his exquisite sensibility to human suffering, had ever attended the practice of his profession : but a still greater effect was to follow. It was from these investigations that he was first led to make those discoveries in the system of the nerves, which are now acknowledged to be the most important contributions of modern times to the science of Physiology.

Before Sir Charles Bell's time, the nerves, which pervade every the minutest portion of our frame, seemed, in the studies of anatomists, a mass of inextricable confusion and a subject of hopeless obscurity ; but he believed that in the works of the Creator there is nothing imperfect, or unnecessarily complex, and that the solution of this apparent confusion was not beyond the reach of human inquiry. In tracing the causes of movements in the countenance and in the frame of the body under the influence of passion or emotion, he engaged in a very careful inquiry into the origin, course, and destination of the nerves ; and consequent investigations led him to those fundamental truths, hitherto unperceived, by which he, and those who have followed his course, have revealed to the medical world the beautiful simplicity of this part of the animal economy. To the physiologist it will be particularly interesting to trace in this work the steps by which the author was led to the comprehension of that most intricate portion of the nervous system, the class of nerves which he has named respiratory ; a subject so difficult, that it was long before his views were acknowledged by the medical profession.

Meanwhile his labours and his anxiety were relieved by the variety of his pursuits. He was a true lover of nature, and to trace the proofs of perfection and design in all the works of the Creator was to him a source of ever new delight. Constantly he had some useful, some noble purpose in view, whether in following up scientific inquiry, or in enthusiastically pursuing nature or art. Those who knew him best, and had seen him in the most trying circumstances of life, were most sensible that there never was a man whose mind was more uniformly attuned to grateful happiness.

CONTENTS.

ON EXPRESSION.

INTRODUCTION.

IT is not an easy task to reconcile two subjects so far apart in the minds of most readers as Anatomy and the Fine Arts ; but if prejudices, early imbibed, be thrown off, it will be found that there is no science, taken in a comprehensive sense, more fruitful of instruction, or leading to more interesting subjects of inquiry, than the knowledge of the Animal body.

The academies of Europe, instituted for the improvement of painting, stop short of the science of anatomy, which is so well suited to enlarge the mind, and to train the eye for observing the forms of Nature ; or if they enforce the study at all, it is only in its more obvious application, that of assisting the drawing of the human figure. But my design in this volume goes further :—I purpose to direct attention to the characteristic forms of man and brutes, by an inquiry into the natural functions, with a view to comprehend the *rationale* of those changes in the countenance and figure which are indicative of Passion.

A just feeling in the fine arts is an elegant acquire-

ment, and capable of cultivation. Drawing is necessary
to many pursuits and useful arts: Locke has included it
amongst the accomplishments becoming a gentleman, and,
we may add, it is much more useful to the artisan. Good
taste and execution in design are necessary to manufactures;
and consequently they contribute to the resources of a
country.

I am not without hope that a new impulse may be given
to the cultivation of the fine arts, by explaining their relation
to the natural history of man and animals; and by shewing
how a knowledge of outward form, and the accuracy of
drawing which is a consequence of it, are related to the
interior structure and functions.

Anatomy, in its relation to the arts of design, is, in truth,
the grammar of that language in which they address us.
The expressions, attitudes, and movements of the human
figure are the characters of this language, adapted to convey
the effect of historical narration, as well as to shew the
working of human passion, and to give the most striking and
lively indications of intellectual power and energy.

The art of the painter, considered with a view to these
interesting representations, assumes a high character. Every
lesser embellishment and minuteness of detail is regarded by
an artist who has those more enlarged views of his profession
as foreign to the main design, distracting and hurtful to the
grand effect, admired only as accurate imitations, almost
appearing to be what they are not. This distinction must be
felt, or we shall never see the grand style in painting receive
that encouragement which results from public feeling and
good taste. The painter must not be satisfied to copy and
represent what he sees; he must cultivate this talent of

imitation merely as bestowing those facilities which are to give scope to the exertions of his genius; as the instruments and means only which he is to employ for communicating his thoughts, and presenting to others the creations of his fancy; it is by his creative powers alone that he can become truly a painter; and for these he is to trust to original genius, cultivated and enriched by a constant observation of nature. Till he has acquired a poet's eye for nature, and can seize with intuitive quickness the appearances of passion, and all the effects produced upon the body by the operations of the mind, he has not raised himself above the mechanism of his art, nor does he rank with the poet or historian.

It is a happy characteristic of the present times, that a love of the fine arts is becoming more and more prevalent among the affluent; but still, rich furniture, mere ornamental painting and gilding, usurp the place of art properly so called. The mansion of an English nobleman and that of a Roman of the same rank present a singular contrast. The former exhibits carpets, silk hangings, lamps, mirrors, china, and perhaps books. The palazzo, on the other hand, in its general aspect, may betray antiquity and decay; yet respect for ancestry retains on its walls the proofs of former grandeur and taste; *there* hang many pictures, each of which would purchase an English villa or furnish a London mansion in all the extravagance of fashion. Vulgar curiosity may seek admittance to the finery of the one, while princes are gratified by admission to the other.

Original genius seems peculiarly necessary to excellence in design. Good taste may be acquired by familiarity with statues and paintings, and by the conversation of the ingenious;

but the power of execution depends on deeper sources. In reading Vasari, we are struck by the difficulties with which the famous painters had to struggle. There is hardly one of them who had not to combat parental authority before obtaining leave to give up his days to painting ; nor is it surprising that there should be an unwillingness to permit a youth to dedicate his life to an art so little gainful, where extraordinary excellence alone obtains notice, and hardly ever an adequate reward. I speak of the higher department of art.

Much has been done at home by the force of genius alone. Our native artists have vindicated us from the aspersion of Winckelman, that genius for the fine arts is stinted in these northern climes,—a notion which has prevailed so extensively as even to have influenced our own Milton :—

> " Unless an age too late, or cold
> Climate, or years, damp my intended wing."

In his history of ancient art, Winckelman seems to attribute all to climate ; not only the perfection of form in the inhabitants of Greece, but their serenity of mind, sweetness, and love of beauty. Such a theory would imply that the people of Sparta and Athens were characterized by the same qualities. But when Sparta triumphed, it was in pride and rapacity. Neither the general intercourse between nations, nor commerce, nor intellectual nor moral excellence, derived any benefit from her ascendancy.* Athens was the mistress of the world ; and she has left examples of the greatest virtues and excellence in philosophy, eloquence, poetry, and art ; yet she has also shown humiliating instances of tyranny,

* Arnold's " History of Rome.".

put.

cruelty, and blood. The history of Greece is the record of incessant wars, of towns sacked, and of citizens inhumanly massacred. And in Athens war was always justified, if it promised advantage; when tried by misfortune, she was found wanting: during pestilence, every affection was blunted; and licentiousness abounded to such a degree, that the people became brutalized. It is strange that Winckelman should attribute so much to the influence of climate, seeing that where the olive still ripens, in the long summer of Greece, not a vestige of those virtues which were the admiration of the world now exists: and centuries have passed without a poet or philosopher appearing, in the country of Homer and Plato.

In the soil and climate of Italy, there have existed together states of society the most dissimilar. Among the Etruscans, and in the cities of Central Italy, the arts and civilization of Egypt and Phœnicia had taken root, long before Rome *

* A more just estimate is now made, than formerly, of the early Romans, and of the virtues of the surrounding tribes. (Dr. Arnold's "History of Rome.") The remains discovered in the tombs of Tarquinii, Tuscania, Argyllæ, Veii, and Clusium, leave no doubt of the high advancement of art in these cities, centuries before the foundation of Rome—at least of its fabled rise under Romulus. These cities were the adversaries of the early Romans; and, though subdued, furnished to their masters the elements of government and of civil policy. Rome had conquered the surrounding states, and sought to blot out all memory of them; when new settlements of Greeks (giving name to the district of Magna Græcia) again offered to her a more extended field of enterprise, in which the arts of peace were once more subjugated under her iron sway.

If I did not believe that Providence rules in the march of nations, I should say, that the world would have advanced in philosophy, literature, and art, more rapidly but for that stern, remorseless people, obstinate against instruction. We are biassed in favour of Rome from her language containing the only record of much that, but for her conquests, would have spread with earlier, and happier influence, over the western world.

arose to crush them. Her policy, and the leaning of her
most virtuous citizens, were adverse to the arts. They feared
that whilst they refined they should soften away those rugged
and sterner qualities of the Roman soldiers which were
bestowing on them the empire of the world. But the old
virtues at length declined, and the Romans came to covet the
luxuries of conquered nations, whom they could not rival
in refinement or the arts ; so that Rome became the centre
and the common receptacle of the spoils of Egypt, Greece,
and Italy.

The inquiry into the history of ancient art were an idle
one, if it did not lead to the conviction, that institutions,
much more than climate, influence the faculties of man.
Indolence steals upon communities as upon individuals. In
the same regions, and in the same climate, the inhabitants
are at one time overwhelmed in ignorance and superstition,
and at another, elevated to the most admired intellectual
exertions. When the energies of a people are roused, there
is an improvement in the arts of peace, however gloomy and
foreboding the struggle may at first appear. The mind
excited by public events does not subside into indolence. In
Athens the struggle for power, and the desire of independence,
forced the highest talents to the highest station. It was
during the contests of the free states of Italy that the arts
revived.*

Perhaps we should attribute the cultivation of literature
and the arts in Italy more to the smallness of the states than
to the forms of their governments, for these were of every
kind. While in Rome the Pope was an absolute sovereign,

* See Roscoe's introductory chapter to the " Life of Lorenzo di Medici."

in Venice the nobility had raised an oligarchic authority on the necks of the people ; and both were distinguished from the democratic turbulence of Florence.

In the great kingdoms of Modern Europe, princes are surrounded by a dense body of courtiers, political agents, and soldiers, numerous and clamorous in proportion to the offices of command and places to be bestowed. All who are distinguished by excellence in liberal studies are jostled aside, and the prince knows little of men of genius, far less does he think of making them friends. But in the smaller states of Italy, princes sought the acquaintance of men remarkable for their talents, for the cultivation of philosophy, of the language of Greece, or of Ancient Rome, for the improvement of their native Italian, and of poetry, or of the fine arts : and it is pleasant to notice how easily the presence or absence of such men affected the splendour of the court. Amidst the more than barbaric magnificence and riches of modern courts, certainly of our own, the exit or entrance of such men would be unmarked.

Perhaps the circumstance that all negotiations were formerly conducted in Latin, and the consequent necessity for courtiers being acquainted with the learned languages, gave a liberal tone to the men of influence in the several states, and a disposition to promote literature and science.

Some authors have attributed the genius of the Greeks, and their love of philosophy and art, to the conformation of the brain,—to the form of the skull ! On this subject I may have occasion to touch hereafter. But does not history determine the question ? The Greeks were not extirpated by the Roman conquests. The skulls of a people do not change. During all the period of the Byzantine Empire, between the reigns of Constantine and Palæologus, luxury, sloth, and effeminacy prevailed, whilst the people of the West of Europe were rising in moral and intellectual energy, and in the cultivation of the mind.*

During the latter periods of Ancient Rome, a fashion arose which conduced much to the advancement of art, and filled the city with its thousand statues. The Romans, like the Greeks, sought a species of immortality by the erection of their busts and statues; they consecrated their friends by setting up their busts in their temples. These being given in honour of the divinity whom they worshipped, were preserved even when the personages they represented had incurred the odium of the people, and when their statues placed in public were cast down. This desire of obtaining the busts of illustrious men † explains the reason of the multitude of those found collected in the Vatican : they are chiefly in marble ; for the statues and busts in bronze and other metals, tempted the cupidity of men in the middle ages, and were melted down. We are struck, too, with the number of the busts of celebrated men in proportion to those of princes ; which Visconti believes to have been owing to the desire which prevailed among private citizens in the better ages of Greece and Rome, to have them copied, as appropriate ornaments for their libraries, porticos, and gardens.

The remains of antiquity in Italy, the presence, though in ruins, of temples, statues, sarcophagi, altars, and relievos, account for the early revival of art in that country. These

---

* See Prichard's "Physical History of Man." He justly controverts the idea of Blumenbach.

† On this subject, see the Preface to Visconti's "Iconographie."

must have been the studies of Donatello* and Ghibert, as afterwards of Buonarotti ; for sculpture led the way to painting. Our countrymen, pursuing their studies there, are placed under similar influences, and give proof that it is neither genius nor devotion to the imitative arts which is wanting in the north. But the time is past when the people knelt down before the works of a sculptor's hands ; when the Amphictyons, the council of all Greece, gave him solemn thanks, and assigned him a dwelling at the public expense in every city ! †

It is in vain that we dream of equalling the great works of antiquity ; they were raised under tyranny and false religions. We must hope for excellence, in a different condition, as the fruit of a religion of love, joy, and peace. If the arts of design bear no relation to that which has the greatest influence on mankind ; if they stand related neither to religion, nor to the records of history, nor to the progress of empire,—·

* If all the great works of Grecian art had been at once disclosed, it might not have produced the happy effect of the successive exhumations of the splendid works of antiquity ; the excitement, or, as Cicognara has expressed it, "un certo fermento," kept up by the contest of princes for these works of art, gave importance to all who sought to imitate them, and raised them in the estimation of even the most vulgar minds. The progress in the history of art seems to have been—First, the establishment of new families ; then, the erection of splendid palaces and the necessity or convenience of digging for materials in the foundation of ancient buildings; next, the exhumation of fine statues, and the emulation thence arising ; lastly, the desire of having professors and universities arose, and this took place at a time when the pontiffs were banished from Rome.

† Tiraboschi refers to an ancient chronicle regarding the Dominican church of Reggio, erected in 1233, for an example of the enthusiasm under which great edifices were built, and where all grades of society wrought as common labourers, like emmets in an ant-hill. "Tam parvi, quam magni, tam nobiles, quam pedites, tam rustici, quam cives, ferebant lapides, sablonem, et calcinam, supra dorsum eorum . . . . et beatus ille qui plus portare potarat," &c.

C

they must be ever, as a dead language, associated with ancient times; and with us, nothing more than a handmaid ↶ to ᴧ domestic ornament and individual refinement and enjoyment.

Our artists should be brought to consider the changed frame of society. No one in these modern times, however much he may deserve the gratitude of mankind, is exalted, as they would desire to see the proficient in art. The young artists madden themselves by the contemplation of antiquity, which leads to disappointment and repining age. The last conversation I had with Flaxman, whose genius was better estimated abroad than at home, was whilst the old man was elevated on a great block of marble, in his studio (*Anglicè*, a shed). "Ay," says he, "we shall see what is thought of these things two hundred years hence." Yes, but they will record these things in stereotype, not in marble. Printing banished sculpture, and no man now, or hereafter, in addressing the people, will, like Fabius Maximus, or Scipio, point to the statues of his ancestors.

Without cherishing vain regrets, there is a source of infinite delight in art, even as cultivated among us; and we may hold the remains of antiquity as superlative models. Gods and goddesses we shall not again see in marble, but the human figure in its perfection we certainly may. The Greeks gave prizes for excelling beauty. Among them a youth might be celebrated for the perfection of his eyebrow; and the proportions of an Aspasia were transferred to the statue of a goddess. The forms of strength and the proportions of the victor in the games were scientifically noted and recorded, whether it was for wrestling, running, or pitching the discus. Here, then, were studies for the sculptor, and a public to judge of the perfection of his work. Our connoisseurs never see the naked figure, or, if they do, it is an academy figure,— probably some hired artisan, with his muscles unequally developed by the labour of his trade,—pale and shivering, and offering none of those fine carnations which more constant exposure gives to the body, as we see in the face, nor having that elegant freedom of limb, which youth, under a genial climate and the various exercises of the gymnasium, acquired.*

For the improvement of art, there must be a feeling in the public in correspondence with the artist's aspirations. † In visiting the Sistine Chapel, I said to the celebrated artist who accompanied me, "How could Michael Angelo venture to do such things? Were such a man to arise amongst us, he would meet with ridicule, or live in neglect." But my friend said, "Do you not remember the impatience of Julius to see these paintings during their execution? For Michael Angelo

* So conscious were some of the Grecian states of the advantages derived from exercise, that they denied them to their slaves.

† I cannot withhold the following instance of public feeling in England : —When Lord Elgin brought to London the figures of the beautiful frieze from the Parthenon of Athens, and while they remained in his court-yard in Piccadilly, he proposed a great treat to his friends. He had entertained an ingenious notion that, by exposing the natural figures of some of our modern athletics in contrast with the marbles, the perfection of the antique would be felt, and that we should see that the sculptors of the best time of Greece did not deviate from nature. The noblemen and gentlemen whom he conceived would take an interest in this display were invited. He had the boxers, the choice men of what is termed "the fancy." They stripped and sparred before the ancient statues, and for one instant it was a very fine exhibition ; but no sooner was the bulky form of Jackson, no longer young, opposed to the fine elastic figure of the champion of all England, than a cry arose, and "the ring" pressed forward, and ancient art and the works of Phidias were forgotten. Such I fear is the feeling of even the better part of the English public. Let not the young sculptor be too sanguine of support.

being unwilling to let his unfinished work be seen, the
Pope threatened to break down the whole scaffolding on
which the painting was raised." It was by such enthusiasm,
and the consequent encouragement of art, that Julius has
justly participated in the fame of those who made his days
an era in the world.

It is perhaps favourable to painting, that it has not to con-
tend with the excellence of antiquity. In visiting the schools
of Florence and Bologna, and the galleries of the Vatican,
we can trace the successive works of the early painters and
the progress of modern painting. In the commencement, the
subjects are such as could only be suggested by monkish
superstition and enthusiasm. They are the representations
of the wasted figures of anchorites, or if of women they are
suffering martyrdom. Even the Saviour, represented so full
of beauty in after-time, is painted from the dead of the lazar-
house or hospital. The purpose must have been to subdue
the mind.* With better times the influence of the Church
was more happily exercised, and finer feelings prevailed.
The subjects were from the Scriptures, and noble efforts
were made, attesting a deep feeling of every condition of
humanity. What we see in the churches of Italy, and

---

* " In the old library in Basle there is a remarkable painting of Christ
by the younger Holbein. The painter must have been where anatomy
was to be learned ; for I am much mistaken if he has not painted from
the dead body in an hospital. It is horribly true. There is here the true
colour of the dead body : (the Italian painters generally paint the dead of
an ivory white). Here is the rigid, stringy appearance of the muscles
about the knee. The wounds where the nails have penetrated the hands
and feet are dark red, with extravasation round the wound, and the hand
itself of the livid colour of mortification. The eyes, too, shew from whence
he drew ; the eyelids are open, the pupil raised, and a little turned out.
Holbein born here, in 1498."—*Note from Journal.*

3

almost in every church, is the representation of innocence and tenderness in the Madonna and Child, and in the young St. John. Contrasted with the truth, and beauty, and innocence of the Virgin, there is the mature beauty and abandonment of the Magdalen. In the dead Christ, in the swooning of the Mother of the Saviour, and in the Marys, there is the utmost scope for the genius of the painter. We see there, also, the grave character of mature years in the Prophets and Evangelists, and the grandeur of expression in Moses. In short, we have the whole range of human character and expression, from the divine loveliness and purity of the Infant Saviour, of Angels and of Saints, to the strength, fierceness, and brutality of the executioners. There, also, we may see the effort made, the greatest of all, in imitation of the ancients, to infuse divinity into the human beauty of that countenance, which, though not without feeling, was superior to passion, and in which benevolence was to be represented unclouded by human infirmity. These were the subjects to call forth the exertions of genius, while the rewards were the riches of the church, and the public exhibition, in unison with the deep feelings of the people. Thus did religion at a later period tend to restore what it had almost destroyed on the overthrow of Pagan idolatry. For the new-born zeal of the first Christians sought to efface every monument of the antique religion, throwing down the statues, destroying the mosaics and pictures, effacing every memorial, and razing the ancient temples, or converting them into Christian churches.

The Church of Rome has favoured the arts in a remarkable manner. The ceremonial and decorations of the altar, have been contrived with great felicity. He is insensible to beauty

who, being a painter, does not catch their ideas of light and
shade, and colour. The Gothic or rich Roman architecture,
the carved skreen, the statues softened by a subdued light,
form altogether a magnificent scene. The effects of light
and colour are not matters of accident. The painted glass
of the high window represents to the superficial observer no
more than the rich garments of the figures there painted.
But the combination of colours evinces science; the yellows
and greens, in due proportion with the crimsons and blues,
throw beams of an autumnal tint among the shafts and
pillars, and colour the volumes of rising incense. The
officials of the altar, the priests in rich vestments, borrowed
from the Levites under the old law, are somewhat removed
from the spectator and obscured by the smoke of the incense.* The young men flinging the silver censers, in
themselves beautiful, and making the volumes of incense
rise, give the effect of a tableau, defying imitation; for
where can there be such a combination to the eye, joined
to the emotions inspired by the pealing organ, the deep
chant, and the response of the youthful choristers, whose
voices seem to come from the vaulted roof? There is
something too in the belief that the chant of the psalms
is the early Jewish measure.

---

* If the painter requires to know these vestments, he will find an
account of them in Eustace's "Classical Tour through Italy," vol. ii.
Antiquity characterises every thing in the Roman Church; and to the
English traveller this affords additional interest. The ceremonies are
ancient; the language of the service is that which prevailed at the period
of the introduction of Christianity; the vestments are Jewish—at all
events very ancient and majestic. Like every thing else in painting, the
artist should know the origin and uses of the drapery, or his lines and
folds will be unmeaning.—(See *Preface to Vasari*.)

It was scarcely possible, during the struggles of the Reformation, to keep the middle course; and in rejecting the corrupt and superstitious parts of its ceremonial, to retain the better part of the Roman Church. Enthusiasm would have the recesses of each man's breast to be the only sanctuary; that, even while on earth, and burdened with the weakness, and subject to the influences, of an earth-born creature, he should attain that state of purity and holiness, when, as in the Apocalypse, there is "no temple." Philosophy came to countenance the poverty and the meanness of our places of public worship. Climate, it was inferred, influenced the genius of a people, and, therefore, their government, and mode of worship. The offices of religion in hot climates were said to require some sensible object before the eyes, and hence the veneration paid to statues and paintings; whilst in the colder climes we were to substitute internal contemplation and the exercise of reason for passion.*

We trust, or hope, that in the breasts of those who fill the family pew, in these northern churches, there may be more genuine devotion; but to appearance all is pale and cold: while to the subject we are now considering, at least, no aid is afforded. What a contrast is offered to the eye of the painter by the figures seen in the churches of the Roman Catholic countries of the south, as compared with those in our own! There are seen men in the remote aisles or chapels, cast down in prayer, and abandoned to

---

* Some such thoughts must have come early into my mind, in trying my pencil on the ruins of an ancient abbey; and when, afterwards within the *kirk*, I looked to the rafters, as of a barn, and saw the swallows flying about during divine service.

their feelings with that unrestrained expression which belongs to the Italian from his infancy: and even the beggars who creep about the porches of the churches are like nothing we see nearer home. In them we recognise the figures familiar to us in the paintings of the great masters. In visiting the church of the Annunziata in Genoa, I found a beggar lying in my way, the precise figure of the lame man in the cartoon of Raphael. He lay extended at full length upon the steps, crawling with the aid of a short crutch, on which he rested with both his hands. In Roman Catholic countries the church-door is open, and a heavy curtain excludes the light and heat; and there lie about those figures in rags, singularly picturesque.

In short, the priests in their rich habiliments, studiously arranged for effect,—the costume of the monks of the order of St. Francis and the Capuchins,—the men and women from the country, and the mendicants prostrate in the churches, and in circumstances as to light and shade, and colour, nowhere else to be seen,—have been, and are, the studies of the Italian painters.

Again, in passing from the galleries of Rome to the country and villages around, we cannot doubt where Raphael and Domenichino found their studies and prettiest models. The holyday dress of the young women in the villages is the same with that which we see in their paintings; and as each village has something distinguishing and characteristic, and still picturesque in its costume, much is left for good taste to select and combine.

When a man of genius, nurtured in his art at Rome, where every thing conspires to make him value his occupations, returns home to comparative neglect, he is not to be envied. He wants sympathy and associates. David Allan, the Scottish Hogarth,* in a letter to Gavin Hamilton, whom he had left in Rome, laments the want of living models, and the defective sensibility of his countrymen. He says, we rarely see in this country a countenance like that of a Franciscan or an Italian beggar, so full of character, so useful to the study of history painting. But, he adds, we have nature, and with the assistance of ancient models and casts from the Greek statues, much may be accomplished.

* See his beautiful edition of the "Gentle Shepherd." While a child, I remember him as a kind and somewhat facetious old gentleman, but chiefly because he gave me drawings to copy and called me "Brother Brush."

ESSAY I.

OF THE PERMANENT FORM OF THE HEAD AND FACE, IN
CONTRADISTINCTION TO EXPRESSION.

MUCH has been written, and gracefully and agreeably
written, on the sources of Beauty; yet I cannot help thinking that, by losing sight of nature, and what may be justly
called the philosophy of the subject, the right principle has
not been attained.

Beauty of countenance may be defined in words, as well
as demonstrated in art.

A face may be beautiful in sleep, and a statue without
expression may be highly beautiful. On the other hand,
expression may give charm to a face the most ordinary.
Hence it appears that our inquiry divides itself into —the
permanent form of the head and face; and the motion of
the features, or the expression.

But it will be said, there is expression in the sleeping
figure, or in the statue. Is it not rather that we see in these
the capacity for expression? that our minds are active in
imagining what may be the motions of these features when
awake or animated? Thus we speak of an expressive face
before we have seen a movement grave or cheerful, or any
indication in the features of what prevails in the heart.
Avoiding a mere distinction of words, let us consider first,

Why a certain proportion and form of face is beautiful, and conveys the notion of capacity of expression ; and, secondly, the movements or the actual expression of emotion. I believe that it is the confusion between the capacity of expression, and the actual indication of thought, which is the cause of the extraordinary difficulty in which the subject is involved, and which has made it to be called a mystery : *La beauté est un des plus grands mystères de la nature.*

A countenance may be distinguished by being expressive of thought ; that is, it may indicate the possession of the intellectual powers. It is manly, it is human ; and yet not a motion is seen to show what feeling of sentiment prevails. On the other hand, there may be a movement of the features, and the quality of thought,—affection, love, joy, sorrow, gratitude, or sympathy with suffering,—is immediately declared. A countenance which, in ordinary conditions, has nothing remarkable, may become beautiful in expression. It is expression which raises affection, which dwells pleasantly or painfully on the memory. When we look forward to the meeting with those we love, it is the illuminated face we hurry to meet ; and none who have lost a friend but must acknowledge that it is the evanescent expression, more than the permanent form, which is painfully dear to them.

It is a prevailing opinion that beauty of countenance consists in the capacity of expression, and in the harmony of the features consenting to that expression.* The author of

---

* Great names may be quoted—Plato, Cicero, and St. Augustin, down to our own professors. " Et ut corporis est quædam apta figura membrorum, cum coloris quadam suavitate, eaque dicitur pulchritudo : Sic in animo opinionum judiciorumque æquabilitas, et constantia, cum firmitate quadam

the "Essays on the Nature and Principles of Taste" denies any original or positive beauty to the human countenance. Those who have professedly written on the antique say, that, to arrive at the perfection of the ancient statue, the artist must avoid what is human, and aim at the divine.* But we speak of what stands materially before us, to be seen, touched, and measured. With what *divine* essence is the comparison to be made? When the artist models his clay, he must have recourse to some abstract idea of perfection in his own mind; whence has he drawn his idea of perfection? This brings us to the right path in the inquiry : the idea of representing divinity is palpably absurd; we know nothing of form but from the contemplation of *man*.

The only interpretation of *divinity* in the human figure, as represented by the ancient sculptors, is, that the artists avoided individuality; that they studied to keep free of resemblance to any individual; giving no indication of the spirit, or of the sentiments or affections; conceiving that all these movements destroy the unity of the features, and are foreign to beauty in the abstract.

In proceeding to define beauty, all that the writers on art have been able to affirm is, that it is the reverse of deformity. Albert Dürer so expresses himself. If we intend the repre-

---

et stabilitate . . . . . pulchritudo vocatur."—*Cicero*. Burton, in the Objects of Love, quotes thus :—"Pulchritudo est perfectio compositi, ex congruente ordine, mensura et ratione partium consurgens."

* "Se la figura era humana, vi facevano tutto quello, que appartiene alla proprieta, e qualita dell' uomo. Se poi era divina, esse tralasciavano la qualità umane e sceglievano unicamente le divine."—*Mengs*. Again, Winckelman, "La beauté suprême réside en Dieu. L'idée de la beauté humaine se perfectionne à raison de sa conformité et de son harmonie avec l'Etre Suprême," &c.—*Winckelman, Histoire de l'Art.*

sentation of beauty, then let us mark deformity, and teach
ourselves to avoid it. The more remote from deformity,
the nearer the approach to beauty. So Mengs : " *La bellezza
e l' opposito della bruttezza.*" Leonardo da Vinci attributed
much to comparison. He searched for ugliness. If he saw
an uncommon face,—if it were a caricature of expression,—
he would follow it, and contrive to look at the individual
in all aspects. He would pursue a curiosity of this kind
for a whole day, until he was able to go home and draw it.*
We have here the practical result of the theory, which is, to
study the deformities, in order to learn to avoid them ; and
certainly the effect was admirable, since we know, as his
biographer has written, that his painting of beauty raised
love in all beholders.†

---

* " Piglìò tanto gusto nel dipingere cose bizzarre et alterate, che s' egli
s' imbatteva in qualche villano che con viso strano et alquanto fuor del
ordinario, dasse un poco nel ridiculo invaghito dalla bizzarria dell' obbietto,
l' haverebbe sequitato un giorno intiero, fin a tanto c' havendone una per-
fetta idea, ritornato a casa lo disegnava come se l'havesse havuto presente."
—*Vasari.*

† This great painter ascribed much importance to contrast in painting,
bringing extremes together,—*ch' il brutto sia vicina al bello, et il vecchio al
giovane, et il debole al forte ;* and such appears, on many occasions, to have
been the principle which directed the old masters. " The statue of Venus
may stand alone; but not so the painting of the goddess by Titian,—there
are two hideous old women introduced for contrast.—*The Florentine
Gallery.* We may take a further illustration from the finest picture in
Italy—the Archangel Michael subduing Satan, which is in the convent of
the Capuchins in Rome. The beauty of the angel is perfect ; the face is
undisturbed by passion. It conveys to us with how little effort the superior
nature subdues the monster who lies howling, and on which he puts his
feet. The expansion of the wings is grand ; and the manner in which the
drapery encircles him indicates the motion of descent,—that he has alighted !
We have all the contrast between a face convulsed by bad passion, and the
serenity and beauty of virtue."—*Notes from Journal.*

If a painter entertains the idea that there is some undefined beauty, distinct from nature, which is in his own mind, his works will want that variety which is in nature, and we shall see in his paintings the same countenance continually reproduced. We are informed that Raphael, in painting the head of Galatea, found no beauty deserving to be his model; he is reported to have said, that there is nothing so rare as perfect beauty in woman; and that he substituted for nature a certain idea inspired by his own fancy. This is a mistake : painters have nothing in their heads but what has been put there. There is no power in us " to disengage ourselves from material things, and to rise into a sphere of intellectual ideas," and least of all in what regards man. In the Farnesina, there are frescoes by Raphael and his scholars, demonstrating to me the nature of those studies which at length enabled him to compose, not to copy, the beautiful Galatea; that he first drew from what he saw, and finally avoided imperfections, and combined excellencies.* •

We shall arrive at a better understanding of this subject, by inquiring into the peculiar form and beauty of the antique.

* " Palazzo Farnesina. Saw the Frescoes of Raphael. Some, finished by his scholars from his outline—only one finished by himself. What I most admire is the beauty and variety of his female heads, especially the different manner in which he has bound up the hair and let it flow about the neck and shoulders; and yet he may have found all this, selecting from what may be seen in the streets. Here is the Galatea!"—*Note from Journal.*

OF THE PERMANENT FORM OF THE HEAD, AND THE
PROPORTIONS OF THE HEAD AND FACE.

PLEASED as all are with the variety in the human countenance, and desirous of discovering why, in the antique
statue, that is beautiful, which is not found in nature, we
seek for some means of more accurate survey, some rule
by which we may measure proportions.

The scientific principle is deducible from this,—that the
outward forms result from the degree of development of
the contained organs. The most obvious plan, and that
which has been most generally adopted, of examining the
proportions, is by a comparison of the size of the head with
that of the face; understanding by the head, the brain-
case, as containing the organ of intellect; and by the face,
the seat of the collected organs of the senses.

But we are not prompted, naturally, to institute this
comparison, or estimate the dimensions of the whole head.
Both nature and custom teach us, every moment, to scan
the features; and to look there for what is to animate, to
charm, or to grieve us. Every scheme by which it shall
be proposed to elicit the reasons of our feelings of admiration, love, or disgust, by measuring the comparative areas
of the head and face, will fail.

Nor will that comparison enable us to mark the gradations in the heads of animals; because the peculiarities in
the skulls of brutes either result from, or are connected
with, the development of particular organs. Those organs
have relation to the existence of the animal, to its means of
procuring nourishment, the pursuit of its prey, or the mode

of avoiding its enemies ; and the difference in the relative
size of their instruments of prehension, or in that of their
ears, eyes, or organs of smelling, will entirely disturb the
line of demarcation between the brain-case and the face.
The vast mass of the brain in man, must have an effect on
the conformation of the whole head ; it causes the upper
part of the face to be thrown forwards : thus at once distinguishing him from the brute, and marking superiority of
intellect. But when we consider the condition of the lower
animals, we must take into our calculation, not intellectual
properties, but the instincts of brutes ; and the measurement
of the face, as compared with the size of the brain, fails us
altogether.

I must speak with respect of this suggestion of measuring
the face against the head, since it has been entertained by
John Hunter, Camper, Blumenbach, and Cuvier. I shall,
however, direct what I have to say on the subject principally
to the works of Camper.

If we are to study the form of the human head, seen in
profile, we must obtain a line, which shall be permanent, on
which we can raise a perpendicular, and so commence a more
accurate survey than by the unassisted eye.

If we present a skull in profile, or draw it thus with the

E

pen, we may begin by tracing a horizontal line, which shall pass through the foramen of the ear and the alveoli or sockets of the front or incisor teeth of the upper jaw. On this we can raise an oblique line, touching the sockets of the teeth and the most prominent point of the forehead, or of the frontal bone. This is the facial line of Camper; and by its obliquity it will be, to a certain degree, the measure of the relative proportion of the areas or spaces occupied by the brain and the face. Another line may be drawn, which will divide the brain-case from the face; commencing at the foramen of the ear, it will touch the upper margin of the orbit.

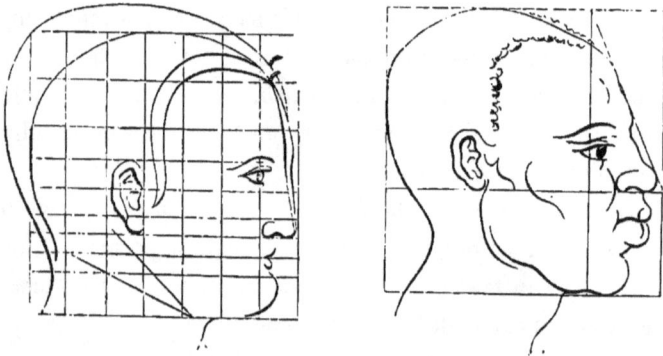

On looking to these illustrations of Albert Dürer, it is apparent that he entertained and practised this mode of distinguishing the forms of the head.

But the idea of the facial line was suggested to Camper on examining certain antique gems. He observed that, in imitating these, the artists failed, from neglecting to throw forward the head, so as to make the line which touched the forehead and teeth nearly perpendicular. For by this line he thought that he had got the key to the whole difficulty, as marking the distinctions in the natural head, compared with the antique. He conceived that when he drew a profile so that the forehead and lips touched the perpendicular line, he obtained the characters of an antique head. If, on the

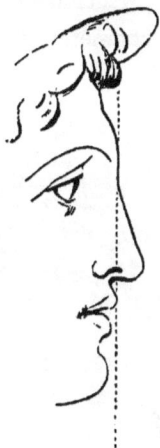

other hand, he let this line fall back, and accommodated the outline of the head to it, he diminished the beauty and perfection of the form. For example, if the line formed an angle of seventy, it became the head of a Negro ; if declining backwards still farther, by the depression of the brain-case, say to sixty, it declared the face of an orang-outang; and so, down to the dog.

To a certain extent, this ingenious mode will be found useful. Had the Count Caylus been guided by it in his great work on Antiquities, his figures, in many instances, would have been better drawn. But even in respect to the state of the human brain, this line does not fully answer the purpose. In the skulls of certain nations the depression of the forehead is so great, that the line drawn from the alveolar processes to the frontal sinus, does not even touch the frontal bone.

Camper's position is this,—that as, by the diminution of the cranium and the further inclination of the facial line, the head is depressed in character to that of the Negro; so, by

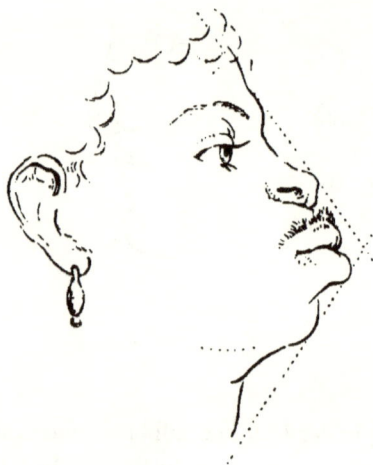

raising and throwing the skull upwards and forwards, until the facial line reaches the perpendicular, as in the preceding page, the great object is attained of resemblance to the antique head.

But his own figures contradict his conclusion; for, although he has thrown the head forward in them, even beyond the perpendicular of the facial line, yet, as he has preserved the features of common nature, we refuse to acknowledge their

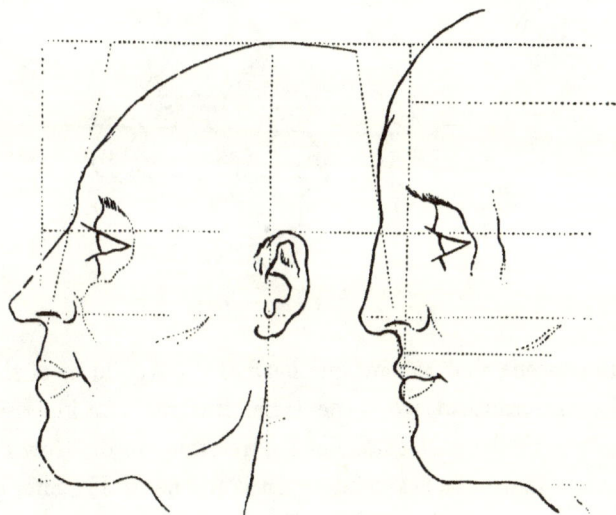

similarity to the beautiful forms of the antique marbles. It is true, that, by advancing the forehead, it is raised; the face is shortened, and the eye brought to the centre of the head. But with all this, there is much wanting,—that which measurement or a mere line will not shew us.

The truth is, that we are more moved by the features than by the form of the whole head. Unless there be a conformity in every feature to the general shape of the head, throwing the forehead forward on the face produces deformity; * and

* On the following page I have sketched the profile of a poor begging Negro in contrast with the head of M. Agrippa, in which the artist has dignified the character on the principle stated by Camper; but, it is here

the question returns with full force :—How is it that we are

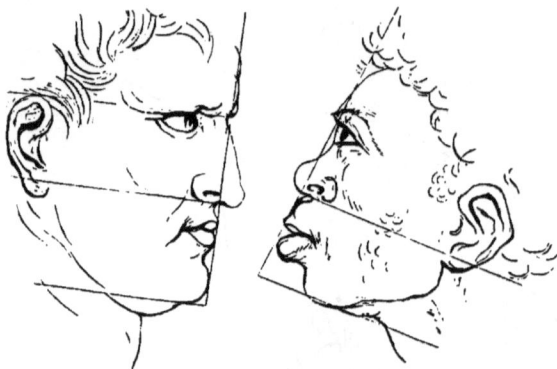

led to concede that the antique head of the Apollo or of the Jupiter is beautiful, when the facial line makes a hundred degrees with the horizontal line? In other words, How do we admit that to be beautiful which is not natural? Simply for the same reason that if we discover a broken portion of an antique, a nose, or a chin, of marble, we can say, without deliberation, this must have belonged to a work of antiquity ; which proves that the character is distinguishable in every part,—in each feature, as well as in the whole head.

We must assume a new principle, and it is this—that in the face there is a character of nobleness observable, depending on the development of certain organs which indicate the prevalence of the higher qualities allied to thought, and therefore human. A great mistake has prevailed in supposing that the expansion of some organs in the face of man,

apparent that the manly dignity results from the character of each feature, even more than from the facial line. It is seen in the eye, in the nose, mouth, and chin ; each of which are in as much contrast with those of the Negro, as is the shape of the whole head.

marks a participation in the character of the brute : that the
fully developed nose indicates the grovelling propensities,
and the extended mouth, the ferocity of the lower animals.
Let us correct this misconception by considering the properties or uses of the mouth. It is for feeding certainly, but
it is also for speech. Extend the jaws, project the teeth,
widen the mouth, and a carnivorous propensity is declared ;
but concentrate the mouth, give to the chin fulness and
roundness, and due form to the lips ; shew through them the
quality of eloquence, of intelligence, and of human sentiments,
—and the nobleness is enhanced, which was only in part indicated, by the projection of the forehead. Now, look to the
antique head and say, is the mouth for masticating, or for
speech and expression of sentiment ? So of the nose. Here,
even Cuvier mistook the principle. The nose on a man's face
has nothing in common with the snout of a beast. The
prominence of the nose, and of the lower part of the forehead, and the developement of the cavities in the centre of
the face, are all concerned in the *voice*. This is ascertained
by the manliness of voice coming with the full developement
of these parts.* Nothing sensual is indicated by the form
of the human nose ; although, by depressing it and joining
it to the lip,—the condition of the brute,—as in the satyr,
the idea of something sensual is conveyed.

A comparison of the eye and the ear brings out the principle more distinctly. Enlarge the orbit, magnify the eyes ;
let them be full, clear, piercing, full of fire, still they combine
with the animated human countenance ; they imply a
capacity consistent with human thought, a vivacity and

* These cavities do not exist in the child, and only attain their full
size in the adult.

intelligence partaking of mind.   But large pendulous ears, or projecting and sharp ears, belong to the satyr ; for man is not to be perpetually watchful, or to be startled and alarmed by every noise.

If we consider for a moment what is the great mark of distinction between man and brutes, we shall perceive that it is SPEECH ; for it corresponds to his exalted intellectual and moral endowments.   Speech implies certain inward propensities, a conformity of internal organs, and a peculiarity of nervous distribution ; but it also implies a particular outward character or physiognomy, a peculiar form of the nostrils, jaws, mouth, and lips.   These latter are the visible signs of this high endowment.

Then again, as to sentiment,—laughter and weeping, and sympathy with those in pleasure or in pain, characterise human beings, and are indicated by the same organs.   Hence, the capacity of expression in the nostril and mouth, are peculiar attributes of the human countenance.

SOME FURTHER OBSERVATIONS ON THE FORM AND PROPORTIONS OF THE SKULL, AND BONES OF THE FACE.

LET us return with more just principles to the study of the lines marking the regions of the face and head.

A line drawn from the tube of the ear to the eyebrow, or prominence of the frontal bone, and one from the same point to the chin, include the face in a triangle.   If another line be drawn to the lowest point of the nose, we divide the face into two regions; the lower occupied by the masticating apparatus of teeth, jaws, and their muscles.   If this alone be enlarged, the effect is an encroachment on the nose and orbit, and the face loses all dignity and form. The eye is especially diminutive, and the nose misshapen.

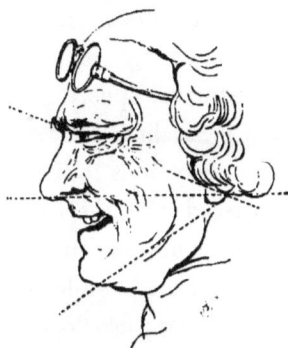

It will be found that the jaws correspond with the general skeleton; very tall men, especially if gigantic, have large jaws, and comparatively small heads. In ricketty deformity

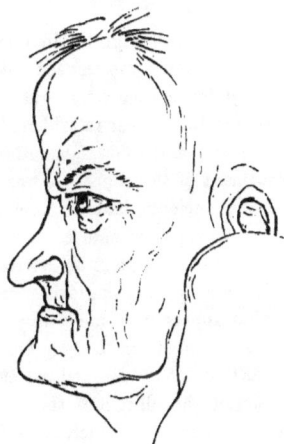

of the bones, the character of the face is exhibited, as in this sketch, by a defect in the size of the jaw-bones, which have

F

yielded to the action of their muscles. The qualities of mind, evinced in expression, may redeem any degree of deformity; but the peculiarity of the countenance here, is that of rickets; the prominence of the forehead arises merely from the accumulation of bone, and not from a superior developement of the brain. We have a further opportunity of observing that the projection of the facial line, unaccompanied with due conformity of features, only adds to the deformity.*

Blumenbach, dissatisfied with the facial line of Camper, contrived a different mode of distinguishing the capacities of the head and face. He selected two bones of the skull; the frontal bone as representing the developement of the cranium or brain-case; and the superior maxillary bone, as the seat of the organs of sense, which are considered as opposite to the intellectual properties. He placed the vertex of the skull towards him, so as to look over the brow or forehead;

---

* "In visiting the Villa Albani, among the indescribable beauties which are everywhere around us, the party was amused with my attention being fixed upon the statue of a deformed person. I was indeed struck with the truth of the representation : the manner in which the ribs are distorted, the head sunk upon the breast, and the exaggeration of certain muscles, consequent upon displacement of the bones. I was thinking of the accurate conception which the ancients had of human anatomy, and the precision with which they copied from nature.

"This is said to be a statue of Æsop, and on referring to Visconti, where he treats of the fabulist, I see that his engraving of the statue, beautiful as it is, is deficient in what appeared to me a due correspondence in the countenance, and the distortion of the body. On comparing it with a sketch I had made, I find that I have marked more distinctly the position of the head, the projection of the chin, and the fulness of the forehead characteristic of that defect in the face which arises from the jaw yielding to the action of the muscles during the age when the bones are soft.

"Visconti discovers in the face a spirituality quite in contrast with that expression which the ancients give to buffoons, and dwarfs, whose physiognomy they always made ridiculous."—*Note from Journal.*

and then he noted how much the bones of the cheek, the nose, and the upper jaw projected beyond the level of the frontal bone. This method he used as better suited to mark the peculiarities of the national head ; and to be employed in the skull rather than in the living head. It may be useful, but it is manifestly imperfect. The breadth of the face may be noted in this manner; but it will better serve the purpose of the artist to draw the face in front, and to apply the principle already explained, in the profile.

It was observed in the preceding pages, that the different plans of measuring the head might assist in pointing out the varieties in the form of the head ; but that none of them proceeded on a just principle for distinguishing what is acknowledged by all to be beautiful in the antique. A circumstance to which Professor Gibson, of Philadelphia, then my pupil, first drew my attention, convinced me that the methods which physiologists had practised were very incorrect. He placed before me the skull of an European and of a Negro ; and resting them both on the condyles of the occipital bone, as the head is supported on the spine, it appeared that the European fell forward, and the African backward. This seemed remarkable, when both physiologists and physiognomists were describing the greater comparative size of the face, as the grand peculiarity of the African head. I was desirous of investigating this matter further.

The difficulty of finding a line by which to measure the inclination of the face would be removed, if we were to take the head as fairly balanced on the articulating surfaces of the atlas, or first bone of the spine ; but in the living body, it will not be easy to fix the head in the equipoise. Something may be attained by comparing the general position of the head, in the European and the Negro ; but nothing approaching to the accuracy which observation pretending to science, requires.

To find a line which should not vary, but enable us to measure with correctness the angles both of the facial line, and of the line intermediate between the cranium and the face, I poised the skull upon a perpendicular rod, by passing the point through the foramen magnum into the interior of the skull, so that the upper part of the cranium rested on the point. By shifting the skull till the rod was exactly betwixt the condyles of the occipital bone, and in the centre of the foramen magnum, I procured the line which was wanted.

I now divided into degrees, or equal parts, the great convexity of the cranium, from the setting on of the nose on the fore part, to the margin of the foramen magnum behind ; and having so prepared several skulls for adjustment on the rod, I began to make my observations.

In comparing the European skull with that of the Negro, the point of the rod in the latter, touched the inside of the cranium several degrees nearer to the bones of the face, or more forward on the cranium, than the former.

On measuring the angle of the facial line of Camper with this perpendicular line, in a European skull the most perfect in form of any I possessed, I found the difference to be ten degrees.

The cause of the difference being much greater between the European and African skull, in this way of measuring, than by Camper's plan is, that here the facial line has reference to the whole form and proportion of the head ;

whereas in Camper's measurement it marks only the inclination of the face.

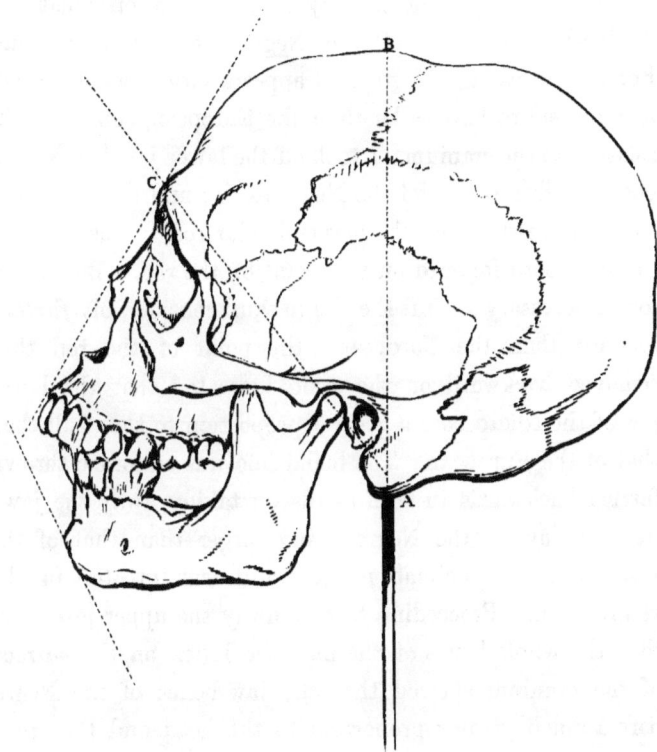

We have now an explanation of the peculiarity in the position of the Negro's head, the upward inclination of the face, and the falling back of the occiput. And here too we have it proved, that it is an error to suppose the Negro head to be remarkable in character on account of any increase in the proportion of the bones of the face, to the cranium; for the area of the bones of the face is in this way shewn to bear a less proportion to that of the bones of the cranium, in the Negro than in the European head.

My next object of inquiry was to find on what the distinctive character of the Negro face really depends. For to the eye the Negro face appears larger, while in fact it is proved to be smaller than the European, considered in relation to the cranium. I took off the lower jaw-bones from both the European and the Negro skull; and then, in order to poise the skulls on the perpendicular rod, it was required to move both forward on the point of the rod. But it was found necessary to shift the Negro skull considerably *farther* forward than the European: the point of the rod thus removed backward on the scale, indicated that the lower jaw of the Negro bore a greater proportion to the skull than that of the European. The facial line was of course thrown farther backwards in both skulls on taking away the jaw; but the jaw of the Negro being larger than that of the European, the inclination backward was greater in the Negro skull. Proceeding to take away the upper jaws, and then the whole bones of the face, the index on the surface of the cranium shewed that the jaw-bones of the Negro bore a much greater proportion to the head and the other bones of the face, than those of the European skull; and that the apparent magnitude of the bones of the Negro face resulted from the size and form of the jaw-bones alone, while the upper bones of the face, and indeed all that had not relation to the teeth and mastication, were less than those of the European skull.

In proceeding with these experiments, I changed the manner of noting the variations in the inclination of the cranium; because I perceived that an index, marked on the convexity of the skull, varied according to the form of the head. Preserving the principle, I measured the inclination of the cranium by an angle formed by the perpendicular line (A B) and a line (A C) intermediate between the cranium and the face. On poising the cranium on the rod, after taking away all the bones of the face, it appeared that the Negro cranium had the line elevated nearly ten degrees more than the European. I also found, on comparing the cranium of a child with that of an adult, that it was deficient in the relative proportions of weight and capacity on the fore part—that the line was depressed by the size of the forehead increasing in proportion to the advance in maturity.

On looking attentively to these skulls, it was evident that there were distinctions to be observed in the form of the cranium itself, independently of the proportions between the face and cranium; that these varieties depended on the form of the brain, and proceeded (I think we may conclude) from the more or less complete development of the organ of the mind. In the infant there is a deficiency of weight, and a less ample area in the higher and anterior part of the brain-case. I say less ample, only in comparison with that which we may estimate as the standard, viz. the adult European. In the Negro, besides the greater weakness and lightness in the bones of the whole skull, there is a remarkable deficiency of length in the head forward, producing a narrow and depressed forehead; whereas a large capacious forehead is allowed to be the least equivocal mark of perfection in the head.

Having been brought by this more accurate method of measuring the skull, to observe distinctions not only in the cranium and bones of the face, but in the face itself, and in the cranium independently of the face, I wished, in the next place, to consider more at large the varieties in the form of the face, and the cause of the secret influence of certain forms on our judgment of beauty.

From the examination of the heads, both of men and brutes, and of the skulls of a variety of animals, I think there is reason to conclude, that the external character consists more in the relative proportions of the parts of the face to each other, than has been admitted. On first consideration we are apt to say, that in the beautiful form of the human countenance the likeness of the brute is inadmissible ; that wherever we see a resemblance to the brute in the form of the whole countenance, or in the particular features, it implies degradation. But this is true to a limited extent only : and how far it extends, the examination of the uses of the parts will inform us.

We have therefore again to inquire, which are the nobler features of the face, and which belong to the inferior functions.

In examining the mouth and jaws of animals we shall be convinced that the form of the bones is adapted to the necessities of the creature, independently altogether of the sense of taste ; that in man, whose jaw-bones are smaller than those of other animals, this sense is most perfect, most exquisite in degree, and suited to the greatest variety in its exercise. Turning to the skulls of the horse and the lion, we shall see that the one is fitted for powerful mastication, and the other for tearing and lacerating, not for cutting or grinding ; and if we examine the form of the teeth more narrowly, we shall perceive that there must necessarily be a form of the jaw corresponding to these actions. In the lion, the tiger, and all carnivorous animals, much of the character of the face lies in the depth of the jaw forward; because this depth is necessary for the socketing of the long canine teeth. When, on the contrary, the jaw is deep and strong towards the back part, it is for the firm socketing of the grinding teeth, and is characteristic of the form of the head of the horse, and of all graminivorous animals. There is also a peculiar form of the head and distinct expression, in the rodentia, and such animals as have to pierce shells for their food, as the monkeys, which is produced by their cutting teeth being placed at right angles in their jaws, for the action of gnawing.

Now it is certainly by that unconscious operation of the fancy, that associating power which has a constant influence on our opinions, that a human face with protuberant jaws seems degraded to the brutal character; that the projection of the incisor teeth especially gives a remarkable expression of meanness; while the enlargement of the canine teeth, as we see in the demons of the Last Judgment of Michael Angelo, produces an air of savageness and ferocity.*

When we consider further the muscles appropriated to the motions of the jaws, we may comprehend why it should be thought a deformity when the zygoma (the arch of bone on the temple) is remarkably prominent. It is enlarged to permit the massy temporal muscle by which the jaw is closed to act freely, and its form corresponds with the size of the jaw, and with the canine teeth. This will be very

---

* Fairy Queen, Book IV. cant. vii. 5.

evident if we place the human skull beside the skull of the horse, the lion, the bull, the tiger, the sheep, the dog, &c.

It has already been said that a comparison of the area of the bones of the head and face in different animals will not inform us of the relative perfection of the brain in its exercise. But still we may recognize, in the form of the jaws and bill, the beast or bird of rapine ; in the breadth and extent of the central cavities of the face the seat of the organ of smelling, tribes which hunt their prey ; in the prominent eye placed more laterally, timid animals which are the objects of the chase ; and in the large socket and great eyeball, the character of such as prowl by night. With these variations in the perfection of the outward senses, there are, no doubt, corresponding changes in the brain, and therefore, in the instincts and habits of animals.

In obtaining a line which shows with precision the bearings of all the parts of the head, I think that I have reduced this subject to greater simplicity ; and have been able to make observations more correctly than by the methods hitherto in use :—I have shown that the relative capacity of the cranium or brain-case to that of the face, as containing the organs of the senses, is insufficient to mark the scale of intellect, or to explain the distinctions of character in the human head :—That the perfection of the human head greatly consists in the increase of the cranium forward ; in the full and capacious forehead ; and that the cranium of the Negro, when compared with the perfect cranium of a European, has less capacity at the fore-part.* It has been shewn

---

* In comparing the skulls of men with those of brutes, e.g. the chimpanzee, it cannot be just to measure the proportions of the cranium behind the foramen of the occipital bone ; for that foramen must correspond with the

that in the Negro the whole of the face is actually smaller, instead of being greater, when compared with the brain-case, than that of the European ; but that the jaws, contrasted with the other parts of the face, are larger. The conclusion to which these views lead is, that some principle must be sought for, not yet acknowledged, which shall apply not only to the form of the whole head, but also to the individual parts. This principle, I imagine, is to be found in the form of the face as bearing relation to its various functions ; not those of the senses merely, but of the parts contained in or attached to the face—the organs of Mastication, the organs of Speech, and the organs of Expression.

And here it is to be observed, that it is not necessarily a deformity that a feature resembles that of a lower animal. In our secret thoughts the form has a reference to the function. If the function be allied to intellect, or is connected with mind (as the eye especially is), then there is no incompatibility with the human countenance, though the organ should bear a resemblance to the same part in a brute ; but, if it has a relation to the meaner necessities of animal life, as the jaws, or the teeth, the effect is incompatible, and altogether at variance with human physiognomy.

If we take the antique as the model of beauty in the human head, we shall confess that a prominent cheek-bone, or a jaw-bone large and square behind, is a defect ; that the great depth of face, produced by the length of the teeth, is also a deformity ; that the projecting jaws are still worse ; and, above all, that the monkey-like protrusion of the fore teeth takes away from the dignity of human expression.

spine on which the head rests ; and the position of the animal, monkey, or quadruped, must determine the connexion of the spine and skull.

When the principles that sway our secret thoughts are
discovered, and when by a comparison of the parts of the
head anatomically, a secure foundation is laid for the accurate
observation of nature, the lines of Camper and Blumenbach
will aid us in the examination of character; but these
methods of measurement are, of themselves, imperfect, and,
being founded on a mistaken principle, they lead to unsatis-
factory conclusions.

ESSAY II.

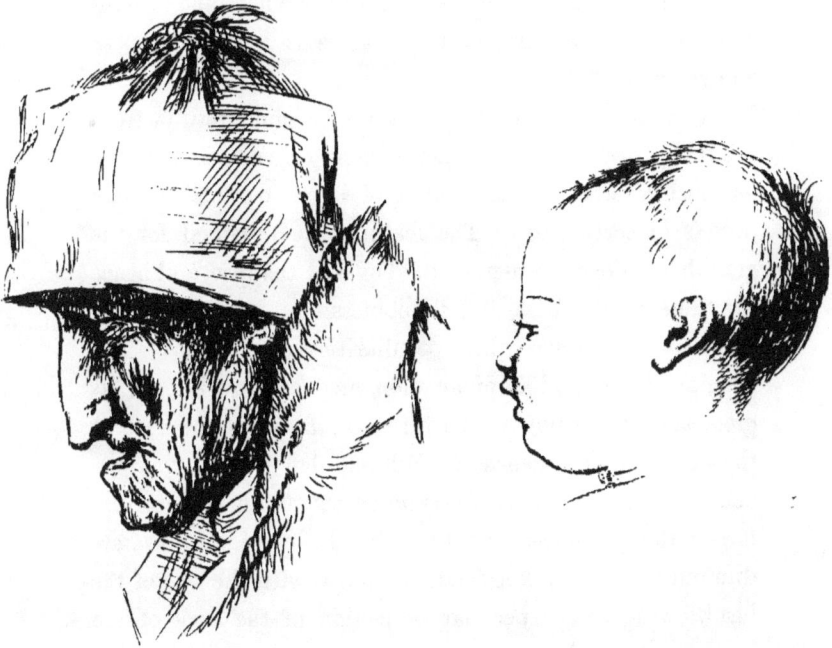

THE bones, and the parts which cover them, or are contained within them, grow, as it were, by one impulse, so
that they correspond together; the fleshy lips of the Negro

are suited to his large protuberant teeth. Among ourselves,
a square jaw-bone is attended by a thickness and heaviness
of the cheeks and lips; and if the canine teeth, the strong
corner teeth, be unusually long and prominent, there is not
only a coarseness and heaviness of a different kind, but a
certain irascibility of expression. In women and young
persons with large incisor teeth, there is a pretty fulness
and ripeness of the lips.

The whole character of the face of a child results from
the fleshy parts and integuments being calculated, if I may
use such a term, for the support of larger bones than they
possess in early years. The features are provided for the
growth and developement of the bones of the face, and hence
the fulness, roundness, and chubbiness of infancy.

There are some other peculiarities in infancy. For
example: the head is of an elongated and oval form, its
greatest length being in the direction from the forehead to
the occiput; the forehead is full, but flat at the eyebrows,
and the whole part which contains the brain is relatively
large; the jaw-bones, and the other bones of the face, are
diminutive; the neck is small compared with the size of the
head, owing to the peculiar projection of the back of the
head (or occiput).

Compare the outline of the infant's head with that of the
boy, and the effect of the expansion of the bones of the face
in bestowing the characteristic form of youth, will be apparent.
The face in the youth is lengthened, and is less round than
that of the infant. The brow, however, is not enlarged in
proportion to the increase of the lower part of the face;
though the form is so far changed that a prominent ridge
is now developed along the course of the eyebrows.

This ridge (the supra-orbitary) is caused by a cavity which is formed in this part of the head by the layers of the frontal bone (or os frontis). It is the enlargement of this cavity (called the frontal sinus) that makes the prominence over -the eyes which is peculiar to manhood.

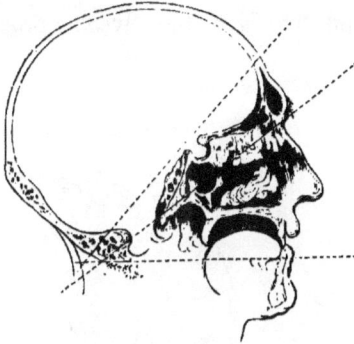

From infancy to adolescence, there is a great increase in the size of the upper jaw-bone (the superior maxillary bone). This is chiefly owing to its containing within it another cavity (the maxillary sinus); which, like the frontal sinus, becomes greatly developed with advancing years. And there are several new characters given to the countenance by the enlargement of the upper jaw-bone, which may be regarded as the centre of the bones of the face. It has the effect of raising and lengthening the bones of the nose, and of making the check-bones (or ossa malæ) project farther.*

* The cavities in the frontal and maxillary bones communicate with the nose, and assist in giving the sonorous, manly tones to the voice. They are very small in women as they are in children.

The growth of the large teeth in the adult, contrasted with the child, adds to the depth, as well as length, of both the upper and lower jaw-bones, and the whole face becomes consequently longer.   Another necessary effect is, that the angle of the lower jaw recedes more towards the ear, and acquires more distinctness.   Thus it is, that by the growth of the teeth and of those processes of the bones which support and fix them (the alveolar processes), and by the

lengthening and receding of the angle of the jaw, a manly squareness of the chin and lower part of the face takes the place of the fulness and roundness of childhood.

This view of the skull at different periods of life suggests another observation, relating to the characters of age. When the teeth fall out in old age, the sockets which grow up along with them waste away. Accordingly, while the depth of the lower jaw-bone, from the hinge to the angle, is undiminished, and its length towards the chin is the same, there remains nothing at the part where the teeth were implanted but the narrow base of the jaw. The effect on the countenance is perceived in this sketch. The jaws are allowed to approach nearer to each other at the forepart; the angle of the lower jaw comes of course more forward, and resembles that of the child, were it not that the chin projects : the chin and the nose approximate, the lips fall in, the mouth is too small for the tongue, and the speech is inarticulate.

Before leaving this subject, we may point out a defect in the sculptures of Fiammingo, who has been justly celebrated for his designs of boys. In his heads of children, it is obvious that he intended to present us with an ideal form, instead of a strict copy from nature. But it will be remarked, that the eyes are too deeply set in his figures. He has made the prominences over the orbits (the supraorbitary ridges), which are peculiar to a more advanced age, distinct features in the child, and has thus produced an unnatural appearance. The only character of the boy which he has kept true to nature is the largeness of the head compared with the face, the fulness of the cheeks, and the falling in of the mouth and chin. In exaggerating

H

the natural peculiarities, the artist has strictly imitated
the antique. But it may remain a question, how far the
principle which is so happy in its effect of heightening
the beauty of the adult countenance, is necessary or allowable in designing the forms of childhood?

OF THE SKULL, AS PROTECTING THE BRAIN.

In touching even slightly on this subject we must attend
to certain principles. It is to be understood, that a
shock or vibration passing through the brain proves more
destructive than a wound penetrating its substance. A
skull stronger, thicker, and more solid than that which
we possess would not have given greater security: it
would have vibrated to a greater degree, and the concussion arising even from trifling blows on the head, would
have effectually benumbed the faculties.

A child bears knocks which would be fatal in old age.
This is owing to the skull being thin, uniform in texture,
and elastic, in childhood; and to the brain being of a
corresponding structure. The brain is at this age soft to
a degree that would be unnatural in mature years. This
resiliency of the skull, and yielding quality of the brain,
explain how the child is uninjured by blows, which would
be attended with fatal concussion in after-life. But there
is also a provision in adults for moderating the effects
of such accidents. In proportion as the brain acquires
firmness during growth, a gradual change takes place in
the structure of the bones of the head; the protecting
cranium is not simply strengthened; it is not merely

thickened; the flat bones which surround the brain are split into layers, an external and an internal one. These layers have each a different density, and a softer substance than either is interposed between them; the effect of which is, to interrupt that vibration which would otherwise ring around the skull, and reach every molecule of the brain.

I have elsewhere* shown that, in brutes, as in man, the processes and joinings of the skull are formed in relation to the forces to which the head is to be exposed; and that they vary according to the habits or mode of existence of the animal. The tearing fangs of the carnivorous animal, and the still more powerful teeth of the hyena, adapted for breaking the hardest bones, are implanted in sockets of corresponding strength. The horns of the bull, the antlers of the stag, are rooted in bones not only capable of supporting their weight, but of receiving the shocks to which such instruments expose the brain; and the firmness of the sutures in the crania of these animals demonstrates the precision with which everything is set in just proportion.

A remark is here suggested by these considerations. The provisions which we have been noticing in the human head are not designed to give absolute security against violence, but to balance duly the chances of life; leaving us still under the conviction that pain and death follow injury; so that our experience of bodily suffering, and fear of incurring it, whilst they protect the life, lay the foundation of important moral qualities in our nature.

Let us now direct our attention especially to the forms

* Paley's "Natural Theology," with illustrative notes by Henry Lord Brougham and Sir Charles Bell.

of the skull. The back of the head is more exposed than
the forehead : we defend the front with our arms and
hands : not so the back, as in falling backwards. There
is, accordingly, a very marked distinction in the strength
of the occipital bone and that of the frontal bone. The
prominence felt at the back part of the head is the centre
of certain groinings, or arched ridges, which strengthen
the bone within. We say groinings, for there is nothing
more resembling the strong arches, or groinings, of an under-
ground story of a building than these projections on the
interior of the occiput. In front, the skull forms, on the
whole, a lighter and more delicate shell than behind; yet
it is not less adapted to protect the brain. The projecting parts of the forehead, which the anatomist calls the
eminentiæ frontales, are, undoubtedly, most exposed ; but
they are, at the same time, the strongest points of the bone,
for here the outer and inner surfaces are not parallel ;
there is an accumulation of bony substance in the two
tables, to give them increased thickness. It has already
been seen that the prominences over the eyebrows, characteristic of the mature or manly forehead, have no relation
to the form of the brain at this part ; they are merely the
anterior walls of the frontal sinuses,—cavities which, it has
been stated, belong principally to the organ of voice; yet
they, and the ridges which project towards the temples,
are a safeguard to the brain. Those latter-raised arches,
called the temporal ridges of the frontal bone, consist of
dense and hard bone, as obviously designed for adding
strength, as is an edging of brass, in carpentry, or a piece
of steel let into a horse-shoe. Imagine a man falling side-
wise, and pitching on the shoulder and side of the head,—

he strikes precisely on that point which is the most convex, the most dense, the thickest, and best protected.

Altogether, independently of phrenology, it has of old time been acknowledged, that fulness of the forehead, combined with those forms which have been noticed, is an indication of intellectual capacity; and, as we have shown, of human character and beauty. All physiologists have agreed in this view; whilst they are equally confident in affirming that anatomy affords no foundation for mapping the cranium into minute subdivisions or regions. As nature, by covering the head, has intimated her intention that we shall not there scan our neighbours' capacities, she has given us the universal language of *expression.* Man is gregarious; he looks for sympathy : it is not good for him to be alone ; he solicits an unity of sentiment ; and the language which expresses it is in the face.

THE CHARACTERISTIC FORMS OF THE LOWER ANIMALS.

Notwithstanding the high authorities in favour of the facial line, we have ventured to say that it is not adapted to give a measure of the capacity or area of the head in contrast with the face, in brutes ; because the peculiarities of face in them depend on their instincts and propensities. These are for the most part indicated by the greater development of some one or more of the organs common to them all, and the subserviency of others, not by the mass of the brain. The head of the horse presents us with an example ; it is an herbivorous or graminivorous animal, and hence the peculiarities of its teeth. Now, it is in accordance with the teeth that the whole character of its form is derived. The incisor teeth or nippers project, that the head may reach the ground for feeding; and they have a peculiar structure, that they may be preserved sharp. The lips also conform to this object; they are not only suited to cover the teeth, but to project and gather the food. Again, the grinders are large, strong, deeply socketed, and adapted to bear the trituration of the food for a term of years corresponding to the natural life of the animal. While the mouth is small, the head is long; and the muscles which operate on the lower jaw, to close it, and to give it the lateral motions necessary for grinding, are proportionably large; therefore the depth of the head behind, and the length and narrowness forwards, are the principal characteristics of the horse.*

Another peculiarity of the horse's head is seen in the construction of his nostril. He does not breathe through the mouth, but only through the nose. Here is an interesting relation of parts, which, though remote in place, are united in function. The nostril is indicative of the state of the lungs: and a large dilateable nostril has descended from the Arabian breed, and marks the capacity of "wind."

---

* Cuvier has been at the pains of measuring the facial line in a great variety of animals, beginning with the ourang-outang and ending with the horse. Let us take the pug-dog, in which the angle is fixed at 35°, and compare it with the horse at 23°; who will not perceive that the difference of the facial angles depends on the extension of the jaws of the horse, necessarily arising from the form and number of the teeth, or in other words, from his mode of feeding?

Veterinary surgeons and naturalists have found it difficult to assign a use for certain cavities at the back part of the horse's head called the Eustachian cells. To me they do not appear to be subservient either to neighing or to the organ of hearing, as supposed; but they are placed in this situation, and filled with air, to occupy the large space intervening between the sides of the jaws, without materially increasing the weight. All jockeys know the defect in a horse of a heavy head and long neck.

It is agreeable to see the young kid in the first hours of existence, impelled by its instincts to mount the cliffs and summits of the hills; or to behold the goat perched high on the scarped rock, his beard tossed by the wind, and browsing fearlessly. These animals, the sheep, and horned cattle generally, congregate, and make a circle to oppose an enemy; and present for their defence a combined front. Their eyes are placed differently from those of the horse; and the nostril wants the expansion necessary for maintaining a continued flight.. The most curious adaptation of the form of an herbivorous animal to its mode of feeding is seen in the giraffe. The whole frame of the creature is formed with the view of enabling it to reach its food, which is not the herbage, but the leaves of trees. The skull is small, and so light, even in comparison with that of the horse, that it is like a thing of paper; and the tongue and the lips protrude, to catch the branches over head. The large prominent eyes, and the limbs formed for flight, betoken the timidity of the creature.

If we compare a carnivorous animal, as the lion, with a horned animal, as the bull, it will be readily perceived that it is from the teeth or the horns that the whole character of the head results. The peculiarity of the skull of the lion, or the tiger, consists chiefly in the breadth of the face, caused by the large zygomatic processes, which are formed of great size to give room to the strong muscles that close the jaw: and it is visible also in the shortness of the muzzle, and the depth of the face in front, where the canine teeth are situated; for these must be deeply socketed in the jaws to sustain the strength of the fangs, and the powerful efforts of the animal. The grinding teeth are small, and formed so as to cut like scissors; for there is here no lateral play of the jaws, as in grinding; the canine teeth overlapping and preventing that motion. The muscles which close the jaws are of tremendous power, commensurate with the length and strength of those fangs, which are for holding or tearing the prey.

See, again, the head of the boar, how all the parts hang, as it were, together, to produce its characteristic form : the snout and the great tusks are for grubbing up roots; yet, from his strength, he is a formidable animal, for he will turn and rend. This very term implies a great deal ; he does not tear with his teeth, he does not *butt*, as with horns; but he runs straight forward, and with his projecting lateral tusk ploughs up the flesh. The whole strength of his body and neck is concentrated to the use of these formidable instruments. Look to the antique boar of the Florentine Gallery. The head rises high and projects behind, to give strong attachment to the powerful muscles constituting his very peculiarly shaped neck, which is large, thick, inflexible, and suited, when he rushes forwards, to convey the impulse to the head, and finally to the tusks.*

It ought to be a pleasing study to the artist to found his designs on an accurate knowledge of the structure and functions of animals. This pursuit unites his art with the liberal sciences of the naturalist and the comparative anatomist. And if he be a lover of the antique, he must have observed that, in the better ages of the arts, the sculptors were remarkable for giving a true and natural character in their representations of brutes. The knowledge of animal form is the only guide to the right conception of the perfection and beauty of the antique.

* Bridgewater Treatise on the Human Hand, 4th edition, p. 400.

FURTHER ILLUSTRATIONS OF THE PRINCIPLE, THAT BEAUTY
IN THE HUMAN FORM HAS RELATION TO THE CHARAC-
TERISTIC ORGANS OF MAN.

WHAT, then, gives nobleness and grace to the human
figure, and how is deformity to be avoided ? In the statues
of antiquity we see that the artists had a perfect knowledge
of the frame, and could represent it in all its natural beauty.
But in many of these remains there is something beyond
an exact copy of nature,—something which, as we have
seen, has been called *divine*. Now the difficulty of explaining why such deviations from real nature should inspire us
with admiration, has forced inquirers into vague surmises
and comparisons. For example, they have applied the principles of harmony in music to the beauty of the human figure.

When the animal frame is surveyed as a whole, or as
composed of parts more or less common to all living
creatures, which is taking the philosophical view of the
subject, an uniform plan is seen to pervade the animal
kingdom. Not only may the skeleton be traced from a
shell up to the complex mechanism in man,[*] but every
organ or individual part, when viewed comparatively, will be
found to undergo a similar development; from the simple
structure of those creatures which enjoy the lowest kind of
sensibility, to that which exists in the human frame. If,
according to this view, we examine the head, and follow
the course of development of the brain, as the part which
occupies the cranium, and then that of the organs of the
senses, which together constitute the face, and include the

* See the author's " Bridgewater Treatise on the Human Hand," which
may be taken as an introduction to the present subject.

apparatus of speech, we shall distinguish what is peculiar to man. We shall learn what forms of parts bear relation to those endowments by which he holds his acknowledged superiority; and the conclusion may be arrived at, that by magnifying, in works of art, what is peculiarly characteristic of man, we may ennoble his countenance, and, without being strictly natural, attain what is better.

No faculties of the mind have been bestowed without the field for their exercise; men's capacities, their thoughts, and their affections, have their counterparts, or objects, to excite or to gratify them. There are beings superior to ourselves, and in a condition of existence different from ourselves, and the mind delights in contemplating them. Even in our enjoyment of beautiful objects, our thoughts rise beyond them. We walk into the country, in the woods and wilds, in love with nature and delighting in solitude. But if we examine our minds, we shall find that we people these solitudes; however we may believe that it is nature and inanimate creation which please us, all is referable to, and concentres in, some reflexion of the voice and features of human kindred.

In admiring the finer works of antiquity, it is admitted that the forms which we regard as models of perfection are unlike what has existed in nature: that no living head ever had the facial line of the Jupiter, the Apollo, the Mercury, or the Venus. Having found reasons to reject the theory of Camper, the question returns, How is that beautiful which is not natural?

Let us take the head of Mercury, which is simply beautiful, and the head of a Satyr, both antique; and contemplate them in succession. In the Mercury, there is a combination of forms and general proportions of the head and face, never seen in all the varieties of living man; yet is the whole and each particular feature perfectly beautiful. In turning to the Satyr, we find every proportion reversed : the forehead narrow and depressed : the eyes near, small, and a little oblique; the nose flattened to the upper lip; the mouth protuberant; the ears large, tipped, and sharp; and the expression of the whole goatish and savage ; and what there is of human expression is lively and humorous, but common and base. Now the principle which has been followed in giving beauty to the head of Mercury is obvious here. Whatever is peculiar to the human countenance, as distinguishing it from the brute, is enhanced. Not only is the forehead expanded and projecting, and the facial line more perpendicular, but every feature is modelled on the same principle: the ear is small and round; the nostril is eminently human, and unlike that of the beast ; the mouth, the teeth, and lips, are not such as belong to the brute, nor are they the mere instruments of mastication, but of speech and human expression. So of every part, take them individually, or as a whole; whatever would lead to the resemblance of the brute is omitted or diminished.

The principle is further extended. It is not in the proportions between the face and the brain-case alone that the contrast is perceived, but in the quality or function of each organ. We have adverted to the theory of Cuvier, that as hunger and the animal passions govern brutes, and as the parts which chiefly minister to them in the face, are the organs of smell and of taste, the unusual development of the nose and the mouth degrades or brutifies the human countenance. But we remarked, in regard to this, that the nose is not elevated in man to increase the organ of smelling : it belongs to the voice, to human voice and speech. And so must we consider the different functions of the mouth. In brutes, it is for prehension, tearing, and mastication ; in man, its more distinguishable office is speech and expression. Model the lips for this, for eloquence and the expression of the softer passions, and it becomes beautiful ; extend the teeth, and make the lips a mere covering for them, and it is brutal, at variance with human physiognomy and detracting from whatever is agreeable in the face.

Our principle will apply with equal force to the motions of the face as to the permanent form. Human sentiments prevailing in the expression of a face, will always make it agreeable or lovely. Expression is even of more consequence than shape : it will light up features otherwise heavy ; it will make us forget all but the quality of the mind. As the natural tones of the voice are understood and felt by all, so it is with the movements of the countenance : on these we are continually intent, and the mind is ever insensibly exercised.

Whether the views which I have here advocated were ever announced by the ancients I know not. But I think it is abundantly evident that their artists acted upon them. They went beyond mere imitation. They advanced to a higher study, that of combining excellencies ; selecting what was indicative of the higher and purer qualities, impassioned thought, and this they exaggerated. Their divinities were of human mould ; but still, as not visibly present, they were creations of their imagination.*

---

* In high art it appears to have been the rule of the sculptor to divest the form of expression. In the Apollo, there is such a stillness of features,

The explanation which I offer differs from what is commonly given by writers on art. They call the "ideal head" that which does not represent individual beauty, but collective beauties, a selection and adaptation of beautiful parts taken from a variety of individuals, and combined in one representation.* I place the superiority of the antique on higher ground, on the more extended study of nature, of brutes as well as of man.

That the true animal character was fully understood by the ancient artists there is sufficient proof. Is there any thing finer than the wolf of the Capitol, or the antique boar, or the dogs in the entrance of the Florentine Gallery, or the horses of the Elgin marbles? It was this study of pure nature that enabled them to undertake such compositions of surprising beauty, as we see in their Fauns,

that every one follows his fancy, and thinks he sees in the statue what is really in his own mind. In the Venus, the form is exquisite and the face perfect, but there is no expression there : it has no human softness, nothing to love. Mrs. —— saw a young gentleman, she thinks an American, kissing the tips of his fingers to the statue, as he left the Tribune (the apartment dedicated to the goddess), but for this the statue gives no licence ; it would not have been unbecoming had he so saluted the Melpomene, for there we see the loveliness which lurks in expression. The authoress of an agreeable work on Rome is disturbed because "she has seen women, real living women, almost as beautiful as the Venus, and far more interesting." We should find more of her way of thinking, if all would confess their first impressions. This, however, cannot detract from the perfection of a statue, which has been admired in all times, as now. It only points to the purity of the design, the high aim of the artist, and its successful execution. Had the Helen of Zeuxis been preserved, I can imagine that it would have been of a more feminine and seducing beauty than the Venus. But we must bear in mind that which I have taken notice of in the text, that all individuality was studiously avoided by the ancient sculptors, in the representation of divinity ; they maintained the beauty of form and proportion, but without expression, which, in their system, belonged exclusively to humanity.

* "Nous dirons donc, que la combinaison des parties peut former un tout, est ce qu'on appelle l'idéal."—WINCKELMAN.

Satyrs, Centaurs, and masks, where the peculiarities of brutes are engrafted on the human form. And it may be remarked that they did not merely give to their sylvan deities hair and cloven feet; they bestowed on them a certain consistency of character very difficult of execution, but necessary to reconcile the eye to the absurdity; a goatish expression of countenance, or a merry festive air, all in conformity with the hair and the hoofs, their embrowned skin, and the savage wildness of their life.*

What, then, was more natural or obvious, in studying the effect of these forms and characters when transferred to the human countenance, than that the artist should perceive that the proportions which distinguish them should be avoided, or even reversed, in representing the dignified and characteristic form of man?

Winckelman would make it appear that the artists of Greece studied the forms of the lower animals for a different purpose:—to join the character of the brute with that of man, in order to embellish him, and to bestow on him new and preternatural properties. And he refers to the heads of Jupiter and of Hercules as instances. "In the former," he says, "we may discover the great eyes, and imposing front, and the mane of the lion; and in the latter, the head and neck of the bull."

I must entertain doubts of this theory, and of the effect

---

* The difficulty of giving these combinations of the human and brute character, is shown in the attempts of modern artists to imitate the ancients in their representations of Fauns and sylvan boys. They do not seem to know how to knit their joints, and their faces are too sober and wise.
> ————"faber imus et ungues
> Exprimet, et molles imitabitur ære capillos,
> Infelix operis summa, quia ponere totum
> Nesciet."

of the excessive exaggeration;—in the head of Jupiter I have not felt its influence. But, if the theory be true, it goes to establish the fact, that the artists studied the form of brutes in comparison with that of man; and I hold it to be an inevitable consequence of such a comparison, that they should discover that the perfection of the human form was to be attained, by avoiding what was characteristic of the inferior animals, and increasing the proportions of those features which belong to man.

I shall not deny ingenuity to the theory of Hogarth, or usefulness to that proposed by Sir Joshua Reynolds. But there is danger to the modern artist, if he is led to conceive that he can bestow beauty by following some fancied curve or gradation of outline. Sir Joshua held that beauty is the medium, or centre, of the various forms of individuals: that every species of animal has a fixed and determinate form, towards which nature is continually inclining, like lines terminating in a centre, or pendulums vibrating in different directions over a single point: as all these lines cut the centre, while only one passes through any other point, so he conceived that perfect beauty is oftener produced than any one kind of deformity. This ingenious idea is well suited to the portrait-painter, who will not be a favourite unless he knows how to soften the features and preserve the likeness. But there is this fatal objection to it; that, as in the antique the artists deviated from nature, the pendulum would never reach the centre.

It is happy for philosophy, science, history, poetry, and eloquence, that the Greeks were a superior people, and happy for our subject that they were an eminently beautiful people. The artists of Greece certainly did not follow a vague line of beauty. They rather imitated some acknowledged beautiful form of age or sex. They even combined the beauty of both sexes, as in the young Bacchus, or more decidedly in the Hermaphrodite.

With them, the highest effort of art was to represent man deified; as it were, purified from the grosser characters of nature. This they did, as we have already seen, by exaggerating whatever is proper to the human form: by increasing what gives dignity, and bestowing features capable of and prone to the expression of the finer emotions; representing them, either as still and imperturbed, or as indicating a superiority to the things of this lower world.

In painting, the representation of the Deity is always a distressing failure. If to represent Him who "became man," and "dwelt among us," be the highest effort of art, how is the Creator to be represented? Michael Angelo painted the Deity boldly, and with the expression of the indignant wrath of man. Raphael represents the Creator plunging into chaos* and separating the elements. But on viewing these paintings, we are brought to feel the insufficiency of the art, and to think of the artist to the exclusion of all sublime contemplations which the subject should inspire. Yet it is foolish to call such attempts impiety, since no other idea is presented than that which is inculcated from our infancy. Our expressions in words are at variance with our just conception of Divine Intelligence, and our tongue as imperfect as the pencil of the painter. The one solitary expression in the Scriptures descriptive of the person of God, is studiously obscure, and the accompaniments of His presence, not the countenance of the Almighty, are described.

* In the Gallery of Raphael, in the Vatican.

The sentiments of Plato, Cicero, and Seneca, are brought to bear on this subject of beauty and ideal perfection. Yet it is fortunate that we have the works of the ancient sculptors before us, to preserve us from the influence of vague theories. Cicero has given us his conception of a perfect orator. "And such an ideal person," he says, "may be the object of imitation; but those who imitate can only approach the model according to the talents which nature has given them. No man can possess all the qualities, or attain to the whole perfection of the model; he must in some one respect be deficient. His knowledge and capacity of research, his acquaintance with human character, his insinuating or commanding language, or his eloquent appeal to the heart, his countenance and expression, his voice, manner, gesture, cannot be all equally balanced so as to constitute the perfect orator." And he illustrates his position by the example of Phidias, who, when he made the statue of Jupiter and Minerva, took no individual for his model, but had an idea of perfection in his own mind.*

Here I conceive is the source and the authority for all

* In the following quotation, Brutus has asked Cicero what constitutes excellence in oratory. He answers, that no man has been perfect ; that there is an ideal perfection which we should attempt to attain, nor resign the effort because to accomplish all is impossible ; just as there is nothing beautiful which may not in imagination be surpassed :—

" Sed ego sic statuo, nihil esse in ullo genere tam pulchrum, quo non pulchrius id sit, unde illud, ut ex ore aliquo, quasi imago, exprimatur, quod neque oculis, neque auribus, neque ullo sensu percipi potest ; cogitatione tantum et mente complectimur. Itaque et Phidiae simulacris, quibus nihil in illo genere perfectius videmus, et his picturis, quas nominavi, cogitare tamen possumus pulchriora. Nec vero ille artifex, cum faceret Jovis formam, aut Minervae, contemplabatur aliquem, e quo similitudinem duceret : sed ipsius in mente insidebat species pulchritudinis eximia-

K

which has been written on this view of the subject. The
great artist had formed a conception of beauty : the
question perpetually returns, By what studies, by what
theory, had he attained this ? The perplexity appears to
me to proceed from a distinction being made between
the pleasures of the mind, and those addressed to the
senses. Plautus says that the poet seeks what nowhere
exists, and yet finds it. His genius supplies it, it is in
his mind.

The novelist who has genius to catch and to represent
the feelings of men, and their motives to action, may give
a truer picture of his period than the historian, even
although he describes what never existed. That is to
say, the incidents, the passions, the prejudices, which he
describes, may never have been combined as he combines
them ; but they are true to nature, and to the state of
society in which he lives, and are, therefore, a record of
the time. But this is not the rationale of the ideal in
painting.

Or we may illustrate this in another manner. When
Zeuxis was employed on his Helen, five of the most
beautiful women were before him, from whom he composed his perfect beauty. But it was not the object of
the artist here to produce ideal beauty, or to give that
repose of sentiment which is the effect of contemplating
the Medicean Venus ; his aim was to represent a beautiful
and seductive woman, whose charms were to lead men to

quædam, quam intuens, in eaque defixus, ad illius similitudinem artem et
manum dirigebat.   Ut igitur in formis et figuris est aliquid perfectum et
excellens, cujus ad cogitatam speciem imitando referuntur ea quæ sub
oculis ipsa cadunt : sic perfectæ eloquentiæ speciem animo videmus,
effigiem auribus quærimus."—CICERO *de Oratore*, cap. 2.

extravagance. And why have not painters with the same means attained to the same perfection? It has been answered, Because they have not had the same genius. On which M. Quatremere De Quincy observes, "What, then, is a model, if genius be still necessary in order to imitate it? Who shall tell whether it is the model that causes genius to see the image of beauty; or, genius that sees its own idea in the model?" *

There has been another theory advanced, that, in the antique statue there is presented to us the grandeur of form and the proportions of man, as he originally proceeded from the Creator: such as he was designed to be before he was subjected to labour, poverty, and sickness.

But in the early times of all people, their gods have been represented by the trunks of trees, or pillars rudely carved; and, when improved, it has been by imitating the human form with simplicity. At first, the head was carved as on a pedestal; then the neck, breast, and shoulders, and the indication of sex; then the arms and the extremities were imperfectly blocked out, until, at length, and after ages had passed, the members were displayed free, and the figure perfected in manly beauty.

I shall once more endeavour to analyse that process

---

* The same author thus expresses himself: " In this we have the enigma of Plautus solved; in every art, whatever comes within the scope of the understanding, of sentiment, and of genius, does not really exist anywhere; has neither substance nor place, and is subjected to no one of the senses, while he who finds it is unable to point out where he has seen the model of it."

This is language which puffs up the young artist to inordinate conceit; and, instead of studying, sets him a dreaming of something for which he is to be beholden to his innate genius.

of thought by which, out of the contemplation of nature, ideal perfection is derived. The idea of the divine form in the mind of any man, whatever may be his genius, has been acquired, and is of human origin; and the attempts of all painters and sculptors to embody the idea in their works, evince that such is the case. That a man of genius has an idea of perfection cannot be the result of pure imagination. Whatever conceptions he may entertain must have been acquired; and the question returns, How ? Let us suppose a painter to have before him the . three Graces; their perfections are not the same; for to have full influence on the heart, we know that, however beautiful, each must be individual; that the form, the attitude, and the expression must be varied, or the interest and grace are injured. The attempt of the painter to combine what is beautiful in each, into one more perfect, would, in my opinion, fail; nature would be lost, and the whole prove inconsistent. At all events, the combination of individual human beauty, however made, and with whatever exercise of genius contrived, would not produce what is aimed at,—ideal beauty, as exhibited in the remains of antiquity; a form which we acknowledge to be beautiful, but which has had no existence in life or in models.

With the view of attaining beauty, the artist is not to slight nature or to avoid it, but to study it deeply, as the only source of improvement. He must not only contemplate those beauties which we may suppose to stand before him, but consider where they differ from others less admirable. How beautiful that smile ! How eloquent those lips! Let him ask himself in what this consists. Smiling and speech are characteristic of man, and are bestowed to express the affections of the heart, and communicate thought. Give to the mouth the capacity for these. Observe the forehead, and the defined eyebrow :—What is there in nature superior? Let him mark them, and then raise and throw forward the forehead, a feature especially human, and elevating to the countenance. Now he sees that depth is given to the eye; that the shadows fall with bold relief, the eyebrow acquires more freedom, stands in a finer arch, and is more expressive of agreeable emotions. And thus he passes from point to point; from one feature to another,—the nose, the ear: exaggerating a little the outline of whatever indicates the higher and purer qualities, and avoiding what is low, or whatever is associated with the baser human passions or with the form of the brutes; and by insensible gradations, and long contemplation of what is highest and best, he acquires, and from nature, that idea which is, in his mind, the perfection of form.

Supposing that a painter so tutored is set with his fellows to copy a model; by his knowledge of what constitutes humanity in its most perfect condition, and of what is indicative of human sentiment, he is enabled to elevate his design ; and then it is acknowledged that, whilst he has preserved the likeness, he has refined it, and has introduced something of the purity of the antique.

Although I have taken the form of the head and the features for illustration, the principle is applicable to the whole figure. In comparing the finer forms of antique statues with those of the Athletæ, Lapithæ, and Fauns,

down to the brutes, we see that the grace, the repose, and
the nobler attitudes of the human body, are preserved in
the former, to the exclusion of whatever belongs to individual character, or partakes by association of what is mean
in condition.

The Satyr and Faun are as mules and hybrids; the
man and the brute are joined; sometimes with the horns
and the hoofs, sometimes with nothing more distinctive
than the tail; and the conception is fulfilled by the gross-
ness of form, the muscular development, and the proportions indicative of activity. But there is neither freedom
nor grace of movement in the position of the body or
limbs, nor in their proportions or contour. In short, we
have the Apollo and Marsyas exhibiting a perfect contrast,
and showing that which is characteristic in the one reversed
in the other.

71

NATIONAL PECULIARITIES IN THE FORM OF THE HEAD.

Sir David Wilkie, whose loss we have had so lately to deplore, was one of my earliest pupils, having attended a course of my lectures on anatomy, as connected with design. On returning from the Continent in August, 1840, I found him preparing for a journey; and he made me guess whither he was going. To Rome?—no. To Greece?—no. Surely not to court fortune in India?—no. He was setting off to the Holy Land, to study there an Eastern people. In this, he displayed that energy which ever accompanies genius. How much of character, in feature and costume, would he not have thrown into his future pictures! Here we have a lesson from one entitled to sway our opinion on his art, of the importance of a knowledge of national forms to the historical painter. It is for this reason that I introduce a slight account of the varieties of the human head, depending on national peculiarities. It may assist the artist in the study of such natives of foreign countries as he may chance to meet with.

Even in the most admired productions of art, I find little to which I can refer for elucidating this subject. Sculptors and painters have been too commonly content to characterize an inhabitant of the East by a tuft of hair on his crown; or an African, by a swarthy face. There is a late publication that illustrates the question of national peculiarities in a very interesting way,—a folio volume which contains accurate portraits of the skulls of all the American races, from the old inhabitants of Mexico and Peru to those of the farthest north.[*]

[*] "Crania Americana," by Dr. Morton, Professor of Anatomy in Pennsylvania College.

In considering the extraordinary collection of skulls in this work, with the view of marking the relation between the form of the head and superiority of mind, in men of cultivated intellect, as contrasted with those leading a savage life, it must be acknowledged that much is wanting. Although there can be no.objection to the mode adopted by the writer of estimating the actual mass of brain; yet his measurements ought to have been made in reference to the dimensions of the whole body. The size of the cranium, and consequently, the volume of the brain, must be relative to the face; and the face can be taken only as an imperfect index of the entire skeleton. If the cavity of the skull is to be gauged,—if the quantity of sand or of seeds, which different crania are capable of containing, is to be measured, the comparison will not be satisfactory, unless the measurement of each be contrasted with that of the face and of the body; and be also examined with respect to the proportions of the brain itself, or its form.

Again, it is taken for granted, that we who exercise our best faculties within the four walls of a house, must have a development of brain beyond what the free-dweller in the plains or forests of, what is termed, a new country can possess. I believe, on the contrary, that man, in his state of nature, has imposed upon him the necessity of bringing into operation quite as many faculties of mind as the man at his desk; and that, from the brain being exercised in every use to which the external senses are put, its volume is not inferior to that of the individual in civilised life. We must take along with us this consideration, that the exercise of our external senses infers an accompanying activity of the brain : that of the nervous apparatus appropriated to the senses, it is the exterior part alone that is given to the eye, ear, nose, tongue : the internal part, forming the sensorium, is in the brain. Remembering this, and that the powers exercised by the savage are not instincts, as in the brutes, but operations of the mind calling the brain into action, I am unwilling to grant that any measurable deficiency in its mass, as a whole, is likely to be perceived. Were it really so, we should find the gamekeeper inferior to his master in a greater degree than my experience warrants.

Every one must have observed among those with whom he lives, that there is as much variety in feature, stature, colour, hair, beard, &c. as there is in expression of countenance : and a very little philosophy will indicate the necessity of such varieties, for the constitution of society. But in regard to national peculiarities, although the distinctions between individuals of a particular country are, doubtless, in many instances as great as between the people of one country compared with another ; yet there are certain forms of head, or casts of feature, or peculiarities of hair, and complexion, which characterise different nations.

We need not here enter into the question, how these distinctions have been produced. It would require much critical examination to decide whether national peculiarities of form are owing to an original provision, by which the structure changes, and acquires distinctive characters under the influence of circumstances—such as of the various climates to which the first families were exposed, on their dispersion from one centre ; or whether there are truly distinct races which had a conformation and constitution from the beginning, suited to the regions for which they were destined, and to which they were blindly driven.

L

All testimony agrees in shewing that mankind was first planted in Western Asia; there, in the valleys, perpetual summer reigns; there the vegetable productions best suited to man's nourishment are most abundant: there are the animals, in a state of nature, which are led by their instincts to yield themselves up to his use—the horse, the ass, the cow, the sheep, the goat, the camel, the dog; and there the climate is so favourable to the human constitution, that even now we look to these countries for examples of perfection, both in feature and colour, of man himself.

From this part of the globe, the varieties of man distinguished as to exterior form and complexion, may be traced divergingly: to this point the sciences and arts may be followed back; and the study of the derivation of tongues, and of the grammatical construction of languages, does not negative the conclusion, but rather indicates that this part of the earth was the centre from which the nations spread.

The grouping of mankind into races has occupied the ingenuity of many naturalists and physiologists, from the time of Buffon and Linnæus to the present day; but we rest principally on the authority of Blumenbach. In the valleys of the Caucasus, between the Black Sea and the Caspian, we may distinguish, in the Caucasian family, those features which, according to the views just presented, we should say were the nearest to perfection. The skull is large and fully developed in front; the face is small, and the features well proportioned; the forehead is elevated; the nose arched, or raised; the teeth perpendicular in their sockets; the chin round, and the lips full of expression; the skin fair; the eyes dark; the eyebrows arched; the eyelashes long; and the hair varied in colour. The Circassians have long been noted for the beauty of the women, and for the imposing stature, elegance, and activity of the men; and the Georgians and other tribes are remarkable for personal beauty.

From this centre, proceeding westward, we recognise the Europeans. The original inhabitants of Thessaly and Greece are designated as the Pelasgic branch: that enterprising and migratory people, who at an early period extended to Italy, and from whom descended the Etruscans. The Hellenes, or Greeks, receiving letters from the Phœnicians, surpassed all the nations of antiquity, in philosophy, literature, and art. The Greek face is a fine oval; the forehead full, and carried forward; the eyes large; the nose straight; the lips and chin finely formed: in short, the forms of the head and face have been the type of the antique, and of all which we most admire. The modern Greeks are still distinguished by athletic proportions and fine features.

The Roman head differs from the Greek, in having a more arched forehead, a nose more aquiline, and features altogether of a more decided character; and this is even apparent in the busts of that people, as exhibited in the two splendid volumes of Visconti. The remarks of Bishop Wiseman on this subject are important, as his lectures were delivered in Rome, and to persons who had only to step out of the college to ascertain their accuracy. Travellers have often stated that the countenances of the population beyond the Tiber exactly resemble those of the Roman soldiers on the column of Trajan; but Dr. Wiseman observes correctly, that any one slightly acquainted with art, will soon be satisfied that the model on these historical monuments is really Grecian, and can give no aid in ascertaining the physiognomy of the ancient inhabitants of Italy. He bids us look to the busts, and reclining statues of the ancient Romans carved on the sarcophagi, or to the series of imperial busts in the Capitol, where we shall discover the true type of the national figure, viz. a large flat head, a low and wide forehead, a face broad and square, a short and thick neck, and a stout and broad trunk : proportions totally at variance with what are generally considered to be those of the ancient Roman. Nor have we to go far, if in Rome, to find their descendants ; they are to be met with every day in the streets, principally among the burgesses or middle class.*

The German race has been spread, from east to west, over a great part of Europe, blending with the Celts. It is separated into the Teutonic and Sclavonian families; their military enterprises form the history of the darker ages, when they came down upon the Roman empire. Other hordes mingled with the Tartars ; and are recognised in history, as the people who broke in upon the Persian and the Roman empires in the east. The Celtic Gaul of the Romans gave residence

---

* " For my part, I looked for the type of the Roman soldier among the Galleotti. There was a body of these condemned men chained together, who were marched every evening from their work of rebuilding the great basilica of St. Paul's, beyond the walls. This church, which was burnt, stands some way out of Rome, and I walked beside and behind these bands ; and finer figures are not to be conceived ; their loose dress, and the gyves upon their legs, gave to their air and attitude something formidable. They seemed fit for the offices of a tyrant, and to subdue the world. I must ever remember one evening, when I saw these men, with their mounted guards, passing under the Arch of Titus, and the broad shadow of the Colosseum. Dr. Wiseman says, in regard to the sculptures on that arch, that the profiles of the soldiers shew that there was a rule, or model, adapted to the common men, and from which the artist might not depart ; while the figure of the emperor, seated in his chariot, forms a strong contrast to them. Though his features are now quite effaced, enough remains of the outline to shew the full heavy face, and bulky head of a true Roman."—*Notes from Journal.*

to a race, which is now diminished to the remnant living in the mountainous districts of the extreme west of Europe.

The Mongolian Tartars occupy great part of the north of Asia and Europe. The eyelids of this people are oblique, the nose is small and flat, broad towards the forehead ; the cheek-bones are high, the chin short, and the lips large and thick ; the ears are flat and square ; the general form of the head round. The Mongol Tartar tribes have become mixed with the neighbouring nations, and exhibit a variety of physiognomy. Hordes of this people invaded China, and settling in the north of that great empire have blended with the original Chinese.

To the north-west, they mingled with the polar races, and have merged in the Kamschatkans and Tungusians ; the Huns, whose incursions into more civilised Europe are recorded in history, were Mongol Tartars. The primitive Turks were also of the same race ; but, by overrunning Circassia, Georgia, Greece, and Arabia, their physical character has been changed, and they have become a handsome people. The open nostril and short nose, which mark the Turkish countenance, still betray their original extraction ; their eyes are dark and animated, and the whole face is expressive and intelligent.

The Chinese skull is oblong, the frontal bone narrow in proportion to the width of the bones of the face. Accordingly the countenance is flat, and the cheeks expanded ; the eyelids are not freely open, and are drawn obliquely up towards the temples ; the eyebrows are black and highly arched ; the nose is small and flattened, with a marked depression separating it from the forehead ; the hair is black, and the complexion sallow.

The Malay race is scattered through the Indian Islands, Sumatra, Java, Borneo, Amboyna, Celebes, the Philippines, Moluccas. The forehead, in the Malay, is prominent and arched, but low; the orbits oblique and oblong; the nasal bones broad and flattened; the cheek-bones high and expanded; the jaws projecting. The head is, altogether, large; the mouth and the lips protrude; the nose is short, depressed, and flattened towards the nostrils; the eyes are small and oblique. They are of a brown complexion, varying in the different tribes.

Some uncertainty prevails as to the race to which the ancient Egyptians belonged. This has arisen from the difficulty of reconciling the early and extensive knowledge of that people, with the acknowledged deficiency of capacity in the Negro. We might expect that the mummies and drawings in their pyramids and tombs should have long since decided the question; but the position of Egypt may account for the obscurity. Being on the confines of two great continents, the Egyptians became early a mixed people. The skull is found to be well formed, and unlike that of the Ethiopian. The probability is, that the Negro was then, as now, a subjugated race.*

The Greek applied the terms Ethiop and Indian to all the dark people of the south. By Ethiopian, we now correctly understand the different races which inhabit the interior of Africa; extending from the south of Mount Atlas and Abyssinia to the country of the Caffres and Hottentots.

---

* Blumenbach thinks that he can discover among the mummies the heads of the Ethiopian, the Indian, and the Besbers. Denon conceives that the female mummies indicate that the women of ancient Egypt had great beauty.

The general character of the Negro countenance is familiar to us. Of the great antiquity of the race there can be no doubt. When, indeed, the effigy of the Negro is found depicted on the ancient walls of Egypt, and vessels are dug up, the characters on which are read by modern Chinese, we may well despair of obtaining any thing like a satisfactory history of the spread of nations, and the settlement of mankind in the different regions of the globe. The depression of the forehead and compression of the temples, which are distinctive of the Africans, although there be splendid examples of fine form among the nations of that continent, mark them as a degraded race.*

Diverging still from the presumed central origin of mankind, we find the Polynesian family in the islands of the Pacific Ocean. The inhabitants of these isles are of middle stature, athletic, with heavy limbs. Their faces are round or delicately oval; the nose is well formed, straight or aquiline, sometimes spread out, but not having the flatness of the Negro; the forehead is low, but not receding; the eyes black, bright, and expressive; the lips full, and the teeth fine.†

* The great families of mankind are distinguished by colour as well as form and features. The Caucasian by white; the African by black; the Mongolian by olive, tending to yellow; the Malay by tawny; the American by brown, or nearly copper hue. The colour of the hair, and that of the iris partake of the colour of the skin. The Caucasian, with fair complexion, has red, brown, or light-coloured hair, and the eyes of different shades of grey and blue. In those of darker complexion, the hair is black and the eyes dark. In the Mongol, the hair is thin, stiff, and straight. In the European, soft, flexible, and flowing. In the Negro, thick-set, strong, short, and curly. But in all races there spring up occasional varieties.

† It is amusing to find voyagers making distinctions here between the

In America, the same difficulties present themselves in relation to the origin and propagation of races as in the Old World. The most recent inquiries authorise the distinction of two families inhabiting America; first, a race called Toltecan, belonging originally to Mexico and Peru, which, from the shapes of the skulls found in the graves, and the accompanying relics, give evidence of greater civilisation than belongs to the present natives; and secondly, a people which extending over the greater portion of the vast continent, embraces all the barbarous nations of the New World, excepting the polar tribes, or Mongolian Americans, which are presumed to be straggling parties from Asia, such as the Esquimaux, Greenlanders, and Fins.

In the native American, there is no trace of the frizzled locks of the Polynesian or the woolly texture on the head of the Negro. The hair is long, lank, and black; the beard is deficient; the cheek-bones are large and prominent; the lower jaw broad and ponderous, truncated in front; the teeth vertical and very large; the nose is decidedly arched, and the nasal cavities of great size. They ought not to be called the copper-coloured race. The colour is brown, or of a cinnamon tint. As in the Old World, the colour varies, and the darkness does not always correspond to the climate or vicinity to the equator.

Of the imperfect sketch of the varieties of mankind which I have here presented, every sentence might be the text of a long essay. But in this, as in the whole volume, I have

plebeian and the aristocratic classes. But so it is every where. Among the Lybians and Moors, as in the countries of Asia and Europe, the comforts and luxuries of life improve the physical condition of man.

attempted only to awaken attention, and to make the reader
an observer of what may pass before him; giving him the
elements on which his ingenuity or acumen is to be
employed in his intercourse with society.

ESSAY III.

ON THOSE SOURCES OF EXPRESSION IN THE HUMAN COUNTE-
NANCE WHICH CANNOT BE EXPLAINED ON THE IDEA OF
A DIRECT INFLUENCE OF THE MIND UPON THE FEATURES.

> "The heart of a man changeth his countenance, whether for
> good or evil."—THE SON OF SIRACH.
>
> "I do believe thee;
> I saw his heart in his face."—SHAKSPEARE.

IN the human countenance, under the influence of passion,
there are characters expressed, and changes of features
produced, which it is impossible to explain on the notion of a
direct operation of the mind upon the features. Ignorance of
the source of these changes of the features, or inattention to
the cause which produces them, has thrown an obscurity over
the whole of this subject, which it is my wish to remove.

If, in the examination of the sources of expression, it should
be found that the mind is dependent on the frame of the
body, the discovery ought not to be considered as humiliating,
or as affecting the belief of a separate existence of that part
of our nature on which the changes wrought in the body are
ultimately impressed. Since we are dwellers in a material
world it is necessary that the spirit should be connected with
it by an organised body, without which it could neither feel

nor re-act, nor manifest itself in any way. It is a fundamental law of our nature that the mind shall have its powers developed through the influence of the body; that the organs of the body shall be the links in the chain of relation between it and the material world, through which the immaterial principle within shall be affected.

As the Creator has established this connexion between the mind and external nature, so has He implanted, or caused to be generated, in us, various higher intellectual faculties. In every intelligent being He has laid the foundation of emotions that point to Him, affections by which we are drawn to Him, and which rest in Him as their object. In the mind of the rudest slave, left to the education of the mere elements around him, sentiments arise which lead him to a Parent and a Creator. These feelings spring up spontaneously; they are universal, and not to be shaken off; and no better example than this can be given of the adaptation of the mind to the various relations in which man is placed, or one that tends more to raise in us a conception of the Author of our being, and increase our estimation of ourselves, as allied to Him.

This it is, perhaps, necessary to premise, when I am about to prove the extensive influence of the corporeal on the intellectual part of man.

In examining the phenomena of the mind, philosophers have too much overlooked this relation between the mental operations and the condition of the bodily frame. It appears to me that the frame of the body, exclusive of the special organs of seeing, hearing, &c. is a complex organ, I shall not say of sense, but which ministers, like the external senses, to the mind; that is to say, as the organs of the five senses serve

to furnish ideas of matter, the framework of the body contributes, in certain conditions, to develope various states of
the mind.*

In the affections which we call passions or emotions, there
is an influence which points to the breast as the part where
they are felt. Some have asserted that they are seated in
the bowels; and the sensations I am about to describe have
been arrayed as proofs that the affections exist in the body.
But that, I affirm, is impossible. They are conditions of the
mind, and cannot be seated in the body, although they both
influence and are influenced by it.

We have learned enough to know that the impressions
communicated by the external organs of sense belong really
to the mind; and there can be no doubt that there is a mutual
influence exercised by the mind and frame on each other.
This is not asserted on the mere grounds that each affection
which is deeply felt, is accompanied by a disturbance in our
breast; nor on the language of mankind, which gives universal
assent to this proposition; but it may be proved by circumstances of expression, in which we cannot be deceived. I
shall make it manifest that what the eye, the ear, or the finger,
is to the mind, as exciting those ideas which have been appointed to correspond with the qualities of the material world,
the organs of the breast are to the developement of our affections; and that without them we might see, hear, and smell,
but we should walk the earth coldly indifferent to all emotions
which may be said in an especial manner to animate us, and
give interest and grace to human thoughts and actions.

By emotions are meant certain changes or affections of the

---

* But since the brain doth lodge the powers of sense,
How makes it in the heart, those passions spring?—DAVIES.

mind, as grief, joy, astonishment. That such states or conditions of the mind should in any degree pertain to the body, may not, perhaps, be willingly admitted, unless we take along with us that the ideas of sense, as light, sound, or taste, are generated by the organs of the senses, and not by any thing received and conveyed by them to the sensorium. It is ascertained that the different organs of the senses can be exercised, and give rise to sensation and perception, when there is no corresponding outward impression; and the ideas thus excited are according to the organ struck or agitated : that is, the same impression conveyed to different organs of sense will give rise to a variety of sensations; as light, when the eye is struck ; sound, when the ear is struck ; and so on with the other organs ; the sensation corresponding with the organ which is exercised, and not with the cause of the impression. A needle passed through the retina, the organ of vision, will produce the sensation of a spark of fire, not of sharpness, or pain ; and the same needle, if applied to the papillæ of the tongue, will give rise to the sense of taste ; while if it prick the skin, pain will follow. This law of the senses is arbitrarily or divinely ordered ; it might have been otherwise. Accordingly, when we observe that the organs of the senses operate in producing specific ideas, independently of their own peculiar exciting causes, we can comprehend better how other organs of the body may have a relation established with the mind, and a control over it, without reference to outward impressions.

Let us consider the heart, in its office of receiving the influence of the mind, and of reflecting that influence.

It may, in the first place, be observed, that there is hardly an organ of the body limited to one function ; all are complex in their operation. How many offices, for example, are performed by the lungs? It is a singular fact in the history of physiological opinions, that the heart, an organ the most susceptible of being excited by the agitations or derangements of the body, should have been considered at one time as insensible. And yet in one sense it is true that it is so. To actual touch the heart is insensible, as was exhibited to the illustrious Harvey, in the person of a young nobleman, who had the heart exposed by disease. This single circumstance, had there been no other evidence, should have earlier directed physiologists to a correct view of the matter; from its proving that the internal organs are affected and united by sensibilities which are altogether different in kind from those bestowed upon the skin. The sensibility of the external surface of the body is a special endowment adapted to the elements around and calculated to protect the interior parts from injury. But though the heart has not this common sense of touch, yet it has an appropriate sensibility, by which it is held united in the closest connexion and sympathy with the other vital organs; so that it participates in all the changes of the general system of the body.

But connected with the heart, and depending on its peculiar and excessive sensibility, there is an extensive apparatus which demands our attention. This is the organ of breathing: a part known obviously as the instrument of speech; but which I shall show to be more. The organ of breathing, in its association with the heart, is the instrument of expression, and is the part of the frame, by the action of which the emotions are developed and made visible to us. Certain strong feelings of the mind produce a disturbed condition of the heart; and through that corporeal influence, directly from the heart, indirectly from the mind, the extensive apparatus constituting the organ of breathing is put in motion and gives us the outward signs which we call expression. The man was wrong who found fault with nature for not placing a window before the heart, in order to render visible human thoughts and intentions. There is, in truth, provision made in the countenance and outward bearing for such discoveries.

One, ignorant of the grounds on which these opinions are founded, has said, "Every strong emotion is directed towards the heart : the heart experiences various kinds of sensation, pleasant or unpleasant, over which it has no control; and from thence the agitated spirits are diffused over the body." The fact is certainly so, although the language be figurative. How are these spirits diffused, and what are their effects ?

We find that the influence of the heart upon the extended organ of respiration has sway at so early a period of our existence, that we must acknowledge that the operation or play of the instrument of expression precedes the mental emotions with which they are to be joined, accompanies them in their first dawn, strengthens them, and directs them. So that it is not, perhaps, too much to conclude that, from these organs moving in sympathy with the mind, the same uniformity is produced among men, in their internal feelings, emotions, or passions, as there exists in their ideas of external nature from the uniform operations of the organs of sense.

Let us place examples before us, and then try whether the received doctrines of the passions will furnish us with an explanation of the phenomena, or whether we must go deeper, and seek the assistance of anatomy.

In the expression of the passions, there is a compound influence in operation. Let us contemplate the appearance

of terror.   We can readily conceive why a man stands with
eyes intently fixed on the object of his fears, the eyebrows
elevated to the utmost, and the eye largely uncovered; or
why, with hesitating and bewildered steps, his eyes are
rapidly and wildly in search of something.   In this, we only
perceive the intent application of his mind to the object of
his apprehensions—its direct influence on the outward organ.
But observe him further : there is a spasm on his breast, he
cannot breathe freely, the chest is elevated, the muscles of
his neck and shoulders are in action, his breathing is short
and rapid, there is a gasping and a convulsive motion of his
lips, a tremor on his hollow cheek, a gulping and catching of
his throat; and why does his heart knock at his ribs, while
yet there is no force of circulation ?—for his lips and cheeks
are ashy pale.

So in grief, if we attend to the same class of phenomena,
we shall be able to draw an exact picture.   Let us imagine
to ourselves the overwhelming influence of grief on woman.
The object in her mind has absorbed all the powers of the
frame, the body is no more regarded, the spirits have left it,
it reclines, and the limbs gravitate ; they are nerveless and
relaxed, and she scarcely breathes ; but why comes at
intervals the long-drawn sigh ?—why are the neck and
throat convulsed ?—what causes the swelling and quivering
of the lips, and the deadly paleness of the face ?—or why is
the hand so pale and earthly cold ?—and why, at intervals,
as the agony returns, does the convulsion spread over the
frame like a paroxysm of suffocation ?

It must, I think, be acknowledged, when we come to
arrange these phenomena, these outward signs of the passions,
that they cannot proceed from the direct influence of the

mind alone. However strange it may sound to unaccustomed ears, it is to the heart and lungs, and all the extended instrument of breathing, that we are to trace these effects.

Over such motions of the body the mind has an unequal control. By a strong effort the outward tokens may be restrained, at least in regard to the general bearing of the body; but who, while suffering, can retain the natural fulness of his features, or the healthful colour of his cheek, the unembarrassed respiration and clearness of the natural voice ? The villain may command his voice, and mask his purpose with light and libertine words, or carry an habitual sneer of contempt of all softer passions ; but his unnatural paleness, and the sinking of his features, will betray that he suffers. Clarence says to his murderers,

> "How deadly dost thou speak !
> Your eyes do menace me : Why look you pale ?" *

But the just feelings of mankind demand respect; men will not have the violence of grief obtruded on them. To preserve the dignity of his character, the actor must permit those uncontrollable signs of suffering alone to escape, which betray how much he feels, and how much he restrains.

Even while asleep, these interior organs of feeling will prevail, and disclose the source of expression. Has my reader seen Mrs. Siddons in Queen Katharine during that solemn scene where the sad note was played which she named her knell ? Who taught the crowd sitting at a play, an audience differing in age, habits, and education, to believe those quivering motions, and that gentle smile,

---

* And troubled blood through his pale face was seen
    To come and go, with tidings from his heart.—*Faëry Queen.*

N

and those slight convulsive twitchings, to be true to nature ?
To see every one hushed to the softest breathing of
sympathy with the silent expression of the actress, exhibits all mankind held together by one universal feeling :
and that feeling, excited by expression, so deeply laid
in our nature, as to have influence, without being obvious
to reason.

To illustrate this curious subject, I shall first explain the
extensive connexions which are established betwixt the great
organs that sustain life and the muscular system of the face,
neck, and chest. I shall then shew that the functions of
these organs are affected by passions of the mind. I shall
prove that this connexion subsists at the moment of birth,
and accompanies us through life ; and, finally, that from
this source are derived those obscure indications of emotion
in the countenance and general frame, which cannot be
explained on the supposition of a direct influence of the
mind on the muscles of expression.

The heart and the lungs may be safely taken as two parts
which are combined in the same function. The action of the
heart, and the motion of the lungs, are equally necessary to
the circulation of that blood which is fitted for the supply of
the body ; and the interruption of their motions threatens
life. Accordingly, these two organs are united by nerves,
and consequently by the closest sympathy ; and in all the
variations to which they are liable, they are still found to
correspond, the accelerated action of the one being directly
followed by the excitement of the other.

The motion of the lungs proceeds from a force altogether
external to them : they themselves are passive, being moved
by a very great number of muscles which lie upon the breast,

back, and neck ; that is, the exterior muscles give play to the ribs, and the lungs follow the motions of the chest. The heart and lungs, though insensible to common impression, yet being acutely alive to their proper stimulus, suffer from the slightest change of posture or exertion of the frame, and also from the changes or affections of the mind. The impression thus made on these internal organs is not visible by its effect upon them, but on the external and remote muscles, associated with them. This law exists in all mankind ; we see the consequence in those susceptible and nervous persons, whom the mere change of position, or the effort of rising, or the slightest emotion of mind, flutters and agitates. But it is when the strong are subdued by this mysterious union of soul and body, when passion tears the breast, that the most afflicting picture of human frailty is presented, and the surest proof afforded, that it is on the respiratory organs that the influence of passion falls with so powerful an expression of agony.

The next circumstance of this detail to which I beg attention, is the extent of the actions of respiration : the remoteness of the parts agitated in sympathy with the heart. The act of respiration is not limited to the trunk ; the actions of certain muscles of the windpipe, the throat, the lips, the nostrils, are necessary to expand those tubes and openings, so that the air may be admitted through them in respiration, with a freedom corresponding with the increased action of the chest. Without this, the sides of these pliant tubes would fall together, and we should be suffocated by exertion or passion. Let us consider how many muscles are combined in the simple act of breathing—how many are added in the act of coughing—how these are changed and modified in

sneezing ;—let us reflect on the various combinations of
muscles of the throat, windpipe, tongue, lips, in speaking and
singing, and we shall be able justly to estimate the extent of
the muscles which are associated with the proper or simple
act of dilating and compressing the chest.   But how much
more numerous are the changes wrought upon these muscles,
when nature employs them in the double capacity of communicating our thoughts and feelings ; not in the language of
sounds merely, but in the language of expression in the countenance also ; for certainly the one is as much their office as
the other.

The nervous system is complex in an extraordinary degree ;
but the reader may not be deterred from attempting to understand at least so much, that there is a class of nerves appropriated to respiration.   These nerves arise from the same
part of the brain ; the great central nerve descends into the
chest, to be distributed to the heart and lungs ; and the others
extend to the exterior muscles of the chest, neck, and face.
Under the influence of the central nerve, the diverging external ones become the instruments of breathing and of expres- ·
sion.   The labour of many months discloses to the anatomist
but a part of these nervous cords ; and the consideration of
the uses they serve presents the most overwhelming proof of
the excellence of design,—but a design made manifest by the
results, rather than comprehensible in its means.

Can we perfectly understand how tickling the throat should
produce a convulsion over the whole frame, in which a hundred
muscles are finely adjusted and proportioned in their actions
to expel what irritates the windpipe ? or, how tickling the
nostril should make a change in these muscles, throw some
out, and bring others into action, to the effect of sending the

air through a different tube to remove what is offensive, and all this without the act of the will.

Let us see how the machine works. Observe a man threatened with suffocation : remark the sudden and wild energy that pervades every feature; the contractions of his throat, the gasping and the spasmodic twitchings of his face, the heaving of his chest and shoulders, and how he stretches his hands, and catches like a drowning man. These are efforts made under the oppressive, intolerable sensation at his heart; and the means which nature employs, to guard and preserve the animal machine, giving to the vital organ a sensibility that irresistibly excites to the utmost exertion.

It is this painful sensation that introduces us to "this breathing world;" which guards the vital functions through life, as it draws us into existence. Pain is the agent which most effectually rouses the dormant faculties of both mind and body. While the child slumbers in the womb it does not live by breathing, it possesses an organ which performs the office of the lungs. In the birth there is a short interval, betwixt the loss of the one organ, and the substitution of the other; nor would the breath ever be drawn, or the lungs perform their function, but for this painful and irresistible *nisus*, which calls the whole corresponding muscles into action. Spasms and contractions are seen to extend over the infant's chest; the features are working, and the muscles of the face agitated, probably for the first time; at last, air is admitted into the lungs, a feeble cry is heard, the air in successive inspirations fully dilates the chest, and the child cries lustily. Now the regular respiration is established, and the animal machinery subsides into repose.

> " We came crying hither.
> Thou know'st, the first time that we smell the air

> We wawl and cry :—I will preach to thee : mark,
> When we are born, we cry, that we are come
> To this great stage of fools !"—*Lear.*

With the revolution which the whole economy has undergone, new wants are engendered, new appetites; these are
again lulled by the mother's breast.   During all this no one
sympathises with the little sufferer : the grimace with which
he enters the world excites only smiles.

> " On parent's knees, a naked new-born child,
>   Weeping thou sat'st, while all around thee smiled—
>   So live, that sinking in thy last long sleep
>   Calm thou may'st smile, when all around thee weep."
>
> *From the Persian.*

"Anger," says Lord Bacon, " is certainly a kind of baseness,
as it appears well in the weakness of those subjects in whom
it reigns—children, women, old folks, sick folks."   But this I
may say, that anger is at no period of life so strongly impressed upon human features, as in the first moment of our
visiting the light.   At the instant of our birth, an association
of muscles is formed, and at the same time put in operation,
stamping a character of expression which betrays the wants
of the body in early infancy, and the sufferings of the mind
in the after period.   The frame of the body, constituted for
the support of the vital functions, becomes the instrument of
expression; and an extensive class of passions, by influencing
the heart, by affecting that sensibility which governs the
muscles of respiration, calls them into co-operation, so that
they become an undeviating and sure sign of certain states or
conditions of the mind.   They are the organs of expression.

Returning now to the contemplation of any of the stronger
passions, we comprehend much which was before obscure.
We see why that grief which strikes the heart should affect

the regularity of breathing*—why the muscles of the throat should be affected with spasm—why slight quivering motions pass from time to time over the face, the lips, and cheeks, and nostrils ;—because these are the organs of respiration, organs which have their muscles united to the sensibility of the heart, and moved under its influence.   Now we comprehend, how the passion of rage or terror binds and tightens the chest, how the features are so singularly agitated by the indirect, as well as by the direct influence of the passions—how the words are cut—how the voice sticks in the throat—how the paralysed lips refuse the commands of the will, so that they are held in a mixed state of violence and weakness, which, more than any fixed expression, characterises the influence of the passion.

BLUSHING.—The sudden flushing of the countenance in blushing belongs to expression, as one of the many sources of sympathy which bind us together.   This suffusion serves no purpose of the economy, whilst we must acknowledge the interest which it excites as an indication of mind.   It adds perfection to the features of beauty.†

The colour which attends exertion, or the violent passions, as of rage, arises from general vascular excitement, and differs from blushing.   Blushing is too sudden and too partial to be traced to the heart's action.   That it is a provision for expression may be inferred from the colour extending only to the surface of the face, neck, and breast, the parts most exposed.   It is not acquired ; it is from the beginning.   It

---

*   The grief that does not speak,
    Whispers the o'er-fraught heart, and bids it break.—*Macbeth.*
    † Dr. Burgess, who has written a volume on " Blushing," affirms that a Circassian maid who blushes, brings a higher price in the slave-market !

is unlike the effect of powerful, depressing emotions, which
influence the whole body. The sudden conviction of the
criminal is felt in every pore; but the colour caused by
blushing gives brilliancy and interest to the expression of the
face. In this we perceive an advantage possessed by the
fair family of mankind, and which must be lost to the dark ;
for I can hardly believe that a blush may be seen in the
Negro.* We think of blushes as accompanying shame ; but
it is indicative of excitement. There is no shame when lively
feeling makes a timid youth break through the restraint which
modesty and reserve have imposed. It is becoming in youth,
it is seemly in more advanced years in women. Blushing
assorts well with youthful and with effeminate features ;
whilst nothing is more hateful than a dog-face, that exhibits
no token of sensibility in the variations of colour.

* A wound in the black leaves a scar in which the dark pigment of the
skin is wanting ; and the white spot, formed by such a cicatrix in the face
of the Negro, reddens with passion.

In contrasting, by comparative anatomy, the internal structure of animals,
we find in some classes, parts of the organization apparently useless or
superfluous, to discover the full development and appropriate functions of
which, we must refer to other classes. If the black blushes unseen, it only
shews that the incidental colour does not affect the general structure and
processes.

ESSAY IV.

THE muscular part of the animal frame consists of a peculiar fleshy substance, possessing the power of contraction, and, consequently, of producing motion. In the limbs and trunk, the muscles are attached to the bones, and are distinct and powerful : but as in the face they have merely to operate on the skin, the lips, nostrils, and eyelids, they require less power, and are, therefore, more delicate. And that power is not always directly under the will, like the muscular exertions of the body and limbs ; it is often involuntary, and is inseparably united to the conditions or affections of the mind. The latter consideration gives much interest to the subject; for, by this provision in the muscles, the very spirit by which the body is animated, and the various emotions, shine out in the countenance.

It has been said that the superiority of the human face in expression is an accidental effect of the number of muscles which are provided in man for the faculty of speech. That many of the muscles called into action in speech are also employed in expression will be readily admitted ; but besides these, there are muscles of the human features which have no connexion with the voice, and are purely instrumental in expression. Further, the human countenance is pre-eminent

o

in possessing, not only the muscles proper to man, but also the peculiarities of two great classes of the lower animals, having the muscles which are characteristic of both these classes combined.

To understand what follows, it is not necessary for the reader to know more of the structure of muscles than that they are formed of distinct packets of fibres; that the extremities are called their origins and insertions : the fixed extremity, attached generally to some point of bone, being the origin ; the extremity which is moved, the insertion.   I shall consider the muscles of the face in three groups.   First, those which surround the eye ; secondly, those which move the nostrils ; and lastly, those around the mouth.

And first,

OF THE MUSCLES OF THE FOREHEAD AND EYEBROW.

The forehead is more than any other part characteristic of the human countenance.   It is the seat of thought, a tablet where every emotion is distinctly impressed; and the eyebrow is the moveable type for this fair page.

" Frons hominis tristitiæ, hilaritatis, clementiæ, severitatis, index est."
PLINY.

The eye is the chief feature of expression.   It takes a thousand shades from the relations of the surrounding parts ; and the eyebrow, that dark arch which surmounts it, is itself an eloquent index of the mind.   Some one has called the eyebrow " the rainbow of peace, or the bended bow of discord." *

* Yea, this man's brow, like to a title leaf,
Fortels the nature of a tragic volume ;
So looks the strond, whereon the imperious flood
Hath left a witnessed usurpation.—SHAKSPEARE.

There are four muscles attached to the eyebrow.

1. A muscle, called *occipito frontalis* (A), descends over the forehead, and is inserted into the eyebrow, where it mingles its fibres with the next muscle. The simple action of the frontal portion of the occipito frontalis is to raise or arch the eyebrow, as in surprise or doubt ; or, as if we meant to say, " I must look further into this."

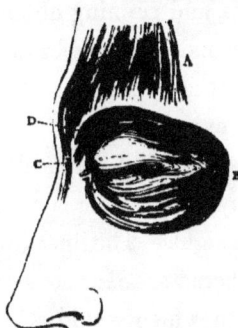

2. The muscle which closes the eyelids, is the *orbicularis palpebrarum* (B). We shall divide this muscle into three parts. Its fibres surround the eye, being spread in a circular direction upon the margin of the orbit and the eyelids. The stronger portion, encircling the orbit, shuts the eyelids with that spasmodic force which is felt when something irritating is thrown into the eye. The paler and more delicate fibres, which lie more immediately upon the eyelids, gently close the eye, as in winking, or in sleep. A third set of fibres is situated directly on the margins of the eyelids.* It is the outer and stronger circle which draws down the eyebrow, and is the direct opponent of the occipito frontalis.

* For the actions of these different portions of the general muscle, see the author's " Practical Essays," Part I. on Squinting.

3. The third muscle (c), is properly a part of the first, and is termed the *descending slip* of the *occipito frontalis*. As it descends on the side of the nose to be attached to the bridge, it has a different effect from the greater part of the muscle : it draws down the inner extremity of the eyebrow.

4. The next muscle is the *corrugator supercilii* (D). It arises from the lowest point of the frontal bone, where it joins the bones of the nose, and running obliquely upwards, is inserted into the skin under the eyebrow. The two muscles acting together knit the eyebrows. These are the muscles of the forehead and eyebrows.

In the arched and polished forehead, terminated by the distinct line of the eyebrow, there is an especial capacity for indicating human thought. The lines drawn here often give meaning of a high character to motions of the features in the lower part of the face, which would otherwise express mere animal activity. And it is not a fleshy brow that is best adapted for expression. The fulness of the forehead and around the eyes, which the artists and poets combined to give to Hercules, conveys the idea of dull, brutal strength, and a lowering expression ; while the forehead of the thin, pale student, may evince intelligence or elevation of thought.

The *levator palpebræ superioris*, the muscle which raises the upper eyelid, and is an opponent of the orbicularis, arises deep within the orbit, and is attached in front to the cartilage which gives form and firmness to the upper eyelid.

There are also within the orbit six other muscles, which are inserted into the eyeball. Their action is a subject of high interest, to discuss which would require a volume. I must limit myself to the question of the expression of the eye; referring the reader for more ample illustrations, to those memoirs which treat of the subserviency of the muscles to vision, and of their action in cleaning the cornea, and protecting the organ.*

OF THE EXPRESSION OF THE HUMAN EYE.

The eye is the most lively feature in the countenance ; the first of our senses to awake, and the last to cease motion. It is indicative of the higher and the holier emotions—of all those feelings which distinguish man from the brutes.

A large eye is not only consistent with beauty, but necessary to it. The eye of the eagle, even of the ox, is familiar in the similes of poets. The Arab expresses his idea of a woman's beauty, by saying, that she has the eye of the gazelle ; it is the burthen of their songs. The timidity, gentleness, and innocent fear, in the eye of the deer tribe, are compared with the modesty of a young girl. " Let her be as the loving hind, and pleasant roe." In the eye we look for meaning, for human sentiment, for reproof.†

Do architects study enough, when arranging the masses of their buildings for effect, how the shadows will fall ? The statuary, at all events, must. " The eye ought to be sunk," says Winkleman.‡ Yes, relatively to the forehead ; but not in reference to the face. That would give a very mean expression. It is the strong shadow produced by the projecting eyebrow, which gives powerful effect to the eye, in sculpture.

---

* See the "Nervous System," 4th edition, p. 145 ; "Bridgewater Treatise on the Hand," 4th edition, p. 329.

† " I gave him," said Dr. Parr, " the chastisement of my eye."

‡ "Aux têtes idéales, les yeux sont toujours plus enfoncés qu'ils ne le sont en général dans la nature."

We have said, that the eye indicates the holier emotions. In all stages of society, and in every clime, the posture and expression of reverence have been the same. The works of the great masters, who have represented the more sublime passions of man, may be adduced as evidences : by the upturned direction of the eyes, and a correspondence of feature and attitude, they address us in language intelligible to all mankind. The humble posture and raised eyes are natural, whether in the darkened chamber, or under the open vault of heaven.

On first consideration, it seems merely consistent, that when pious thoughts prevail, man should turn his eyes from things earthly to the purer objects above. But there is a reason for this, which is every way worthy of attention. When subject to particular influences, the natural position of the eyeball is to be directed upwards. In sleep, languor and depression, or when affected with strong emotions, the eyes naturally and insensibly roll upwards. The action is not a voluntary one ; it is irresistible. Hence, in reverence, in devotion, in agony of mind, in all sentiments of pity, in bodily pain with fear of death, the eyes assume that position.

Let us explain by what muscles the eyes are so revolved. There are two sets of muscles which govern the motions of the eyeball. Four straight muscles, attached at cardinal points by combining their action, move it in every direction required for vision ; and these muscles are subject to the will. When the straight muscles, from weariness or exhaustion, cease to guide the eye, two other muscles operate to roll it upwards under the eyelid : these are the oblique muscles. Accordingly, in sleep, in fainting, in approaching death, when the four voluntary muscles resign their action, and insensibility creeps over the retina, the oblique muscles prevail, and the pupil is revolved, so as to expose only the white of the eye. It is so far consolatory to reflect, that the apparent agony indicated by this direction of the eyes, in fainting or the approach of death, is the effect of encroaching insensibility— of objects impressed on the nerve of vision being no longer perceived.

We thus see that when wrapt in devotional feelings, and when outward impressions are unheeded, the eyes are raised by an action neither taught nor acquired. It is by this instinctive motion we are led to bow with humility—to look upwards in prayer, and to regard the visible heavens as the seat of God.

> "Prayer is the upward glancing of the eye,
> When none but God is near."

Although the savage does not always distinguish God from the heavens above him, this direction of the eye would appear to be the source of the universal belief that the Supreme Being has His throne above. The idolatrous Negro in praying for rice and yams, or that he may be active and swift, lifts up his eyes to the canopy of the sky.[*] So, in intercourse with God, although we are taught that our globe is ever revolving : though religion inculcates that the Almighty is everywhere, yet, under the influence of this position of the eye, which is no doubt designed for a purpose,—we seek Him on high. " I will lift up mine eyes unto the hills from whence cometh my help."[†]

* BARBOT : "Description of Guinea."
† The same influence, which thus induces a posture of the body in accommodation to the eye, makes the attitude of stooping the sign of supplication—of obeisance—and courtesy, among all nations. "And Araunah looked, and saw the king and his servants coming on towards

See, then, how this property of our bodily frame has influenced our opinions, and belief ; our conceptions of the Deity—our religious observances—our poetry, and daily habits.

Although the geologist may think that the account in the Scriptures of the formation of the earth, is contradicted by his

him : and Araunah went out, and bowed himself before the king, on his face upon the ground." So, Abraham : " And he lift up his eyes and looked, and lo, three men stood by him ; and when he saw them he ran to meet them from the tent door, and bowed himself toward the ground."

The Mahomedans, in acts of devotion, cross their hands on their bosom and incline the head.

theories, we perceive in our present investigation a strict
agreement in man's inmost structure with the book of life :
and we may say with Kepler, that man should not resign his
natural feelings and thoughts in pursuit of philosophy, "but
that, lifting up his natural eyes, with which alone he can see,
he should from his own heart pour himself out in worship to
the Creator ; being certain that he gives no less worship to
God than the astronomer."

By this physical conformation, combined with our highest
quality of mind, we are led to the expression of devotion.
The design of man's being was, that he might praise and
honour his Maker.   Gratitude is the debt of our nature, and
in this property of the eye there is pointed out to us how
that gratitude, which is the distinguishing character of our
minds, is to be directed.

The orbicularis muscle of the eyelids acts powerfully in
certain kinds of expression.   In laughing and crying, the
outer circle of this muscle, as it contracts, gathers up the
skin about the eye ; and at the same time it compresses the
eyeball.   A new interest is given to the subject when we inquire into the object of that compression.   It has a distinct
relation to the circulation of the blood within the eye.   During
every violent act of expiration, whether in hearty laughter,
weeping, coughing, or sneezing, the eyeball is firmly compressed by the fibres of the orbicularis ; and this is a provision
for supporting and defending the vascular system of the interior of the eye from a retrograde impulse communicated to
the blood in the veins at that time.   When we contract the
chest, and expel the air, there is a retardation of the blood in
the veins of the neck and head ; and in the more powerful
acts of expulsion, the blood not only distends the vessels, but

P

is even regurgitated into the minute branches. Were the eye not properly compressed at that time, and a resistance given to the shock, irreparable injury might be inflicted on the delicate textures of the interior of the eye.* Hence we see a reason for the closed state of the eyelids, and wrinkling of the surrounding skin, and twinkling of the eye, in hearty laughter.

In the drunkard, there is a heaviness of eye, a disposition to squint, and to see double, and a forcible elevation of the eyebrow to counteract the dropping of the upper eyelid, and preserve the eyes from closing. Hogarth has very happily caught this hanging of the eyelid, with the effort in the muscles of the forehead to prevent it from actually falling. The peculiar expression may be thus explained. In the stupor of inebriation, the voluntary muscles of the eyeball resign their action to the oblique muscles, which, as we have seen, instinctively revolve the eye upwards when insensibility comes on : at the same time, the muscle which elevates the upper lid yields, in sympathy with the oblique muscles, to the action of the orbicularis which closes the eyes, and the eyelid drops. The condition is, in short, the same as that of falling asleep ; when the eyeball revolves as the lids close. It is the struggle of the drunkard to resist, with his half-conscious efforts, the rapid turning up of the eye, and to preserve it under the control of the voluntary muscles, that makes him see objects distorted, and strive, by arching his eyebrows, to keep the upper lid from descending. The puzzled appearance which

---

* "If we separate the eyelids of a child, to examine the eye while it cries and struggles with passion, by taking off the natural support to the vascular system of the eye, and the means of guarding it against the rush of blood then occurring, the conjunctiva becomes suddenly filled with blood, and the eyelids everted."—*Nervous System*, p. 175.

this gives rise to, along with the relaxation of the lower part of the face, and the slight paralytic obliquity of the mouth, complete the degrading expression.

OF THE MUSCLES OF THE NOSTRILS.

The nostrils are features which have a powerful effect in expression. The breath being drawn through them, and their structure formed for alternate expansion and contraction in correspondence with the motions of the chest, they are an index of the condition of respiration, when affected by emotion. As they consist of cartilages moved by appropriate muscles, acting in strict sympathy with the drawing of the breath, they become expressive of animal excitement.

We may enumerate four muscles which move the cartilages of the nostrils.

Levator labii superioris et alæ nasi (A).—This muscle arises from the upper jawbone, and descends to the lip ; but a part of it stops short, to be attached to the moveable cartilage of the nostril; it raises the nostril along with the upper lip.

The *Depressor alæ nasi* (B) arises from the upper jawbone, close to the sockets of the front teeth; it ascends and is inserted into the lateral cartilage of the nostril, and pulls down that cartilage.

The *Compressor nasi* (C) arises from the cartilaginous bridge of the nose,* and is inserted into the lateral cartilage of the nostril. The name would imply that this muscle compresses the membraneous part of the nose, which it does; but its principal action must be to expand the nostril, by raising the lateral cartilage.

The next muscle is a slip of the *Orbicularis oris* (D), which, detaching itself from that mass of the muscle, runs up to the edge of the septum of the nose.

Thus we see how Nature has provided for the motions of the nostrils. The actions of these muscles are controlled by a nerve of the class which has been distinguished as subservient to the apparatus of breathing; and it is owing to this that the sympathy is established between the general act of drawing the breath and the expansion of the nostrils. As the motions of the nostrils, however, are intimately connected with those of the lips, I shall defer making any further observations upon them, until the muscles of the mouth have been described.

MUSCLES OF THE LIPS AND CHEEKS.

The fleshy structure of the lips is in a great measure owing to a circular muscle which surrounds the mouth. This muscle

---

* That is certainly its most fixed extremity.

closes the lips, and is the opponent of many other muscles, which, taking their origin from the prominent points of the bones of the face, are concentred towards the mouth, and, besides opening it, move the lips in various directions. We must look upon the whole of these muscles in three points of view. 1, as belonging to mastication, turning the morsel, and placing it under the action of the teeth; 2, as part of the organ of speech; and 3, as powerful agents in expression.

Orbicularis oris (A).—The fibres of this circular muscle can be traced continuously round the lips, and have properly no origin. We have already taken notice of the *Levator labii superioris et alæ nasi* (B), some fibres of which are inserted into the upper lip.

The *Levator labii proprius* (C) arises from the upper jaw, near the orbit. It is attached exclusively to the upper lip, and raises it.

Levator anguli oris (D).—This muscle lies under the last, and is, of course, shorter; it raises the angle of the mouth.

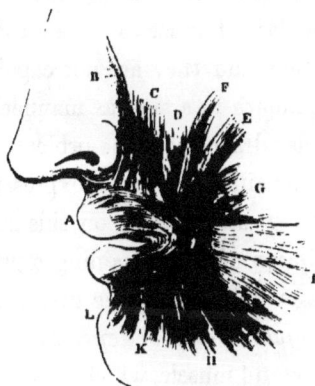

The *Zygomaticus* (E) arises from the zygoma, a process of

the cheekbone, which joins the temporal bone ; it is inserted into the angle of the mouth.

There is sometimes an additional muscle, arising and inserted in a similar manner, called the *zygomaticus minor* (F).

The *Buccinator* (some of the fibres of which are represented by G) is a flat muscle, which lines the inside of the cheek, and, arising from the sockets of the back teeth of both jawbones, is inserted into the angle of the mouth.

As the teeth of man indicate that he is omnivorous, and intermediate between the two great tribes of animals—the carnivorous and herbivorous, we expect the muscles also to exhibit the same middle state and to partake the characters of both these classes. And such is found to be the case. The three muscles last enumerated combine to raise and retract the angle of the mouth, and by doing so, they expose the canine teeth. Now this group of muscles is especially powerful in the carnivorous animal ; they lift the fleshy lips off the long tearing fangs of the lion or tiger, and produce a fierceness of expression. But in the milder graminivorous animals the same class of muscles have a different direction given to their action, and they are not capable of elevating the angles of the mouth in a similar manner. In ourselves, when these muscles draw upon the orbicularis, and disclose the angular teeth, a painful and bitter expression is the effect. But before we can speak correctly on this subject, we must pursue the description of the remaining muscles.

Of the muscles which depress the lips, there is,

1st. The *Triangularis oris*, or *depressor anguli oris* (H), a comparatively powerful muscle, which arises from the base of the lower jaw, and is inserted into the angle of the mouth.

In the drawing, some muscular fibres (I) may be seen,

which join the triangularis oris, and pass to the angle of the mouth. These are part of a superficial muscle of the neck,— the *platysma-myoides:* the fibres of which mount over the jaw to terminate on the cheek. The uppermost fasciculus, represented in the drawing, has been described by Santorini as a distinct muscle, and from its action in laughter, has obtained the name *Risorius Santorini.*

The *Quadratus menti* (K), a small square muscle, situated on the chin, depresses the lower lip.

The *Levator menti* (L) is a small muscle, which arises from the lower jaw, near the sockets of the front teeth, and passes to be inserted into the centre of the integument of the chin. When both muscles act, they throw up the chin, and project the lower lip.

The angle of the mouth is full of expression ; and much is implied, according to the prevailing action of the superior or inferior class of muscles. The triangularis oris and the levator menti combine to produce a kind of expression which is peculiar to man. The angle of the mouth is drawn down by the former, while the lower lip is arched and elevated, with a contemptuous effect, by the latter ; whence the levator menti has sometimes been called *superbus.* The union of so many muscles at the angle of the lips produces that fulness about the mouth remarkable in those who are both thin and muscular. In the child, or youth, whose face is plump, they make the dimple in the cheek. It is perceived that the orbicularis is the opponent of all the muscles which are concentred from various points to the lips ; and it is by the successive action and relaxation of these antagonising muscles that so much and so varied expression is given to the mouth. This circular muscle is affected in various emotions ; it tremblingly yields to the superior force of its counteracting muscles, both in joy and grief : it relaxes pleasantly in smiling ; it is drawn more powerfully by its opponent muscles in weeping.

We can have no better illustration of how much depends on the function exercised by the mouth, for the particular character impressed on the lower part of the face, when the lips are in motion, than by watching the features of a preacher or advocate engaged in his vocation, and afterwards, if opportunity offers, looking at the play of the same jaws and lips, when over a trencher. The whole machinery from the temple downwards, and from the angle of the jaw to the chin, is in operation during mastication; whereas, in the most impassioned discourse, the action is concentrated to the lips.

In speaking, there is much motion of the lower lip, and consequently, activity in those muscles which form the fulness of the chin : yet a remarkable variety is produced in the lines which mark the features about the upper lip, by the play of the different muscles which converge to the mouth from the margins of the orbits. But this subject has further interest.

The organization necessary to speech, the great instrument of human thought, is widely dispersed : that is, for the utterance of sound there must conform, a motion of the lungs or chest, an adjustment of the larynx and pharynx, and a fine modulation of the lips. It is more directly from the motions of the tongue and lips that articulate sounds proceed ; and the connexion of the numerous muscles brought into operation in these actions, is congenital with the awakening intellect. Long before a child is taught to speak, we may see an imperfect agitation of the lips and cheeks ; and sounds are uttered which wait only for the effort of imitation to become language.

These remarks bear out our former statement, that beauty in the lips and lower part of the countenance of a well-formed face, has relation to the perfection of the structure viewed in connexion with speech, and in contrast with the apparatus for mastication. The possession of an instrument of speech is instinctively associated in our thoughts with the most exalted endowments of man, moral and intellectual.

OF THE BEARD.

" Vidi presso di me un veglio solo,
  Degno di tanta riverenza in vista,
  Che più non dee a padre alcun figliolo.
  Lunga la barba e di pel bianco mista,
  Portava a' suoi capegli simigliante
  De quai cadeva al petto doppia lista."

DANTE.

The stages of man's life are outwardly characterised. An opinion prevails, that the form and lineaments of old age are a consequence of the deterioration of the material of our frame ; and that the resemblance so often drawn between an aged man leaning on his staff, and a ruin tottering to its fall, is a perfect one. It is not so ; the material of the frame is ever the same : years affect it not; but infancy, youth, maturity, and old age, have their appropriate outward characters. Why should the forehead be bald, and the beard luxuriant, if not to mark the latest epoch of man's life? or what reason can be given for the hair not growing on the chin during the vascular fulness of youth, but that it would be inconsistent with the characters of that time of life to be provided with a beard ?

When these Essays were first written, there was not a

Q

beard to be seen in England, unless joined with squalor and neglect : and I had the conviction that this appendage concealed the finest features. Being in Rome, however, during the procession of the Corpus Domini, I saw that the expression was not injured by the beard ; but that it added to the dignity and character of years. It was evident that the fine heads by the old masters were copies of what were then seen in nature, though now but rarely. There were beards which nearly equalled that of the " Moses" of Michael Angelo, in length ; and which flowed like those in the paintings of Domenichino and Correggio.*

The beard is characteristic of nations. In the East, it is honoured ; and to be shaved, is the mark of a slave.† A beard of three hands' breadth is a goodly show : but to exceed that, requires a life of repose : violent exercise in the field shortens the beard. The Turks have a very poor beard. The Persians have noble beards, and are proud of the distinction. The beard of Futteh Ali Shah, the late king of Persia, reached below his girdle, was full and fine, and remarkable in a nation of beards, for having no division in the middle. Such a beard, during the active period of life, shews finely on horseback ; being tossed over the shoulders in the wind, and indicating speed. In the natural

* " In the procession of the Corpus Domini, the Pope is attended by bishops from all parts of Christendom : from Mount Lebanon and the East, as well as from Roman Catholic Ireland. These dignitaries, with the cardinals, the superiors of convents, the friars of various orders, and the cavalcade of the guarda nobile, form a pageant far beyond what royalty can attain, or can anywhere else be witnessed, whether we consider the place and accompaniments, or the actors and their costumes. Then it was, that age, with bald head, and flowing beard, and appropriate robes, surpassed youth and beauty, with all the trappings of the cavalier."—*Note from Journal.*
† 2 Samuel x. 4.

beard, the hair has a peculiarity depending on the place from which it grows. The hair of the upper lip is more profuse, and even in the oldest man is of a darker hue, than that of the under lip; so that falling on the lower part, it can still be distinguished as it mixes with the purer white. Again, the hair descending from the sides of the face attains a greater length than that which comes from the chin : and this is more especially the character of age.

In the French regiments they set frightful fellows, with axes over their shoulders, to march in front : on their heads is a black bear-skin cap, of the form and dimensions of a drum, and they select men with beards of the same hue, which grow in a bush, the counterpart of that on their heads. But the face, as seen between the two black masses, is more ludicrous than terrible, and has an effect very different from what is intended. A common fellow's beard, like a common fellow's countenance, is coarse.

Even in the Franciscan and Capuchin monks, the beard has not always the fine character displayed in the works of the old painters. Their models are gone with their times. Something excessive and ideal may be represented by the beard. Michael Angelo has, perhaps, followed Scripture, in the beard of his "Moses," which floats below the girdle ; and in the fresco of Jeremiah, in the Sistine Chapel. The finest painting of the beard that I have seen, is by Correggio, in the Scala of the Albergo dei Poveri, in Genoa,— a fresco of the Saviour, in the arms of the Almighty, where the beard of the Father flows beautifully. In short, the beard may become, with knowledge and taste, the most characteristic part in a figure.*

* "Our northern artists are unfavourably situated, not owing to the

Expression in the Lips and Moustaches.—Things familiar do not always give rise to their natural association. I was led to attend more particularly to the moustaches as a feature of expression, in meeting a handsome young French soldier, coming up a long ascent in the Coté d'Or, and breathing hard, although with a good-humoured, innocent expression. His sharp-pointed black moustaches rose and fell with a cata-mountain look that set me to think on the cause.

Every one must have observed how the nostrils play in hard breathing.* We have seen that there is a muscle which is the principal agent in this action; and it may be felt swelling during inspiration, when the finger is pressed on the upper lip, just under the nostril. It is the *depressor alæ nasi.* The action of this muscle, under the roots of the hairs on the lip, sensibly moves them; and as all passionate excitements influence the respiratory actions, the nostrils and moustaches necessarily participate in the movement in violent passions. Thus, although the hair of the upper lip does conceal the finer modulations of the mouth, as in woman, it adds to the character of the stronger and harsher emotions.

direct influence of cold, as Winckelman imagined, but an indirect cause. In historical painting, they draw from copies of nature, and paint beards, as they do the naked figure, without seeing it, or being familiar with the form and colour of the one or the other. But in Rome also they make mistakes. I found the artists supporting a fellow, whose beard was their model. The hair of the head, and the beard of this man, had grown to an extraordinary length, showing what an uncouth mass it may become. He had been painted so often as the Father of the gods, that in his craze he had believed himself to be no less. I said, if they would plunge him in the Tiber, and study him as he rose, he might pass for a river god. No; the beard is a mere mass of hair, but admits of much character."—*Note from Journal.*

* Physiognomists make a wide nostril the sign of a fiery disposition. It may be expressive of passion, without being the cause. The idea of its being the seat of passion, is undoubtedly taken from animal expression. "There went a smoke out of His nostrils," is hardly descriptive of human excitement.

I continued to think of this in descending the Rhone in company with some French officers; they were merry with wine, and I saw their moustaches, black, red, and white, animated in their songs and laughter; and although with a *farouche* character, these appendages rather added to, than concealed expression. We see the pictorial effect in the hilarity of the Dutch boor.

The lower lip moves more than the upper. With this, too, we are so familiar as not to be sensible of it; but if we try the experiment of looking on the face of a friend, in a reversed position, we shall be convinced that it is so. The expression of speaking results very much from the modulation of the lower lip; and the rising and falling of the jaw, which takes place at the same time, and more especially in singing, adds to the motion. Passion, however, is expressed more in the upper lip.

In compassionating a fellow-creature, it is not natural to look on the face reversed. Yet I have seen in a modern picture, a soldier regarding his wounded comrade, *dessus dessous*, the mouth to the forehead, the eye to the mouth. The immediate effect was a want of sympathy,—of proper feeling. Even the nurse turns her head in correspondence with the face of the infant. Is the same not meant by the Psalmist, "*My heart said unto thee, Let my face seek thy face?*" This was in my mind in looking on a picture of the Saviour, dead, lying on the knees of the Madonna; she turns her head, bringing her face nearly parallel with that of the Redeemer; which produces infinite grace and tenderness.*

The drawing of the head of a man, thrown to the ground, being to our eye reversed, has not the same effect as when

* In the Gallery of the Academia delle Belle Arte, Bologna.

represented upright. Certain features must be exaggerated. That is, if the painter were to draw the face accurately, and then turn the picture the contrary way, the head downwards, it would have no force. This arises from the reversed features being deficient in the accustomed harmony, and from the altered relation of the upper and lower lips. Michael Angelo, with his other excellencies, was a master of expression. There is a *Pieta* by him in alto-relievo,* which gives proof of this. The piece of marble does not exceed three feet; and nothing but expression could have given to it its celebrity.

I was never more sensible of the action of the lower lip, as expressive of speech, than in looking on a picture by that very extraordinary painter, Zurbaran. It represents St. Francis. He is kneeling, his hands locked together energetically, his eyes raised, and his lower lip has the expression of moving in prayer.†

Among the many advantages which the artist has in the southern countries of Europe, the service of the Roman Catholic Church affords him the chief. At all seasons, as well as during the service of the altar, there are in the cathedrals and churches groups and single figures; the lady in rich attire, not more picturesque than the country girl; the beggar, and the monk, on their knees, muttering their prayers. In the family pew of the Reformed Church there may be as holy a frame of mind, but never the expression

* In the Albergo dei Poveri, in Genoa. " A Pieta is the representation of Christ resting on the lap of the mother. The eyes of the mother are shut, the mouth not open, but in the lips a form that implies she is about to kiss the cheek. The angles of the mouth are in the slightest degree depressed, and the lips must open when next she draws breath."—*Note from Journal.*
† The picture is in the Spanish School of the Musée Royale of the Louvre.

· of those rapt and solitary figures, whom we see prostrate on the bare stones in the solemn light of these churches. But my object was to advert to their inaudible mutterings, in which the amount of expression capable of being thrown into the lips during speech may be well observed. Nor can a stranger go from the church to the picture-galleries, and mistake for a moment where the great painters found their studies, where they gained those conceptions of devotion, of enthusiasm and abandonment, which we see in the portraits of their saints and martyrs.*

* "St. Siro, Genoa. It is a new thing to see those beggars crawling on the stairs. There is one who, lying on his belly, drags himself along with a short stick; the precise figure that is in the cartoons of Raphael. They are squalid, distorted, and strange. One fellow among them I should have in my sketch-book. He is on his knees, and, whilst receiving a soldo from a very poor and very old woman, counts his beads, and crosses himself with an indifference that hardly can be real. In entering a church in health, and the enjoyment of life, to step through amongst the 'poveri' is no bad preparation. It is impossible to witness the countryman, whose coarse dress marks the lowness of his condition,—to see him apart, in an obscure aisle, cast down, and in prayer, with such perfect abstraction and abandonment, without the words of the publican being suggested, 'God be merciful to me a sinner.' In this respect, amidst all the blazon and show of worship which belong to the Roman Catholic, it is still the church of the poor. There is no respect for rank or condition within the precincts of a place of worship."—*Note from Journal.*

ESSAY V.

⸺

OF THE EXPRESSION OF PASSION, AS ILLUSTRATED BY A COM-
PARISON OF THE MUSCLES OF THE FACE IN MAN AND IN
ANIMALS ; AND OF THE MUSCLES PECULIAR TO MAN, AND
THEIR EFFECTS IN BESTOWING HUMAN EXPRESSION.

THE violent passions are exhibited so distinctly in the
countenance of both man and animals, that we are led to
consider the movements by which they are made obvious,
as characteristic signs provided by nature for the express
purpose of intimating the inward emotions : that they may
be interpreted by a peculiar and intuitive faculty in the
observer.

This view, however, so natural at first, is not altogether
satisfactory ; and an opposite theory has been proposed, in
which such special provision is denied, and the appearances
are accounted for, as the effect of certain actions which are
performed in obedience to the common laws of the animal
economy. It is also said, that we are taught by experience
alone to distinguish the signs of the passion in man : that in
infancy we learn that smiles are expressive of kindness, because
accompanied by endearments, and that frowns are the reverse,
because they are followed by blows. The expression of anger
in a brute is alleged to be merely the cast of features which
precedes his biting ; and the character of fondness, that which

is seen in his fawning and licking of the hand. In short, it has been maintained that what are called the external signs of passion, are only the concomitants of those voluntary movements which the structure renders necessary. That, for example, the glare of the lion's eye proceeds from his effort to see his prey more clearly; and his grin or snarl from the natural act of unsheathing his fangs before using them.

But, if we attend to the evidence of anatomical investigation, we shall perceive a remarkable difference between the provision for giving motion to the features in animals, and that for bestowing expression in man. In the lower creatures, there is no expression, but what may be referred, more or less plainly, to their acts of volition, or necessary instincts; while in man there seems to be a special apparatus, for the purpose of enabling him to communicate with his fellow-creatures, by that natural language, which is read in the changes of his countenance. There exist in his face, not only all those parts, which by their action produce expression in the several classes of quadrupeds, but there is added a peculiar set of muscles to which no other office can be assigned than to serve for expression.

OF EXPRESSION IN ANIMALS.

In brutes the most marked expression is that of rage; the object of which is opposition, resistance, and defence. But on examination it will be found that the force of the expression is in proportion to the strength of the principal action in the creature when thus excited.

R

The graminivorous animals, which seek their subsistence, not by preying upon others, or by the ferocity, contest, and victory, which supply the carnivorous with food, have in their features no strong expression of rage; it is chiefly confined to the effect produced on the general system. Thus the inflamed eye and the breathing nostrils of the bull are induced by the excitement of the whole frame; his only proper expression of rage is in the position of the head, with the horns turned obliquely to the ground, ready to strike; and indeed it may be observed, that animals which strike with the horns shew little indication either of fear or rage, except in the position of the head; for the breath ejected from the expanded nostril is the effect of mere exertion, and may belong to different conditions of the frame. In all graminivorous animals, the skin of the head is closely attached to the skull, and capable of very limited motion: the eye is almost uniformly mild, and the lips are unmoved by passion.

It is in the carnivorous animals, with whose habits and manner of life ferocity is instinctively connected, as suited to their mode of subsistence, that rage is distinguished by remarkable strength of expression. The eyeball is terrible, and the retraction of the flesh of the lips indicates the most savage fury. The action of the respiratory organs, the heaving and agony of breathing, the deep and harsh motion of the air drawn through the throat in the growl, declare the universal excitement of the animal. It is wrong to imagine that all this is a mere preparatory exposure of the canine teeth. Brutes may have expression, properly so called, as well as man, though in a more limited degree; but in them, expression is so moulded to their natures and their necessities, that it seems accessory to their needful and voluntary actions.

The horse is universally held to be a noble animal, as he possesses the expression of courage, without the ferociousness of the beast of prey ; and as there is a consent between the motions of the ear and the eye, which resembles the exertion of mind, and the movements of the human countenance. But even this expression is the result of an incidental consent of animal motions ; and no more proves intelligence, than the diminutive eye and the unexpressive face of the elephant denote the contrary. We admire it, because there is as much animation as in the tiger, without the ferocity. The consent of motions between the eye and the ear of the horse is a physical consequence of the necessities of the animal. His defence lies in the hind feet, and there is an arrangement both in the muscles, and in the form of the skull, for that retroverted direction of the eye, which seems so expressive in the horse, but which merely serves to guide the blow. The inflation of the nostrils, and the fleshiness of the lips, belong to the peculiar provision for his respiration and mode of feeding.

The head of a lion is taken to show the muscular apparatus of a carnivorous animal.

A A. The circular fibres, which surround the eyelids, and which are common to all animals.

B C D. Accessory muscles, which draw back the eyelids from the eyeball, and give a sparkling fierceness to the eye.

Artists bestow an expression on the eye of the lion which they suppose gives dignity—a kind of knitting of the eyebrows, whilst the eyelids are straining wide. This is quite incompatible with the powers of expression in brutes. When the lion closes his eyes in repose, the fleshiness about the eyelids and the hair of the skin produce the effect of a morose human expression, but when he is excited, and the eye is fixed, there is no such character.

E F. The mass of muscular fibres, with those concealed under them, is very strong in this class of animals. They

raise and expose the teeth, with the savage expression peculiar to the carnivora.

G. The muscles which move the nostril in smelling.

H. A muscle which answers to the *zygomaticus* in man, and which must have great power in this animal, as it reaches from the ear to the angle of the mouth. It opens the mouth, retracts the lips, and disengages them from the teeth, as in seizing their prey.

I. The buccinator muscle.

K. Insertion of part of the masseter muscle, one of the powerful muscles that close the jaws.

I observed above, that some painters have thought it allowable to give human expression to the heads of lions, and others have presented it in their heads of horses. I think this is done on a mistaken view, and that it will never enhance the peculiar beauty of any animal to engraft upon it some part of human expression. Rubens, in his picture of Daniel in the lions' den, has given this character to the heads of the lions. It is more than doubtful whether it be in the true spirit of that principle of association which should govern the adaptation of expression and character in producing an ideal form, thus to mingle human expression with the features of the savage animals. It seems, however, that a distinction is to be made when the lion is represented in its natural state and when sculptured emblematically. Represented in his den, or in the forest, the picture should possess all the natural character; when couched amidst the insignia of empire, there may be a difference.

A horse's head is added in illustration; it is taken from Giulio Romano. The painter has here produced an ideal head: we say that it is a horse rather on account of the bridle in the mouth than because we recognise the natural character of that animal. Instead of the full clear eye standing prominent upon the temple, there is an eye sunk deep, with an overhanging eyebrow; the character entirely human, and the expression thoughtful and suspicious. In the hair of the forehead, and in the ears, in the roundness of the head and neck, the artist has preferred the model of the antique to what, in this instance, we must consider to be the finer forms

of nature.   Here are the nostrils of the horse, but they want
expansion ; and there are thick and fleshy lips, with an open
mouth, which no power of association can ever teach us to
admire.

There is a spirit in the expanded nostril, a fire in the eye,
a kind of intelligence in the horse's head taken altogether ;
there is a beauty in the form of the neck, and an ease and
grandeur in the carriage of the head, where strength and
freedom are combined, which cannot be excelled by the substitution of an ideal form.   No doubt the painter in this
instance wished to avoid that commonness of form, which
represses sentiment in the beholder, and destroys the poetical
effect of a picture ; but it is attempted at the expense of truth
of character.   In the utmost excitement, animals of this class
do not open the mouth ; they cannot breathe through the
mouth,—a valve in the throat prevents it,—so that animation
is exhibited only in the nostril and the eye.   The open mouth

is from the checking of the bit between the teeth, and is never seen when the horse is untrammelled and free.

Such were the opinions delivered in the first edition of this work, and they were drawn from observation of nature, on which I always rest with absolute reliance. Since that time, the Elgin collection of sculptures has arrived. These remains of antiquity are of great value to the arts of this country, as they obviously tend to turn the artist's attention to nature, and exhibit to him the consistency of natural form and beauty. The horses' heads in that collection are perfectly natural, and if there be exaggeration, it is only in the stronger marking of that which is the characteristic distinction of the animal.

The next drawing represents the muscles of the horse's head.

A A. The orbicular muscle of the eyelids.

B. An accessory muscle to raise the eyelid.

C. A very peculiar muscle. It pulls down the eyelid.

D. A muscle connected also with the eye, and arising from the cartilages of the ear.

E. A muscle answering to the zygomatic muscle in man.

These muscles, surrounding the eyelids of the horse, account for the superior expression of the eye. The muscle D seems calculated to operate upon the outer angle of the eyelids, and to enable the animal to direct the eye backwards; in this it is probably assisted by the muscle E.

F. This forms a class of muscles which descend on the side of the face, and are inserted into the nostril.

G G. Muscular fibres, also operating in the distension of the tube of the nostril.

H. A strong muscle, which acts upon the cartilage, and distends the nostril with great power.

There is something in the distribution of these muscles which illustrates the character of the class, and accounts for the peculiarity of expression. We cannot fail to observe the difference in the general direction and classing of the muscles of the face in the horse and in the lion. In the carnivorous animal, they all tend to lift the lips from the canine teeth, so that they cannot act without shewing the teeth, with a snarling expression : in the graminivorous animal, on the contrary, muscles, having the same place and origin, pass to the cartilages of the nose, and inflate it the instant they are excited. It is these muscles, therefore, more than any thing else, which produce the very different character and expression in the two classes of animals.

I I. A strong muscle, which lies under that of the nostril F. Its tendon passes forward over the nose, and unites with its fellow of the other side. These together form a broad tendon K, which is inserted into the upper lip. There is a similar muscle moving the lower lip, which cannot be seen in this view.

L M. The circular fibres of the lips, which in the horse are particularly strong and fleshy.

N. A web of muscle, which is extended from the cutaneous muscle of the neck.

The last-named muscles have all great power, and give extensive motion to the lips. They take a course over the nose in a manner quite peculiar to this class of animals, to raise and project the upper lip, as in gathering food. Any one who feeds his horse from his hand may feel the singular sensitiveness and mobility of his lips.

Looking to these muscles, and contrasting them with the animated sketch by Mr. Northcote, we cannot fail to see how much the form of the head depends upon the teeth being small in front, and large and deep-set at the back part of the jaw; how much the peculiarity of expression in the animal is owing to its breathing through the nostril, and not through the mouth, and to its brilliant eye being placed on the utmost projection of the head, so that, by the slightest turn of the pliant neck, it may be directed backward. Finally, we perceive how the muscles are adapted to draw back the eyelids, to expand the nostrils, and project the lips from the incisor

S

teeth, and also to place the food under the operation of the grinding teeth.

OF THE MUSCLES OF ANIMALS COMPARED WITH THOSE OF MAN.

Referring to the remarkable difference between the range of expression in man and in animals, and considering that in brutes it proceeds from necessity or voluntary action, while in man there is a special provision for bestowing it,—a peculiar set of muscles to which no other office can be assigned, it is proper to reduce the muscles of several quadrupeds into classes, that we may distinguish the characteristics of mere animal expression from those in man.

They may be distinguished as, 1st. Those which raise the lips from the teeth; 2d. Those which surround the eyelids ; and 3d. Those which move the nostrils.

1. The first of these classes, viz. *the muscles which raise the lips from the teeth*, admit of a subdivision. In the carnivorous animals the muscles of the lips are so directed as to raise the lip from the canine teeth. In the graminivorous they are directed so as to raise the lips from the incisor teeth. The former I would distinguish by the name *ringentes*, snarling muscles : the latter by the name *depascentes*, muscles simply for feeding.

The snarling muscles arise from the margin of the orbit, and from the upper jaw ; they are inserted into that part of the upper lip from which the moustaches grow, and which is opposite to the canine teeth. Their sole office is to raise the upper lip from the canine teeth ; and although they are assisted in this by others (the masticating muscles), I have ventured to distinguish them particularly as the muscles of snarling. This action of snarling is quite peculiar to the ferocious and canivorous animals. The graminivorous are incapable of it, and consequently these muscles are to be found largely developed only in the former class, not in the latter. In the carnivorous animals it can scarcely be said that there is a perfect or regular orbicular muscle, as in man, for contracting the lips ; the lips hang loose and relaxed, unless when drawn aside by the snarling muscles, and they fall back into this state of relaxation, with the remission of the action of these muscles.

The chief muscles of the lips, which in carnivorous animals are directed to the side of the mouth, are, in graminivorous animals, directed to the middle of the lip over the front teeth. I call them *depascentes*, from their use, which is to enable the creature to open its lips so as to gather food, and to bite the grass. They are long muscles; one set come down upon each side of the face, and joining in a broad tendon, pass over the nose to be inserted into the upper lip. Another set run along the lower jaw, to be inserted by a peculiar feathered tendon into the under lip. These muscles are very strong in the horse. They give a peculiar and characteristic expression to the stallion, when he snuffs the breeze, with his head high in air ; when he bites, the expression is entirely different from that of the carnivorous animal ; instead of exposing the teeth corresponding with the canine, he lifts the lips from the fore teeth, and protrudes them. The carnivorous animals have not these muscles of the fore part of the lip ; in them, the lips covering the incisor teeth are not fleshy like those of the graminivorous animals, but are tied down to the gums, and the fore teeth are exposed only in consequence of the straining occasioned by retraction of the side of the mouth.

Although the graminivorous animals do not possess those muscles which so powerfully retract the lips in the carnivorous class, they have a more perfect orbicular muscle surrounding the mouth, and regulating the motion of their fleshy lips.

2. *Muscles which surround the eyelid.*—In man, the upper eyelid is raised by a muscle coming from the back of the orbit. But animals of prey, in whose eyes there is the peculiar and

ferocious splendour, which distinguishes the tiger or the lion,
have, in addition to this muscle, three others attached to the
eyelids, which, stretching the coats and drawing the eyelids
backward upon the prominent eyeball, produce a fixed straining of the eye, and a greater brightness. These muscles I
have termed *scintillantes*, because by retracting the eyelids,
they expose the brilliant white of the eye, which reflects a
sparkling light. In the sheep, besides the proper muscle
coming from the bottom of the orbit, there is only a web of
fibres to assist in raising the eyelid. In the horse, there is a
muscle to pull down the lower eyelid ; and another, which,
passing from the ear to the outer angle of the eyelid, retracts
it, and enables the animal to direct the pupil backward, where
his defence lies. In the feline tribe light is reflected from the
bottom of the eye, when the pupil is dilated ; and as the pupil
dilates in obscure light, there is a brilliant reflection from the
cat's eye, which we mistake for indication of passion. All
these may be partially displayed in the human eye, as in the
bloodshot redness combined with the circle of reflected light
from the margin of the corner, like a flame or angry spark,
as Charon is described by Dante,—

> " Ch' intorno agli occhi avea di fiamme ruote,"

Or as lighted charcoal, from the bottom of the eye,—

> " Caron demonio con occhi di bragia."

It is in this way that a touch of true expression will illustrate a whole passage ; so Milton,

> " With head uplift above the wave, and eyes
> That sparkling blazed." *

* So also Spenser, B. vi. cant. 7, stanza 42.

3. *Muscles of the Nostrils.*—These are not less distinct and peculiar, in different classes of animals, than the muscles of the eye and lips. In the carnivorous animals, the nose is comparatively insignificant, provision being made in the open mouth for any occasional increase of respiration above the uniform play of the lungs ; while in the inoffensive animals, which are the prey of the more ferocious, the inflation of the nostril is provided for by the action of another set of muscles.

For example, in the horse " the glory of whose nostrils is terrible," the muscles which inflate the nostril are very peculiar. They arise like the *ringentes;* but instead of being fixed into the lips, as in carnivorous animals, whose lips are to be raised from the canine teeth, they pass to the nostrils, and in combination with some lesser muscles, powerfully inflate them when the animal is pushed to his speed, excited by fear, or inflamed to rage.

In the gallery of Florence, there is the head of a horse in bronze, and antique ; it is very fine, and in all respects as natural as those of the Elgin Marbles ; the mouth is open, but there is a bit in it.

Over the fountain, in the Piazza of the Grand Duke, is placed a group of Neptune, drawn by four horses ; the mouths of all the horses are open, and as they are free agents, without bit or harness, they seem to be of one mind, and to be expressing the same thing, whatever that may be. They would have been much finer, had the artist given them animation through the eye and nostril, without opening the mouth.*

The horse's mouth is never seen open when the animal is

* " Milan. The four horses in the triumphal arch have their mouths gaping wide ; not so the coursers last night in the Circus."—*Note from Journal.*

free. Nothing can be finer than the action of a charger in the field : but though he should snort and neigh and throw up his head and mane, with all his excitement he does not open his mouth. In the antiquities of Count Caylus, the horse's head is represented naturally.

We may notice here, that most of the carnivorous animals hunt their prey. For this object, they not only require a peculiar and extended organ of smelling, but the air must be drawn forcibly over the surface on which the olfactory nerve is spread. It appears to me, that this accounts for their small confined nostril, and their breathing freely through the mouth. In smelling, an action of the nostrils takes place which directs the stream of air upwards into the cells of the nose, where the olfactory nerve is distributed. This is especially the case in the conformation of the dog's nostrils.

Returning now to the muscles in the human countenance, we perceive that, although the motions of the lips and nostrils in man may not be so extensive as in other classes of animals, there is in his face a capacity for all the varieties of expression which distinguish these creatures. He stands, as we have said, between the carnivorous and graminivorous animals; or, rather, he partakes the nature of both. He has the snarling muscles which so peculiarly distinguish the carnivorous class, while he is able to protrude the lips, and uncover the teeth, like the graminivorous. We have seen that in the carnivorous animals, the muscles descending from the cheek-bones and upper jaw to raise the lip are strong, and that the orbicular or circular fibres of the mouth are feeble, the lip being attached to the forepart of the gums. In the graminivorous animals, on the contrary, the orbicular muscle has great power ; while the elevating and depressing muscles of the side of the mouth are weak. But in man, both classes of muscles are combined; the elevating and depressing muscles are fully developed, while the orbicular muscle completely antagonises them, modulating and qualifying their actions, and bestowing the utmost perfection on the motions of the lips.

Whether we look to the form of the features or to their power of expression, the consideration of these two classes of muscles alone will account for certain varieties in the human face. In one man, the excitement of passion may be indicated chiefly by the prevalence of one class, while in a second, another class will predominate in the expression.

If it be allowable to give examples, I would say that in the countenance of Mrs. Siddons or Mr. John Kemble, there was presented the highest character of beauty which belongs to the true English face. In that family the upper lip and nostrils were very expressive: the class of muscles which operate on the nostrils was especially powerful, and both these great tragedians had a remarkable capacity for the expression of. the nobler passions. In their cast of features there was never seen that blood-thirsty look which Cooke could throw into his face. In him, the *ringentes* prevailed: and what determined hate could he express, when, combined with the oblique cast of his eyes, he drew up the outer part of the upper lip, and disclosed a sharp angular tooth! And is it not this lateral drawing of the lips, and stretching them upon the closed teeth, which make the blood start from them, in remorseless hate and rancour?

But besides the muscles analogous to those of brutes, others are introduced into the human face, which indicate emotions and sympathies of which the lower animals are not susceptible; and as they are peculiar to man, they may be considered as the index of mental energy, in opposition to mere animal expression.

The most moveable and expressive features are the inner extremity of the eyebrow and the angle of the mouth ; and these are precisely the parts which have least expression in brutes ; for they have no eyebrows, and no power of elevating or depressing the angle of the mouth. It is therefore in these features that we should expect to find the muscles of expression peculiar to man.

The most remarkable muscle of the human face is the corrugator supercilii (D, fig. p. 99), arising from the frontal bone, near its union with the nasal bones, and inserted into the skin of the eyebrow ; it knits the eyebrows with an energetic effect, which unaccountably, but irresistibly, conveys the idea of mind.

The frontal portion of the occipito-frontalis muscle (A, fig. p. 99), is the antagonist of the orbicular muscle of the eyelids. It is wanting in the animals which we have examined ; and in its stead, fibres, more or less strong, are found to be inserted directly into the eyelids.

The motion of the features which, next to that produced by the corrugator supercilii, is most expressive of human passion and sentiment, is to be seen in the angle of the mouth. At one time I conceived that this distinctive expression was chiefly owing to the superbus (L, fig. p. 109), which elevates and protrudes the under lip, but I was deceived. The character of human expression in the mouth is given by the *triangularis oris,* or *depressor anguli oris* (H, fig. p. 109), a muscle which I have not found in any of the lower animals; I believe it to be peculiar to man, and I can assign no other use for it than that which belongs to expression. It arises

T

from the base of the lower jaw, and passes up to be inserted, with the converging fibres of almost all the muscles of the side of the face, into the corner of the mouth : it produces that arching of the lip so expressive of contempt, hatred, jealousy ; and in combination with the elevator of the under lip, or superbus, and the orbicularis, it has a larger share than any other muscle in producing the infinite variety of motions in the mouth, expressive of sentiment.

When we compare the muscles of the human head with those of animals, we perceive many smaller distinctions, which I shall not at present discuss. The *depressor alœ nasi* (D, fig. p. 107), the *nasalis labii superioris* (B, fig. p. 109), the anterior fibres of the *occipito-frontalis* (A, fig. p. 99), are not found in the brute ; and in general, the more minute and fasciculated structure of all the muscles of the lips, in the face of man, shows a decided superiority in the provision for motion of the features.

We have already observed, that the faces of animals seem chiefly capable of expressing rage and fear; even pain is indicated more in the voice, and in writhing and struggling.

The rage of the graminivorous animal is chiefly visible in the eye, in the inflation of the nostril, and in the disturbed state of the body. It is expressed most strongly by the carnivorous animals : in them it is wild, ferocious, and terrifying. Their expression of rage, so far as it appears in the face, is shown by the strong action of the *ringentes,* or snarling muscles, the exposure of the canine teeth, the gnashing of the tusks, and the brilliant excitement of the eye. The expression of human rage partakes of both ; the corresponding muscles of the lips and nostrils producing a similar action to that in animals ; an exposure and clenching of the teeth ;

a degree of sparkling of the eye, and an inflation of the
nostrils. Of a face under the influence of such actions, a
spectator would infallibly say, that the aspect was brutal,
savage, and cruel. But when the corrugator supercilii, a
muscle peculiar to human expression, is brought into action,
the sign is altered. The eyebrows are knit, the energy of
mind is apparent, and there is the mingling of thought and
emotion with the savage and brutal rage of the mere animal.

In man, the actions of the frontal muscle of the corrugator
supercilii, and of the orbicular muscle of the mouth, give
much expression. If instead of the retraction of the lips and
the exposure of the teeth, as in the rage or pain of animals,
the mouth is half closed, the lips inflected by the circular
fibres, and drawn down by the action of the peculiarly human
muscle, the depressor anguli oris, then there is expressed
more agony of mind than of mere bodily suffering, by a combination of muscular actions of which animals are incapable.

The action of the orbicular muscle of the lips is, indeed,
the most characteristic of agony of mind, and of all those
passions which partake of sentiment ; in grief, in vexation
of spirit, in weeping, it modifies the effect of the muscles of
animal expression, and produces human character.

Fear is characterised in animals by a mingling of anger,
and of preparation for defence, with a shrinking of alarm in
the more ferocious, and a straining of the eye and inflation
of the nostril, with trembling, in the milder. In human fear
and suspicion, the nostril is inflated, and the eye has that
backward, jealous, and timid character which we see in the
horse, and in the gentler classes of animals.

The orbicular muscle of the lips, with the system of elevating and depressing muscles in man, lead to expressions

peculiarly human. And here I may observe, that expression is not always the effect of a contraction of the muscles of the face, either general or partial. It proceeds rather from a combined action of the muscles when under passion : for it is often the relaxation of a certain class, more than their excitement, which gives expression ; and of this, smiling and laughter furnish the most apposite examples.

The capacity of receiving ludicrous ideas is as completely denied to animals as they are utterly incapable of the accompanying action of laughter. Dogs, in their expression of fondness, have a slight eversion of the lips, and grin and snuff amidst their frolic and gambols, in a way that resembles laughter ; but in all this there is nothing which truly approaches to human expression. That is produced by the relaxation of the orbicular muscle of the lips, and the consequent preponderating action of the elevating muscles ; and, of course, it can exist only in a face which possesses both the orbicular and the straight muscles of the lips in perfection.

In the emotions of contempt, pride, suspicion, and jealousy, the orbicular muscle and the triangularis oris, produce by their combination the arching of the lips, and the depression of the angle of the mouth. The horizontal drawing of the lips, which just discloses the teeth, and betrays the severe or bitter and malignant passions, is owing to a more general action of the muscles overcoming the opposition of the orbicularis.

In grief, the muscles of the eyebrow and those of the lips are combined in expression ; hence the union of that upward direction of the extremity of the eyebrow characterising peevishness, discontent, and sinking of the spirits, with the depression of the angle of the mouth, which so distinctly indicates the harassed and subdued state of mind.

By the combination of those muscles of expression, much of that various play of the features expressive of human passions, as joy, hope, admiration, anxiety, fear, horror, despair, is produced ; and thus, while the human countenance is capable of expressing both the rage of the more ferocious animals, and the timidity of the milder, it possesses, by the consentaneous action of a few superadded muscles, powers of expression varying almost to infinity.

It is curious to observe how the muscles thus afford a new occasion of distinguishing the classes of animals ; and how, as signs of superior intelligence, they give proofs of the endowments of man, and the excellence of his nature. The full clear eye ; the arched and moveable eyebrow ; the smooth and polished forehead ; as indicating susceptibility of emotion, and power of expression, are grand features of human character and beauty ; and it is the perfection of beauty when the spectator is made sensible of this inherent, this latent power, even while no prevailing passion affects the features. But a great portion of the beauty of the human face is in the nose and the mouth ; in a nostril which has a capacity for expression, without being too membranous and inflatable, for that produces a mean and imbecile kind of fierceness ; and in lips, at once full and capable of those various modulations of form which are necessary to speech and the indication of human feeling.

ESSAY VI.

"Grief laments the absence, and fear apprehends the loss of what we love; desire pursues it; hope has it in view; and joy triumphs in possession."*

OF EXPRESSION (CONTINUED).

WE advance to the interesting subject of variable expression in the human face. It is by the habit of expression that the countenance is improved or degraded, and that the characters of virtue or vice are imprinted. If hardship, misfortune, care, and, still more, vice, are there habitually impressed, then all that we admire is lost.

Peace, comfort, society, and agreeable studies, preserve the features mobile, and ready to conform, as an index of the mind, to the sentiments we love. Petrarch, Boccaccio, and Dante, dwell on the expression of their mistresses.† Addison

---

* Heylin, vol. i. p. 5.
† " Poi guardo l'amorosa e bella bocca—
    La spaziosa fronte, e il vago piglio
    Li bianchi denti, e il dritto naso, e il ciglio
    Polito e brun tal che depinto pare."—DANTE.

" Soave va a guisa di un bel pavone."
                                 Decamerone Giornata, iv.

has justly said, "No woman can be handsome by the force
of features alone, any more than she can be witty only by
the help of speech."

The form of the face and the features are but the ground-
work of expression. The influence of passion on the body is
a subject which has been discussed from the first dawnings
of philosophy. The Greeks did not confine their study to the
outward form of man; they also speculated on the habit of
the body as affecting the mind : and we insensibly use their
language, although the course of their ideas may be rejected
or forgotten. There are varieties in the forms, strength,
temper, and capacities of man. It has been well said that
you cannot tread on a man's toe without learning something
of his temper. One man will have his joke, although it may
hurt his dearest friend, and another has so little imagination,
that even in the delirium of fever he is dull. Some are
generous to profligacy, or frugal to meanness, or gallant and
true, or cowardly and insincere : these varieties are a part of
human nature, and necessary to the constitution of society.
But the ingenious reasoners of Ancient Greece ascribed the
diversity of disposition to the texture of the frame; not to
the features, nor to the proportions or shape of the skull, but
rather to the mixture of the elements of the body; and more
to the fluids than to the solids. Those distinctions, familiar
to all, have in every succeeding age been attributed to the
humours. When we speak of the constitution, the temper,
the humour of a man, we are in truth adopting the language
of Hippocrates, who treated of the four radical humours,—
the sanguineous, phlegmatic, choleric, and melancholic.

Other philosophers have imagined that the dispositions of
man might have their source in his greater or less resemblance

to the brutes. It was then allowable to fancy that a lion-like frame, strong hair, deep voice, and powerful limbs, were combined with courage. But our heroes are not of that mould. To be collected amidst fire and smoke, and the deafening sounds of battle—to marshal thousands—or to direct the vessel's course, whilst exposed not only to wounds but to death, is true courage; and, in these days, it is witnessed in the pale and fragile, more than in the strong and sanguineous, or the bulky and hairy savage. We can better estimate true courage since combatants have been divested of the helmet and mail.*

That the features indicate the disposition by resembling those of animals, is an unjust and dangerous theory. The comparison which we have made of the human form and features with those of certain classes of animals, is very different from those speculations which would lead us to condemn a man because of some resemblance in face to a brute.†

Notwithstanding the attraction of the engravings in Lavater's work, the study of physiognomy is now abandoned for that of the cranium. But I must repeat, that the brain and the skull are constructed in strict relation,—a perfect

* Sir G. N., in the assault of ——, killed his opponent. "The soldier thrust at me with his bayonet. I parried, and passed my sword through his body. In withdrawing it, I experienced a sensation which will only leave me with life." A kindred spirit expresses himself well. "The modern soldier is not the stern, bloody-handed man the ancient soldier was;" the ancient warrior, fighting with the sword, and reaping the harvest of death when the enemy was in flight, became habituated to the art of slaying. "The modern soldier sees not his peculiar victims fall, and exults not over them as proof of personal prowess." Homer represents Achilles as driving over the dead, till his chariot-wheels are dyed in blood.

† This was the theory of Giambatista Porta, in his "Humana Physiognomia." He was equally successful in detecting the qualities of plants by their resemblance to animals.

brain and a perfect skull are formed together. And what is the perfection of the skull? The cranium is as a helmet, constituted for the protection of the brain; and if so, must it not be adapted to the forces it has to sustain or resist? The skull is most perfect when its forms indicate the best possible provision for its peculiar use, the defence of the brain.

Let us attend more especially to the human passions. I do not mean to treat of all those conditions of mind which are considered under the head of the passions, sentiments, or emotions; but to limit my inquiry to that kind or degree of mental excitement, which draws the frame into action, and which is interpreted by its agitation; when the spirits, by their vehemence, produce uncontrollable movements of the body, not determined by the will, but spontaneously arising with the state of feeling, which they strengthen and direct.*

We shall begin, by marking the most extreme expression of the passions,—*laughter* and *weeping*. They suit our purpose as being peculiarly human, arising from sentiments not participated by the brutes.

It is vain to inquire into the sources of these emotions; but I hope my reader consents to believe that the capacity of expression is bestowed as a boon, a mark of superior intelligence, and a source of enjoyment; and that its very nature is to excite sympathy; that it radiates, and is understood by all; that it is the bond of the human family.

* Were we not to limit our inquiry to the agitations of the body, we should be embarrassed with the ambiguity of such words as passion, emotion, desire, inclination, appetite, the generous passions, the passion of pride or of avarice; even the mere state of suffering is called passion.

U

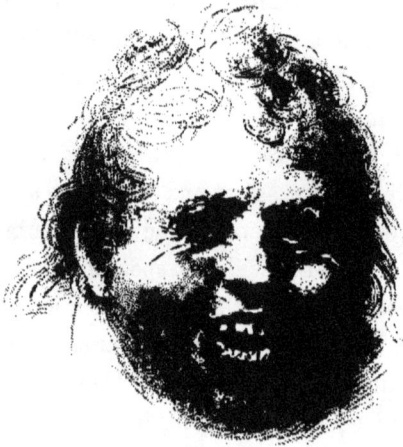

We have seen that the muscles which operate upon the mouth are distinguishable into two classes,—those which surround and control the lips, and those which oppose them, and draw the mouth widely open. The effect of a ludicrous idea is to relax the former, and to contract the latter; hence, by a lateral stretching of the mouth, and a raising of the cheek to the lower eyelid, a smile is produced. The lips are, of all the features, the most susceptible of action, and the most direct index of the feelings.

If the idea be exceedingly ridiculous, it is in vain that we endeavour to restrain this relaxation, and to compress the lips. The muscles concentring to the mouth prevail; they become more and more influenced; they retract the lips, and display the teeth. The cheeks are more powerfully drawn up, the eyelids wrinkled, and the eye almost concealed. The lacrymal gland within the orbit is compressed by the pressure on the eyeball, and the eye suffused with tears.

Simple and passive pleasures, the delight of meeting or the contemplation of innocence, relax the lips and dimple the cheek, whilst the eyes are bright and intelligent. The dimple is formed by the muscles which are inserted in the angle of the mouth acting on the plump integument of infancy and youth.

Observe the condition of a man convulsed with laughter, and consider what are the organs or system of parts affected. He draws a full breath, and throws it out in interrupted, short, and audible cachinnations; the muscles of his throat, neck, and chest, are agitated; the diaphragm is especially convulsed. He holds his sides, and, from the violent agitation, he is incapable of a voluntary act.

It is impossible to avoid the conclusion, that it is the respiratory organs and their muscles which are affected during the paroxysm of laughter. Physiologists, in all former times, attributed the line of sympathetic relations which draw these remote parts into action, to a nerve called the sympathetic. But I have proved, that there is a machinery altogether distinct; and that the expression, not only of this, but of all the other passions, arises from that system of nerves, which, from their great office, I have called *respiratory*.

The respiratory nerves spring from a common centre in

the medulla oblongata,* and pass off divergingly to all the parts just enumerated, and to every organ employed in respiration. They combine these distant parts in the ordinary action of breathing ; and they are the agents in all the effects of passion, when these organs give the outward signs of the condition of the mind.

WEEPING.†

* The medulla oblongata is that part of the nervous system which is traced from the brain into the tube of the spine ; it is, consequently, the upper part of the spinal marrow.

† I have thrown the expression of weeping, from pain, into the face of a Faun ; for such expression is inexpressibly mean and ludicrous in the countenance of a man.

Weeping is another state of the features, proceeding, as we have before observed, from sensibility; and, therefore, human. Though the organs affected are the same as in laughter, viz., the respiratory muscles, the expression is as much opposed as the nature of the emotion which produces it. Were the condition of the features the effect of mere excitement, why should there be an association of the same class of muscles, so different from that in laughter? Is not this variety of expression a proof of *design*, and that all our emotions are intended to have their appropriate outward characters?

According to Homer, the expression of weeping is not confined to babes; Ulysses is made to feel that sensation in his nose which precedes the shedding of tears.

The lacrymal glands are the first to be affected; then the eyelids; and finally, the whole converging muscles of the cheeks. The lips are drawn aside, not from their circular fibres relaxing, as in laughter, but from their being forcibly retracted by the superior influence of their antagonist muscles. Instead of the joyous elevation of the cheeks, the muscle which pulls down the angle of the mouth, *triangularis oris*, is more under influence, and the angle is depressed. The cheeks are thus drawn between two adverse powers: the muscles which surround the eyelids, and that which depresses the lower lip.

The same cause which drew the diaphragm and muscles of the chest into action in laughing is perceived here. The diaphragm is spasmodically and irregularly affected; the chest and throat are influenced; the breathing is cut by sobbing; the inspiration is hurried, and the expiration is slow with a melancholy note. In the violence of weeping, accompanied with lamentation, the face is flushed, or rather suffused by stagnant blood, and the veins of the forehead

distended.   In this we see the effect of the impeded action
of the chest; a proof, not only that it is the respiratory
system of nerves which is affected, but also of the condition
of the heart, and its influence in respiration, of which we
have spoken in a former essay.   This expression of emotion
may be introduced even in the highest walks of art; but it
requires great taste to pourtray it without offensive exaggeration.*

The depression of the angle of the mouth gives an air of
despondence and languor when accompanied by a general
relaxation of the features, or, in other words, of the muscles.
When the *corrugator* which knits the brows co-operates
with it, there is mingled in the expression something of
mental energy, of moroseness, or pain.   If the frontal
muscle adds its operation, there is an acute turning upwards of the inner part of the eyebrow, characteristic of
anguish, debilitating pain, or of discontent, according to the
prevailing cast of the rest of the countenance.

But while languor and despondency are indicated by
depression of the angle of the mouth, the depression must
be slight, not violent : for the *depressor anguli oris* cannot
act strongly without the combination of the *levator menti*

* "The finest possible example of this condition of suffering is in the
picture of Guercino (in the Gallery of Milan), the 'Departure of Hagar and
Ishmael.' Those who have seen only the engraving can have little conception
of the beauty of the picture, for the perfection is in the colouring. Hagar
has been weeping ; her eyes are red and swollen, but not so as to destroy
her beauty; she turns again on hearing Abraham once more addressing her;
she suspends her breath, you persuade yourself that you hear her short convulsive sobs; for in the elevated shoulders and in the form of the open lips,
this is plainly indicated. The suffering expressed in the condition of the
chest, the misery in the forehead, and the colouring of the eyelids, make this
the finest example of expression which I have seen."—*Note from Journal.*

or *superbus*, which quickly produces a change in the expression, by making the nether lip pout contemptuously.

In sorrow, a general languor pervades the whole countenance. The violence and tension of grief, the lamentations, and the tumult, like all strong excitements, gradually exhaust the frame. Sadness and regret, with depression of spirits and fond recollections, succeed ; and lassitude of the whole body, with dejection of the face and heaviness of the eyes, are the most striking characteristics. The lips are relaxed and the lower jaw drops ; the upper eyelid falls and half covers the pupil of the eye. The eye is frequently filled with tears, and the eyebrows take an inclination similar to that which the depressors of the angles of the lips give to the mouth.*

I am not quite sure that in the distress of Constance there is not an unnatural mixture of the tumult and violence of grief with the contemplative recollections of sorrow. Her impatience and turbulence, which make her tear her hair, defy all counsel and redress, and call on death or madness as her sole relief, seem ill assorted with that calmness of spirit which can stop to recollect and enumerate in detail the figure and endearing manners of her son.

> " Grief fills the room up of my absent child,
> Lies in his bed, walks up and down with me ;
> Puts on his pretty looks, repeats his words,
> Remembers me of all his gracious parts,
> Stuffs out his vacant garments with his form :
> Then, have I reason to be fond of grief.
> Fare you well ! had you had such a loss as I,
> I could give better comfort than you do.—

---

* Some have been so far deceived by the effect of this raising of the eyebrows towards the centre of the forehead as to give the same oblique line to the eyes ; but the canthus or angle of the eye is fixed immoveably, and no working of passion can alter it.

I will not keep this form upon my head [*tearing off her head-dress.*]
When there is such disorder in my wit.
O Lord! my boy, my Arthur, my fair son!
My life, my joy, my food, my all the world!
My widow's comfort, and my sorrows' cure!" *

This appears rather to be the stage of the passion which is called sorrow; the indulgence of which is attended with a melancholy delight which can sanction the conclusion, " Then have I reason to be fond of grief." Yet, as conviction returns at intervals upon the mind, a period of quiet and sorrowful resignation is succeeded by starts and violent bursts of grief.

Though grief is in general distinguished by its violence, lamentation, and tumult, while sorrow is silent, deep brooding, and full of depression, there is a stupefaction which sometimes characterises grief, " the lethargy of woe."

We have already had occasion to remark, that expressions, peculiarly human, chiefly affect the angle of the mouth and the inner extremity of the eyebrow; and to these points we must principally attend in all our observations concerning the expression of passion. They are the most moveable parts of the face; in them, the muscles concentre, and upon the changes which they undergo, expression is acknowledged chiefly to depend. To demonstrate their importance, we have only to repeat the experiment made by Peter of Cortona; to sketch a placid countenance, and touch lightly with the pencil the angle of the lips and the inner extremity of the eyebrows. By elevating or depressing these, we shall quickly convey the expression of grief or of laughter.

These parts, however, and all the features of an impassioned countenance, have an accordance with each other. When

* King John, Act III. Scene 4.

the angles of the mouth are depressed in grief, the eyebrows are not elevated at the outer angles as in laughter. When a smile plays around the mouth, or the cheek is raised in laughter, the brows are not ruffled as in grief. The characters of such opposite passions are so distinct, that they cannot be combined where there is true and genuine emotion. When we see them combined, it is by those who have an unnatural control over their muscles, and the expression is farcical and ridiculous. It is an unworthy conceit to give to one side of the face comedy and to the other tragedy.

In the features of an impassioned countenance there is a consent and accordance of expression. It is not upon a single feature that the emotion operates ; but the whole face is marked with expression, all the movements of which are consentaneous. This is referable to some cause acting gene-rally on the tone and state of the frame : the peculiar ex-pression of individual emotion being distinguished by the action and determination of certain features.

Taking indifference as the line of distinction between the two great classes of pain and of pleasure, the sensations above this line are weak compared with those below it. The simple sensations of pleasure, before they are heightened and diver-sified by the multiplied associations of mental affection, are soft and gentle in their nature. The class of painful sensations is powerful and overwhelming ; they are meant as our guardians and protectors against danger and death, and they operate with resistless force. The pleasureable sensations induce a languor and delight, partaking of the quality of indulgence and relaxation ; the painful excite to the most violent tension, and make the muscular frame start into con-vulsive action.

x

The emotions and passions, grounded on these great classes
of sensation, raised and increased by the mingling of hopes
and fears, and the combination of analogous and associated
images of delight or of danger, derive their most important
traits of expression from the general tone of pleasure or of
pain.

In pain, the body is exerted to violent tension, and all the
emotions and passions allied to pain, or having their origin
and foundation in painful sensations, have this general distinction of character, that there is an energetic action or
tremor, the effect of universal and great excitement. It must
at the same time be remembered, that all the passions of this
class, some more immediately, others more indirectly, produce
in the second stage exhaustion, debility, and loss of tone,
from over-exertion.

On the other hand, as pleasure is characterised by languor,
tranquillity, and relaxation, all the emotions related to it, or
deducible from pleasureable sensations, are felt in the prevailing state of the system—a degree of inaction, and as it
were forgetfulness of bodily exertion, and an indulgence in
mental contemplation.* The contemplation of beauty, or the

---

* "Here (Academia delle Belle Arte, Bologna) are two pictures which
one naturally compares.   On the one side is the St. Cecilia ; on the other,
the Murder of the Innocents.   In the St. Cecilia of Raphael, in ecstasy,
there is not only great beauty, but very fine expression.   She hears the
music of angels ; her face is turned upwards ; the features composed and
fine.   In the lower part of the face there is a gentle relaxation, almost a
smile ; the eyes are directed upwards, but the eyebrow is placid.   She is
so wrapt, that the pipes of the organ are almost falling from the hands,
which hang without exertion.
"In the picture of the Murder of the Innocents, by Guido Reni, there
is an admirable figure of a woman, wild and full of fire, who flies with her
infant pressed to her bosom.   But there is another, whose face is in the

admiration of soft music, produces a sense of languor; the body reclines; the lips are half opened; the eyes have a softened lustre from the falling of the eyelids; the breathing is slow; and from the absolute neglect of bodily sensation, and the temporary interruption of respiration, there is a frequent low-drawn sigh.

very attitude of the Cecilia, yet how different! The murder of her child has been perpetrated; the child lies dead before her; she is on her knees; her hands are clasped, and she looks up to heaven; her mouth is open, and all the features relaxed. The hair and dress are deranged. What, then, is the difference in expression, for there is a certain resemblance in the form and attitude of these heads? What is the difference between the relaxation of despair and of enjoyment? the relaxed jaw, and open mouth, and troubled forehead of the one,—the softness and languor, with a certain firmness in the lips of the other."—*Note from Journal.*

ESSAY VII.

THE further we proceed in this inquiry the more difficult
and delicate does it become. In continuing the subject, I
shall rather indulge in detached remarks than pretend to
follow a regular course; keeping, I hope, still true to the
observation of nature, and, as far as possible, unprejudiced
by theory.

Pain is affirmed to be unqualified evil; yet pain is necessary to our existence; at birth, it rouses the dormant faculties, and gives us consciousness. To imagine the absence
of pain, is not only to imagine a new state of being, but a
change in the earth, and all upon it. As inhabitants of
earth, and as a consequence of the great law of gravitation,
the human body must have weight. It must have bones, as
columns of support, and levers for the action of its muscles;
and this mechanical structure implies a complication and
delicacy of texture beyond our conception. For that fine
texture a sensibility to pain is destined to be the protection;
it is the safeguard of the body; it makes us alive to those
injuries which would otherwise destroy us, and warns us to
avoid them.

When, therefore, the philosopher asks why were not our actions performed at the suggestions of pressure, he imagines man, not constituted as he is, but as if he belonged to a world in which there was neither weight, nor pressure, nor anything injurious, where there were no dangers to apprehend, no difficulties to overcome, and no call for exertion, resolution, or courage. It would, indeed, be a curious speculation to follow out the consequences on the highest qualities of the mind, if we could suppose man thus free from all bodily suffering.

But I return to the position, that pain is the great safeguard of the frame, and now proceed to examine its expression.

In bodily pain the jaws are fixed, and the teeth grind :
the lips are drawn laterally, the nostrils dilated ; the eyes
are largely uncovered and the eyebrows raised; the face is
turgid with blood, and the veins of the temple and forehead
distended ; the breath being checked, and the descent of
blood from the head impeded by the agony of the chest, the
cutaneous muscle of the neck acts strongly, and draws down
the angles of the mouth. But when, joined to this, the man
cries out, the lips are retracted, and the mouth open ; and we
find the muscles of his body rigid, straining, struggling. If
the pain be excessive he becomes insensible, and the chest is
affected by sudden spasms. On recovering consciousness, he
is incoherent, till again roused by suffering. In bodily pain
conjoined with distress of mind, the eyebrows are knit, while
their inner extremities are raised ; the pupils are in part concealed by the upper eyelids, and the nostrils are agitated.

The expression of pain is distinguished from that of weeping not less than from that of laughing. These arise from
mental conditions, independent of physical causes, and are
uncontrollable and sympathetic. But pain is bodily ; that is
to say, there is a positive nervous sensation, which excites to
action, or to acts of volition ; an energy of the whole frame
is produced by suffering, and, from the consciousness of its
place or source, the efforts are directed to remove it. Hence
the struggle, the powerful and voluntary exertions which
accompany it. Yet there is a resemblance and, in some
degree, an alliance between these actions and the spasms
excited by galvanism in experiments on the nerves of animals
apparently dead.

"*He has a Devil.*"—Two of the greatest painters, Raphael
and Domenichino, have painted demoniacal boys. In the
convent of the Grotto Ferrata, in the neighbourhood of Rome,
Domenichino has represented Saint Nilus in the act of reliev-
ing a lad possessed.* The saint, an old man, is on his knees
in prayer; the lad is raised and held up by an aged man;
the mother with a child is waiting the consummation of the
miracle. Convulsions have seized the lad; he is rigidly bent
back; the lower limbs spasmodically extended, so that his
toes only rest on the ground; the eyes are distorted, and the
pupils turned up under the eyelids. This would be the position of Opisthotonos, were not the hands spread abroad, the
palms and fingers open, and the jaw fallen. Had the representation been perfectly true to nature, the jaws would have
been clenched, and the teeth grinding. But then the miracle
could not have been represented, for one, under the direction
of the saint, has the finger of his left hand in the boy's mouth,
and the other holds a vessel of oil, with which the tongue is
to be touched. The drawing and colouring exhibited in the
lad, and the grandeur of the old men, make this one of the
most admired paintings in Italy.

I have here given a sketch of the true Opisthotonos, where
it is seen that all the muscles are rigidly contracted, the more
powerful flexors prevailing over the extensors. Were the

* "Domenichino, in consequence of some peccadillo, took shelter in the
sanctuary of the monks of the Grotto Ferrata, a fortified convent some
miles distant from Rome. The monks, under the threat of delivering him
up, made him paint their walls; and the frescoes are, indeed, beautiful,
particularly the old men. That compartment which is called the Demoniac
Boy, is most admired."—*Note from Journal.*

painter to represent every circumstance faithfully, the effect
might be too painful, and something must be left to his taste
and imagination.*

It may be considered bold to criticise the works of Raphael;
but I venture to say that, if that great master intended, in
his cartoon of the Death of Ananias, to excite horror, the
effect would have been more powerful, if there had been
greater truth in the convulsions of the chief figure, instead
of a mere twisting of the body. Strange it is, but true, that
we are most affected by the more slight, if correct, por-
traiture of a natural condition.

In the same painter's great picture of the Transfiguration,
in the Vatican, there is a lad possessed, and in convulsions.

* The original sketch is in the College of Surgeons of Edinburgh. I
took it from soldiers wounded in the head, at the battle of Corunna. Three
men were similarly hurt, and in short successive intervals similarly affected,
so that the character could not be mistaken.

I hope I am not insensible to the beauties of that picture, nor presumptuous in saying that the figure is not natural. A physician would conclude that this youth was feigning. He is, I presume, convulsed; he is stiffened with contractions, and his eyes turned in their sockets. But no child was ever so affected. In real convulsions, the extensor muscles yield to the more powerful contractions of the flexor muscles; whereas, in the picture, the lad extends his arms; and the fingers of the left hand are stretched unnaturally backwards. Nor do the lower extremities correspond with truth; he stands firm; the eyes are not natural; they should have been turned more inwards, as looking into the head, and partially buried under the forehead. The mouth, too, is open, which is quite at variance with the general condition, and without the apology which Domenichino had. The muscles of the arms are exaggerated to a degree which Michael Angelo never attempted; and still it is the extensors and supinators, and not the flexors, which are thus prominent.

Disease has characteristic symptoms, which we can accurately and scientifically reduce to description; and borrowing from this source, there is no state of suffering from which we can so well infer the nature of the agitation of the frame as from hydrophobia. The patient being sensible of his condition, and calm, and aware of the experiment which is to be made upon him by his physician, when he calls for a glass of water, cannot resist the influence of the disease. He shudders, his face assumes an expression of extreme horror and alarm; convulsive gulpings take place in his throat; he flies to some support, and clings to the bedpost in an agony of suffocation. This I have witnessed in a powerful man. I have had the pain of seeing the disease in a girl of eighteen. The irritability of the skin being increased to an awful degree, so that the touch of her long hair falling on her naked body, excited, as she said, the paroxysms. These recurred with a sense of choking, with sudden and convulsive heavings of the chest, a shuddering, and catching of the muscles of breathing, and an appalling expression of suffering. The paroxysms in such a case becoming more frequent and severe, finally exhaust the

powers of life. In these convulsions it is the nervous and muscular systems belonging to the natural function of respiration which are affected; and as they are also the organs of expression, the condition is seen not only in the countenance, but in the throat and chest, to be that of extreme horror.

163

FEAR.

" Nam Timor unus erat, facies non una timoris,
Pars laniat crines, pars sine mente sedet.
Altera mœsta silet, frustra vocat altera matrem,
Hæc queritur, stupet hæc, hæc fugit, illa manet."
OVID, *De Arte Amandi.*

So Ovid describes the Sabine virgins; and such the
tumultuary and distracted state of mind produced by fear.
" And there is good reason for this, because in a sudden daunt
and onset of an unexpected evil, the spirits which were before orderly carried by their several due motions unto their
natural works, are upon this strange appearance and instant
oppression of danger so disordered, mixed, and stifled, that
there is no power left either in the soul for counsel, or in the
body for execution." In mere bodily fear there is mere
animal expression and meanness. The breath is drawn and
the respiration suspended ; the body fixed, and powerless ;
the eyes riveted, or searching and unsteady ; and the action
undetermined.

Mr. Burke, in his speculations on fear, assimilates it, with
perhaps too little discrimination, to pain. "A man in great
pain," he observes, "has his teeth set ; his eyebrows are
violently contracted ; his forehead is wrinkled ; his eyes are
dragged inwards, and rolled with great vehemence ; his hair
stands on end ; his voice is forced out in short shrieks and
groans ; and the whole fabric totters."—"Fear or terror," he
continues, "which is an apprehension of pain or death, exhibits
exactly the same effects, approaching in violence to those just
mentioned, in proportion to the nearness of the cause, and the
weakness of the subject." *

* Sublime and Beautiful, Part IV. sect. 3.   Cause of Pain and Fear.

But there is one distinguishing feature of the two conditions : the immediate effect of pain is to produce an energetic action and tension of the whole frame ; that of fear is to relax all the energy of mind and of body—to paralyse, as it were, every muscle. Mr. Burke seems to have written loosely, partly from forgetting that pain and fear are often combined, and partly from taking a view of the subject too much limited to the particular conclusion which he wished to enforce. There cannot be great pain without its being attended by the distraction of doubts and fears ; the dread even of death is a natural consequence of extreme pain, and so the expression of fear in the countenance is frequently mingled with that of pain. But, perhaps, there are few passions which may not be assimilated by such combinations ; fear and hatred ; hatred and rage ; rage and vengeance and remorse. On the other hand, confining ourselves to simple bodily fear, there is much truth in the observation of this eloquent writer. The fear of boiling water falling on the legs, gives an expression of the anticipation of scalding, resembling the meaner expression of bodily pain. As Mr. Burke says, fear in the dog will no doubt be that of the lash, and he will yelp and howl as if he actually felt the blows ; and this indeed is the only kind of fear which brutes know. The higher degrees of fear, in which the mind operates, and which we shall see characterised in the countenance by an expression peculiar to mental energy, do not appear in them.

In man, the expression of mere bodily fear is like that of animals, without dignity ; it is the mean anticipation of pain. The eyeball is largely uncovered, the eyes are staring, and the eyebrows elevated to the utmost stretch. There is a spasmodic affection of the diaphragm and muscles of the chest, disturbing the breathing, producing a gasping in the throat, with an inflation of the nostril, convulsive opening of the mouth, and dropping of the jaw ; the lips nearly conceal the teeth, yet allow the tongue to be seen, the space between the nostril and the lip being full. There is a hollowness and convulsive motion of the cheeks, and a trembling of the lips, and

muscles on the side of the neck. The lungs are kept distended, while the breathing is short and rapid. From the connexion of the nerves of the lungs and diaphragm with those of the side of the neck, and with the branches which supply the cutaneous muscle of the cheek and neck, we may comprehend the cause of the convulsive motion of this muscle.*

* See Essay on the Nerves.

The aspect is pale and cadaverous from the receding of the blood.   The hair is lifted up by the creeping of the skin, and action of the occipito-frontalis.

In the preceding sketch, I have endeavoured to express fear mingled with wonder.   But if we should suppose the fear there represented, to have arisen from apprehended

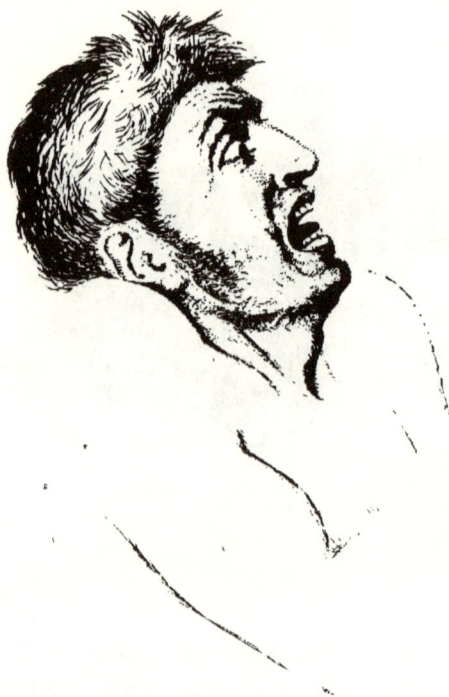

danger still remote, and that the object of fear approaches, and is now about to cleave to the person, he trembles, looks pale, has a cold sweat on his face, and in proportion as the imagination has less room to range in, as the danger is more distinctly visible, the expression partakes more of actual bodily pain. The scream of fear is heard, the eyes start forward, the lips are drawn wide, the hands are clenched, and the expression becomes more strictly animal, and indicative of such fear as is common to brutes.[*]

[*] I shall here transcribe a portion from my brother's volume on Italy. Mr. John Bell travelled in declining health ; and died in Rome, in 1820. He had written a great deal with a pencil, in the course of his journey ; and no less than thirty small volumes of notes, thus jotted down on his knee, were submitted by his widow to Professor Bell and myself. In these we saw much to admire ; but knowing how much would have been changed and corrected had our brother lived, we thought them unfit for publication. Of the many striking passages in the work, the following may be selected as relating to the present subject :—

"*Turin. The Execution of an Assassin.*—I found myself opposite to the distracted criminal whom they were conducting to execution in all the agonies of terror and despair. He was seated in a black car, preceded by arquebusiers, on horseback, carrying their carabines pointed forward. These were followed by a band of priests, clothed in long black robes, singing, in deep and solemn tones, a slow mournful dirge,—part of the service for the dead. A hot burning sun shone with a flood of light ; and, though it was mid-day, such was the silence, and such the power and effect of this solemn chant, that its sound was re-echoed from every distant street. The brothers of the Misericordia, clothed in black, and masked, walked by the side of the car, and joined in the chant. On the steps of the car sat a man bearing a flag, on which Death was represented in the usual forms, and on which was inscribed in Latin (if I read it rightly), 'Death has touched me with his fingers,' or 'Death has laid his hands on me.' On each side of the car, the officiating priests were seated ; and in the centre, sat the criminal himself. It was impossible to witness the condition of this unhappy wretch without terror ; and yet, as if impelled by some strange infatuation, it was equally impossible not to gaze upon an object so wild, so full of horror. He seemed about thirty-five years of age; of large and muscular form; his countenance marked by strong and savage features ; half naked, pale as death, agonised with terror, every limb strained in anguish, his hands clenched convulsively, the sweat breaking out on his bent and contracted brow, he kissed incessantly the figure of our Saviour, painted on the flag which was suspended before him ; but with an agony of wildness and despair, of which, nothing ever exhibited on the stage can give the slightest conception. I could not refrain from moralising upon the scene here presented. The horror that the priest had excited in the soul of this savage, was greater than the fear of the most cruel

I should apply the name of terror to that kind of fear, in which there is a strong working of the imagination, and which is therefore peculiar to man. The eye is bewildered; the inner extremity of the eyebrows is elevated, and strongly knit by the action of the corrugator; thus producing an expression of distracting thought, anxiety, and alarm, and one which does not belong to animals. The cheek is a little raised, and all the muscles which are concentred about the mouth are active; there being a kind of modulating action in the circular muscle of the lips, which keeps the mouth partially open. The cutaneous muscle of the neck, the platysma myoides, is strongly contracted, and its fibres may be seen starting into action like cords, under the skin, and dragging powerfully on the angles of the mouth. The imagination wanders; there is an indecision in the action, the steps are furtive and unequal, there is a spasm which hinders speech, and the colour of the cheeks vanishes.

> " Canst thou quake and change thy colour,
> Murther thy breath in middle of a word,
> And then again begin, and stop again,
> As if thou wast distraught and mad with terror ?" *

When mingled with astonishment, terror is fixed and mute. The fugitive and unnerved steps of mere terror are

death could ever have produced. But the terrors thus raised, were the superstitions of an ignorant and bewildered mind, bereft of animal courage, and impressed with some confused belief, that eternal safety was to be instantly secured by external marks of homage to the image. There was here none of the composed, conscious, awful penitence of a Christian ; and it was evident, that the priest was anxious only to produce a being in the near prospect of death, whose condition should alarm all that looked on him. The attempt was successful."—*Observations on Italy*, p. 48. By the late John Bell. Published by his Widow. Edinburgh, 1825.

* Richard III. Act iii. Scene 5.

then changed for the rooted and motionless figure of a creature appalled and stupified. Spenser characterises well this kind of terror :—

> " He answer'd nought at all : but adding new
> Fear to his first amazement, staring wide
> With stony eyes, and heartless hollow hue,
> Astonish'd stood, as one that had espy'd
> Infernal furies with their chains unty'd.
>
>   *   *   *   *   *
>
> But trembling every joint did inly quake,
> And falt'ring tongue at last these words seem'd forth to shake." *

Horror differs from both fear and terror, although more nearly allied to the last than to the first. It is superior to both in this, that it is less imbued with personal alarm. It is more full of sympathy with the sufferings of others, than engaged with our own. We are struck with horror even at the spectacle of artificial distress, but it is peculiarly excited by the real danger or pain of another. We see a child in the hazard of being crushed by an enormous weight, with sensations of extreme horror. Horror is full of energy ; the body is in the utmost tension, not unnerved, by fear. The flesh creeps, and a sensation of cold seems to chill the blood ; the term is applicable of " damp horror."

Despair is a mingled emotion. While terror is in some measure the balancing and distraction of a mind occupied with an uncertainty of danger, despair is the total wreck of hope, the terrible assurance of ruin having closed around, beyond all power of escape. The expression of despair must vary with the nature of the distress of which it forms the acmé. In certain circumstances it will assume a bewildered, distracted air, as if madness were likely to be the only close

* Faery Queen, Book i. cant. 9, s. 24.

Z

to the mental agony. Sometimes there is at once a wildness in the looks and total relaxation, as if falling into insensibility; or there is upon the countenance of the desperate man a horrid gloom; the eye is fixed, yet he neither sees nor hears aught, nor is sensible of what surrounds him. The features are shrunk and livid, and convulsion and tremors affect the muscles of the face. Hogarth has chosen well the scene of his picture of despair. In a gaming-house, the wreck of all hope affects, in a thousand various ways, the victims of this vice; but in every representation of despair, an inconsolable and total abandonment of those exertions to which hope inspirits and excites a man, forms an essential feature. We have two fine descriptions of despair given in detail by English poets. One is by Spenser:

> "The darksome cave they enter, where they find
> That cursed man, low sitting on the ground,
> Musing full sadly in his sullen mind;
> His greazy locks, long growing and unbound,
> Disorder'd hung about his shoulders round,
> And hid his face; through which his hollow eyne
> Look, deadly dull, and stared as astound;
> His raw-bone cheeks, through penury and pine,
> Were shrunk into his jaws, as he did never dine." *

The other is in the tragedy of the "Gamester," where Beverley, after heart-rending reiteration of hope and disappointment, having staked the last resource of his wife and family on one fatal throw, finds himself suddenly plunged into ruin.

"When all was lost, he fixed his eyes upon the ground, and stood some time with folded arms stupid and motionless: then snatching his sword that hung against the wainscot, he

* Faery Queen, Book i. cant 9, s. 35.

sat him down, and with a look of fixed attention drew figures on the floor. At last he started up; looked wild and trembled; and, like a woman seized with her sex's fits, laughed out aloud, while the tears trickled down his face. So he left the room."

A painter may have to represent terror, despair, astonishment, and supernatural awe, mingled in one powerful expression of emotion. In a mind racked with deep despair, conscious of strength and courage, but withered and subdued by supernatural agency, the expression is quite removed from all meanness; it must be preserved grand and terrific; the hero may still appear, though palpitating and drained of vigour.

Milton has admirably sketched the nerveless stupefaction of mingled astonishment and horror:—

> " On th' other side, Adam, soon as he heard
> The fatal trespass done by Eve, amaz'd,
> Astonied stood and blank, while horror chill
> Ran through his veins, and all his joints relax'd ;
> From his slack hand the garland wreath'd for Eve
> Down dropp'd, and all the faded roses shed :
> Speechless he stood and pale, till thus at length
> First to himself he inward silence broke." *

In admiration, the faculty of sight is enjoyed to the utmost, and all else is forgotten. The brow is expanded and unruffled, the eyebrow gently raised, the eyelid lifted so as to expose the coloured circle of the eye, while the lower part of the face is relaxed in a gentle smile. The mouth is open, the jaw a little fallen, and by the relaxation of the lower lip we just perceive the edge of the lower teeth and the tongue. The posture of the body is most expressive when it seems arrested in some familiar action.

* Paradise Lost, Book ix. ver. 888.

Joy is distinguishable from pleasure. It consists, not so much in the sense of gratification, as in the delight of the conviction that the long-expected pleasure is within our reach, and the lively anticipation of the enjoyment which is now decked out in its most favourite and alluring shape. A certain sensation of want is mingled with joy; a recollection of the alternate hopes and fears which formerly distracted the mind, contrasted with the immediate assurance of gratification.

In joy the eyebrow is raised moderately, but without any angularity; the forehead is smooth; the eye full, lively, and sparkling; the nostril is moderately inflated, and a smile is on the lips. In all the exhilarating emotions, the eyebrow, the eyelid, the nostril, and the angle of the mouth are raised. In the depressing passions it is the reverse. For example, in discontent the brow is clouded, the nose peculiarly arched, and the angle of the mouth drawn down.

Contrasted with joy is the testy, pettish, peevish countenance bred of melancholy; as of one who is incapable of receiving satisfaction from whatever source it may be offered; who cannot endure any man to look steadily upon him, or even speak to him, or laugh, or jest, or be familiar, or hem, or point, without thinking himself contemned, insulted, or neglected.

The arching of the mouth and peculiar form of the wings of the nose are produced by the conjoint action of the triangular muscle which depresses the angles of the mouth, and the superbus, whose individual action protrudes the lower lip. The very peevish turn given to the eyebrows, the acute upward inflection of their inner extremities, and the meeting of the perpendicular and transverse furrows in the middle of the forehead, are produced by the opposed action of part of the frontal muscle and of the corrugator.

Habitual suspicion and jealousy are symptoms and accompaniments of melancholy. Envy may be classed with these expressions; but it is an ungenerous repining, not a momentary passion.* "It consumes a man as a moth does a garment, to be a living anatomy, a skeleton—to be a lean

* "La invidia, crudelissimo dolore di animo, per il bene altrui, fa ritirar tutti i membri, come contraere et offuscar le ciglie, stringere i denti, ritirar le labbra, torcersi con certa passione di sguardo quasi in atto di volere intendere et spiare i fatti altrui," &c.—LOMAZZO, p. 130.

and pale carcass quickened with the fiend—'*intabescetque videndo.*'"

Suspicion is characterised by earnest attention, with a certain timorous obliquity of the eyes :—

> "Foul, ill-favoured and grim,
> Under his eyebrows looking still askance ;
> And ever as Dissemblance laughed on him,
> He lour'd on her with dangerous eye glance,
> Showing his nature in his countenance :
> His rolling eyes did never rest in place,
> But walk'd each where, for fear of hid mischaunce,
> Holding a lattice still before his face,
> Through which he still did peep as forward he did pace." *

Jealousy is marked by a more frowning and dark obliquity of the eyes, as if it said, "I have an eye on you ;" with the lowering eyebrow is combined a cruel expression of the lower part of the face.

Jealousy is a fitful and unsteady passion : its chief character is in the rapid vicissitudes from love to hate ; now absent, moody, and distressed ; now courting love ; now ferocious and revengeful : these changes make it a difficult subject for the painter ; and it is only in poetry that it can be truly presented in the vivid colours of nature. Even among poets, Shakspeare alone seems to have been equal to the task. Sometimes it may be personified in the face of a mean, suspicious, yet oppressed creature ; or again in a lowering expression, the body as if shrunk into itself ; like that of one brooding over his condition, and piecing out a tissue of trifling incidents to abuse his judgment.

In jealousy the eyebrows are knit, and the eyelid so fully lifted as almost to disappear, while the eyeball glares from

* Faery Queen, Book iii. c. 12, s. 15.

under the bushy eyebrow. There is a general tension of the muscles which concentre around the mouth, and the lips retract and shew the teeth with a fierce expression; this depends partly on the turn of the nostril, which accompanies the retraction of the lips. The mouth should express that bitter anguish which the Italian poet has rather too distinctly told :—

> "Trema 'l cor dentro, e treman fuor le labbia,
> Non può la lingua disnodar parola,
> La *bocca amara* e par che tosco v' habbia."

Again:—

> " E per l' ossa un tremor freddo gli scorre,
> Con cor trafitto, e con pallida faccia,
> E con voce tremante, e *bocca amara*."

There seems to be a natural succession in the passions of rage, revenge, and remorse : I do not mean morally, but in regard to our present inquiry concerning the traits of expression. A slight change in the lineaments of rage gives the expression of revenge, while the cruel eye of revenge is tempered by the relaxing energy of the lower part of the countenance in remorse.

Rage is that excess or vehemence of anger that can be no longer restrained—*sæva animi tempestas.* Whether the object be near or remote, the frame is wrought and chafed. It is a brutal passion, in which the body acts with an impetuosity not directed by sense. If we observe it in a beast, we shall better recognise it in man. When the keeper strikes the tiger or the wolf with his pole, there is an instantaneous fire of expression ; the eye, the teeth are in a moment exposed, and accompanied with an excitement of the frame which we cannot see unmoved. If we imagine the human brute strangling helpless age or infancy, it must be with such a rage as this. Lord Kames says, " A stock or a stone by which I am hurt becomes an object of resentment, and I am violently incited to crush it to atoms." This is purely as the wolf bites the stick which is presented to him. In considering those bursts of passion which lead us to wreak our vengeance upon inanimate objects, Dr. Reid supposes we are possessed with the momentary belief that the object is alive :

"There must," he says, "be some momentary notion or conception that the object of our resentment is capable of punishment." I believe the mistake here is in not having a confirmed notion of the intimate connexion between the emotion in the mind and the exertion of the bodily frame. The body and limbs suffer an agitation as the face does, resulting from the passion ; and if a man, half conscious of the frenzy which possesses him, and afraid of being betrayed into an act of cruelty, flings from him the weapon of destruction, it is with the jerk and impetuosity of an outrageous act; whilst his humane sense controls him, it is not capable of arresting that instinctive agency of the body wrought upon by the passion; just as a man, after a long exercise of patience in some work of delicacy or nicety, is at last overcome, dashes the instrument from him, and relieves himself by a burst of impatience and some angry strides.

In rage the features are unsteady; the eyeballs are seen largely; they roll and are inflamed. The front is alternately knit and raised in furrows by the motion of the eyebrows, the nostrils are inflated to the utmost; the lips are swelled, and, being drawn by the muscles, open the corners of the mouth. The whole visage is sometimes pale, sometimes turgid, dark, and almost livid; the words are delivered strongly through the fixed teeth; "the hair is fixed on end like one distracted, and every joint should seem to curse and ban." *

Tasso thus describes the rage of Argante :—

> " Tacque ; e 'l Pagano al sofferir poco uso,
> Morde le labbra, e di furor si strugge.
> Risponder vuol, ma 'l suono esce confuso,
> Siccome strido d' animal, che rugge :
> O come apre le nubi ond' egli è chiuso,
> Impetuoso il fulmine, e sen fugge ;
> Così pareva a forza ogni suo detto
> Tonando uscir dall' infiammato petto."
>
> *Cant.* vi. 38.†

---

* " La furia fa gl' atti stolti e fuor di se ; si comme di quelli che si avvolgono ne i moti offensivi, senza riguardo alcuno, rendendosi vehementi in tutti gl' affetti, con bocca aperta et storta, che par che stridano, ringhino, urlino et si lamentino, stracciandosi le membra et i panni e facendo altre smanie."—LOMAZZO, lib. ii. p. 135.

† If the painter has any imagination and power of delineation, the reading of the combat of Tancred and Argante must inspire him with a grand conception of the sublime ferocity of the human figure in action.

A A

But in representing the passion, it may be much varied : perhaps the eyes are fixed upon the ground ; the countenance pale, troubled, and threatening ; the lip trembling and the breath suppressed, or there is a deep and long inspiration as of inward pain.

In the following sketch I have endeavoured to represent

that expression which succeeds the last horrid act of revenge : the storm has subsided, but the gloom is not yet dissipated. Some compunctious visitings of nature are in the lips, though the eye retains its severity. By the posture and fixed attention, I would indicate that the survey of the now lifeless body carries back the train of thought with regret for past transactions.

To represent the prevailing character and physiognomy of a madman, the body should be strong and the muscles rigid and distinct, the skin bound, the features sharp, the eye sunk; the colour of a dark brownish yellow, tinctured with sallowness, without one spot of enlivening carnation; the hair sooty black, stiff and bushy. Or, perhaps, he might be represented as of a pale sickly yellow, with wiry hair.

> " His burning eyen, whom bloody strakes did stain,
> Stared full wide, and threw forth sparks of fire ;
> And more for rank despight than for great pain,
> Shak'd his long locks, colour'd like copper wire,
> And bit his tawny beard to show his raging ire." *

I do not mean here to trace the progress of the diseases of the mind, but merely to throw out some hints respecting the external character of the outrageous maniac.

You see him lying in his cell regardless of everything, with a death-like settled gloom upon his countenance. When I say it is a death-like gloom, I mean a heaviness of the features without knitting of the brows or action of the muscles. If you watch him in his paroxysm you may see the blood working to his head ; his face acquires a darker red ; he becomes restless; then rising from his couch he paces his cell and tugs his chains; now his inflamed eye is fixed upon you, and his features lighten up into wildness and ferocity.

The error into which a painter may naturally fall, is to represent this expression by the swelling features of passion

* Faery Queen, Book ii. cant. 4, s. 15.

and the frowning eyebrow ; but this would only give the idea
of passion, not of madness.   Or he mistakes melancholia for
madness.   The theory upon which we are to proceed in attempting to convey this peculiar look of ferocity amidst the
utter wreck of the intellect, I conceive to be, that the expression of mental energy should be avoided, and consequently

the action of all those muscles which indicate sentiment.   I
believe this to be true to nature, because I have observed
(contrary to my expectation) that there was not that energy,
that knitting of the brows, that indignant brooding and
thoughtfulness in the face of madmen which is generally
imagined to characterise their expression, and which is so

often given to them in painting. There is a vacancy in their laugh, and a want of meaning in their ferociousness.

To learn the character of the countenance, when devoid of human expression, and reduced to the state of brutality, we must have recourse to the lower animals, and study their looks of timidity, of watchfulness, of excitement, and of ferocity. If these expressions are transferred to the human face, I should conceive that they will irresistibly convey the idea of madness, vacancy of mind, and mere animal passion.

But these discussions are only for the study of the painter. The subject should be full in his mind, without its being for a moment imagined that such painful or humiliating details are suited to the canvass. . If madness is to be represented, it is with a moral aim, to show the consequences of vice and the indulgence of passion.

There is a link of connexion between all liberal professions. The painter may borrow from the physician. He will require something more than his fancy can supply, if he has to represent a priestess or a sybil. It must be the creation of a mind, learned as well as inventive. He may readily conceive a female form full of energy, her imagination at the moment exalted and pregnant, so that things long past are painted in colours as if they stood before her, and her expression becomes bold and poetical. But he will have a more true and precise idea of what is to be depicted, if he reads the history of that melancholia which undoubtedly, in early times, has given the idea of one possessed with a spirit. A young woman is seen constitutionally pale and languid ; and from this inanimate state, no show of affection or entreaty will draw her into conversation with her family. But how changed is her condition, when instead of the lethargy and fixed countenance, the circulation is suddenly restored, the blood mounts to her cheeks, and her eyes sparkle, while both in mind and body she manifests an unwonted energy, and her whole frame is animated. During the continuance of the paroxysm, she delivers herself with a force of thought and language, and in a tone so greatly altered, that even her parents say, "She is not our child, she is not our daughter, a spirit has entered into her." This is in accordance with the prevailing superstition of antiquity; for how natural to suppose, when this girl again falls into a state of torpor, and sits like a marble statue, pale, exhausted, taciturn, that the spirit has left her. The transition is easy; the priests take her under their care, watch her ravings and give them meaning, until she sinks again into a death-like stupor or indifference.

Successive attacks of this kind impress the countenance indelibly. The painter has to represent features powerful, but consistent with the maturity and perfection of feminine beauty. He will show his genius by portraying, not only a fine female form with the grandeur of the antique, but a face of peculiar character; embodying a state of disease often witnessed by the physician, with associations derived from history. If on the dead and uniform paleness of the face he bestows that deep tone of interest which belongs to features inactive, but not incapable of feeling : if he can show something of the imprint of long suffering isolated from human sympathy, throw around her the appropriate mantle, and let the fine hair fall on her shoulders, the picture will require no golden letters to announce her character, as in the old paintings of the Sybil or the Pythoness.

OF DEATH, AS REPRESENTED IN THE PAINTINGS OF THE
OLD MASTERS.

Before proceeding, I must repeat, that the convulsions of the body which sometimes accompany the act of dying, are not the effect of pain, but succeed to insensibility. There may remain, after death, for a time, the expression of suffering; but this soon subsides, and the features become placid and composed. Therefore it is that the sorrowing friends are withdrawn, until Death has had the victory, when the features assume the tranquillity of sleep.

The observation of Leonardo da Vinci, that contrast is essential in painting, has a fine example in the picture of the "Martyrdom of St. Agnes." * Near the martyr lie two soldiers struck down by a miracle : one of these is in the agony, but not yet dead ; the muscles of his neck are convulsed, the mouth extended, and the lips drawn back from the teeth, the brow is furrowed, the eyes almost closed, and the pupils not visible : the other soldier is tumbled over him ; his features are fixed in death : with both of these is contrasted the resignation of the martyr.

When in Rome, I heard much of the fine statue of St. Cecilia Decollata ;† I, therefore, went to the Church of St. Cecilia in Trastevere. Looking for a statue, my surprise was great when it was pointed out where the figure lay, in a crypt or low marble arch, under the great altar.‡ A gold

* In the Academia delle Belle Arte, Bologna.
† Stefano Mademo Sculptor. 1599.
‡ Cardinal Banonius has given us an exact description of the appearance of the body, buried by Pope Paschal (in the 9th century) when exhumed by order of Cardinal Spondati in 1599. "She was lying not in the manner of one dead and buried, that is, on her back, but on her right

case, containing the heart of the saint, hangs from the centre of the arch. St. Cecilia was an early convert to Christianity, and having drawn her brother, and many others to the faith, she suffered martyrdom, and was found in the precise position in which this marble represents her. The body lies on its side, the limbs a little drawn up ; the hands are delicate and fine, they are not locked, but crossed at the wrists ; the arms are stretched out. The drapery is beautifully modelled, and modestly covers the limbs. The head is enveloped in linen, but the general form is seen, and the artist has contrived to convey by its position, though not offensively, that it is separated from the body. A gold circlet is around the neck to conceal the place of *decollation*. It is the statue of a lady, perfect in form, and affecting, from the resemblance to reality in the drapery of white marble, and the unexpected appearance of the statue altogether. It lies, as no living body could lie ; and yet correctly, as the dead, when left to expire,—I mean in the gravitation of the limbs.*

The position of the head will distinguish the dead from the living figure. There is so much difference between fainting and death ; that is to say, it is so possible to mark

side, as one asleep : and in a very modest attitude ; covered with a simple stuff of taffeta, having her head bound with cloth, and at her feet the remains of the cloth of gold and silk which Pope Paschal had found in her tomb." The statue of Mademo agrees exactly with this description.— MRS. JAMESON, *Sacred and Legendary Art.*

 * *Statua di St. Cecilia.*—" Questa graziosa statua giacente, rappresenta un corpo morto come se allora fosse caduto mollemente sul terreno, colle estremità ben disposte e con tutta la decenza nell'assetto dei panneggiamenti, tenendo la testa rivolta all' ingiu e avilluppata in una benda, senza che inopportunamente si scorga l' irrigidire dei corpi freddi per morte. Le pieghe vi sono facile, e tutta la grazia spira dalla persona, che si vede essere giovine e gentile, quantunque asconda la faccia ; le forme generali, e le belle estremità che se mostrano, danno a vedere con quanta grazia e con quanta scelta sia stata imitata la natura in quel posare sì dolcemente."

the difference, that I confess I have been disappointed by the failure of some of the finest painters; for example, in the representation of the Madonna fainting at the foot of the cross, which is a very frequent subject, the colouring is commonly that of death.*

There is sometimes in death a fearful agony in the eye ; but we have said, that it is consolatory to know that this does not indicate suffering, but increasing insensibility. The pupils are turned upwards and inwards. This is especially observed in those who are expiring from loss of blood. It is the *strabismus patheticus orantium* of Boerhaave. Sauvages observes on this rolling up of the eyeball, in dying children, —"Vulgo aiunt hos tenellos suam patriam respicere." 'The vulgar say, that these little ones are looking to their native home.'†

We cannot fail to observe how artfully the poets accommodate their descriptions of death to that kind of interest which they have laboured to excite. The tyrant falls

* *Gesù Cristo Morto.*—"He lies, the head and shoulders resting on the knees of his mother, who has fainted. The posture and abandonment of the Magdalen is the finest representation possible ; her hair, as usual, loose. She is kneeling at the feet of our Saviour, her hands convulsively entwined. The dead body is beautifully drawn ; the anatomy perfect, not exaggerated. But the mother is dead—gone to decay—not in faint, but in death : such is the effect of the colouring."—*Note from Journal.* Parma.

† To express approaching dissolution, the French peasant uses a phrase derived from this upturning of the eye-ball. She arrived—"au moment ou sa mère tourne l'œil."

In the sudden death of the necromancer by the action of Astolfo's sword on his fated hair :—

" Si fece il viso allor pallido e brutto
Travolse gli occhi, e dimostrò a l' occaso
Per manifesti segni esser condutto."

Ariosto, c. 15, st. 65.

B B

convulsed and distorted in agony ; the hero, in whose fate
we have been made to sympathise, expires without the
horrors of death ; his fall is described with all the images
of gentle sinking, where mortal languor is succeeded by
insensibility, unaccompanied by pangs and struggles.

In the episode of Nisus and Euryalus, Virgil gives to the
death of Sulmo all the horror of violent death ; the breath
is convulsively drawn, and the sides palpitate.

> " Hasta volans noctis diverberat umbras,
> Et venit aversi in tergum Sulmonis, ibique
> Frangitur, ac fisso transit præcordia ligno.
> Volvitur ille vomens calidum de pectore flumen
> Frigidus, et longis singultibus ilia pulsat."—*Æneid,* ix. 411.

But in the death of Euryalus the poet recurs to all the
images of languid and gentle decline :—

> " Volvitur Euryalus letho, pulchrosque per artus
> It cruor, inque humeros cervix collapsa recumbit :
> Purpureus veluti quum flos, succisus aratro,
> Languescit moriens ; lassove papavera collo
> Demisere caput, pluvia quum forte gravantur." *
> *Æneid,* ix. 433.

---

* In the death of Dardinel, the simile of Virgil is beautifully imitated
by Ariosto :—

> " Come purpureo fior languendo muore
> Che 'l vomere al passar tagliato lassa ;
> O come carco di soverchio umore
> Il papaver no l' horto, il capo abbassa ;
> Così giù de la faccia ogni colore
> Cadendo, Dardinel di vita passa," &c.
> Cant. xviii. 153.

As a further contrast, we might take the death of the Soldan's page, *Ger.
Lib.* ix. 86. So of Nisus throwing himself upon the body of his friend,

Tasso presents us with some very fine contrasts of the same kind ; in the death of Argante, for example, there is a picture of ferocious impetuosity and savage strength :—

> " Infuriossi allor Tancredi et disse ;
> Cosi abusi, fellon, la pietà mia ?
> Poi la spada gli fisse et gli refisse
> Nella visera, ove accertò la via.
> Moriva Argante, e tal moria qual visse :
> Minacciava 'morendo, e non languia ;
> Superbi, formidabili, e feroci
> Gli ultimi moti fûr, l'ultime voci."
>
> TASSO, *Ger. Lib.* cant, xix. 26.

Sometimes, indeed, death may be represented unaccompanied by the horror with which it is commonly associated. A young creature is seen in death, as if asleep, with the beauty of countenance unobscured by convulsion ; the form remains, but the animation is gone, and the colours of life have given place to the pale tints of death.

> " D' un bel pallore ha il bianco volto asperso,
> Come a' gigli sarian miste viole.
> . . . .
> . . . . . In questa forma
> Passa la bella donna, e par che dorma."
>
> TASSO, *Ger. Lib.* cant. xii. 69.

Again the same poet :—

> " E' quasi un ciel notturno, anco sereno
> Senza splendor la faccia scolorata."

Æneid, ix. 444.   Contrast also the death of Eunæus, *Ib.* xi. 668, with that of Camilla, in the same book.

Sallust thus describes finding the body of Catiline :—" Longe a suis inter hostium cadavera, paululum etiam spirans, ferociamque animi quam habuerit vivus, in voltu retinens."

Or Petrarch :—

> " Non come fiamma che per forza è spenta,
>   Ma che per sè medesma si consume,
>   Se n' andò in pace l' anima contenta:
> A guisa di un soave e chiaro lume,
>   Cui nutrimento a poco a poco manca,
>   Tenendo al fin suo usato costume;
> Pallida no, ma più che neve bianca,
>   Che senza vento in un bel colle fiocchi,
>   Parea posar come persona stanca.
> Quasi un dolce dormir ne' suoi begli occhi,
>   Essendo il spirto gia' da lei diviso,
>   Era quel che morir chiaman gli sciocchi.
> Morte bella parea nel suo bel viso."
>
> *Trionfo della Morte.*

A man who has died in battle lies blanched and very pale ; he has bled to death ; but one strangled, smitten, or crushed by some deadly contusion, has the blood settled in his face. The following picture is truly horrible from its truth and accuracy :—

> " But, see, his face is black, and full of blood ;
>   His eyeballs further out than when he lived,
>   Staring full ghastly like a strangled man ;
>   His hair uprear'd, his nostrils stretch'd with struggling ;
>   His hands abroad display'd as one that grasp'd
>   And tugg'd for life, and was by strength subdued.
>   Look on the sheets ; his hair, you see, is sticking ;
>   His well-proportion'd beard made rough and rugged,
>   Like to the summer's corn by tempest lodged.
>   It cannot be but he was murder'd here ;
>   The least of all these signs were probable."
>
> *King Henry VI.* Part II.

The laws of inquest in England require such things to be witnessed in all their appalling circumstances, since the body lies where it falls, and no weapon or even disorder of dress is removed.

Are such scenes to be painted ?—Certainly not. The impression may be conveyed to the spectator consistently with good taste, and in a manner less obtrusive, so as to awaken the sensations which should attend them, without the detail of the actual scene. It may be allowed in words, as Shakspeare has represented the body of the good Duke Humphrey; but, in painting, the representation becomes too palpable to admit the whole features of horror.

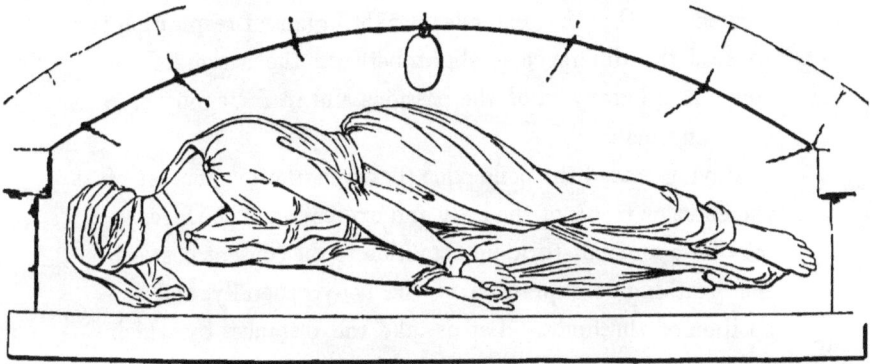

ESSAY VIII.

OF EXPRESSION IN REFERENCE TO THE BODY—THE EMOTIONS
MODIFIED BY CONTROLLING EXPRESSION.

In the preceding essays, it has been shown that the
powerful passions influence the same class of nerves and
muscles which are effected in highly excited or anxious
breathing ; and it was inferred, that the apparatus of respiration is the instrument by which the emotions are manifested.   In fear or in grief, the movements of the nostrils,
the uncontrollable tremor of the lips, the convulsions of the
neck and chest, and the audible sobbing, prove that the
influence of the mind extends over the organs of respiration ;
so that the difference is slight between the action of the
frame in a paroxysm of the passions and in the agony of a
drowning man.

Having traced the connexion between the excitement of
the chest or trunk of the body and expression in the face, we
may for a moment turn our attention to the consent between
the breathing or expression of the body generally, and the
position of the limbs.   Let us take the instances by which
we before illustrated the universal consent of the animal

frame. When the tiger or wolf is struck by the keeper, and suddenly roused to ferocity and activity, the character is seen not only in the glare of the eyes, the retraction of the lips, and the harsh sound of the breath as it is forcibly drawn through the confined throat, but every muscle is in tension, and the lips in an attitude of strained exertion, prepared to spring. In this condition of high animal excitement, observe the manner in which the chest is kept distended and raised ; the inspiration is quick, the expiration slow ; and, as the keeper strikes the jaw, there is at the same instant a start into exertion, and the breath rapidly drawn in. The cause of this expansion of the chest is readily understood, when we recollect that the muscles by which the limbs are exerted have two extremities : one fixed, which is called the origin ; the other moveable, which is called the insertion. The muscles of the arms, in man, and of the forelegs, in brutes, have their origins on the chest. To give power to the further extremities or insertions of these muscles into the limbs, the chest must be fixed : and, to give them their fullest power, it must be raised and expanded, as well as fixed. Hence that most terrible silence in human conflict, when the outcry of terror or pain is stifled in exertion ; for, during the struggle with the arms, the chest must be expanded or in the act of rising and, therefore, the voice, which consists in the expulsion of the breath by the falling or compression of the chest, is suppressed, and the muscles which perform the office of raising and distending the chest, act in aid of the muscles of the arms. The moment of alarm is also that of flight or defence ; the sudden and startled exertion of the hands and arms is attended with a quick inspiration and spasm of the mouth and throat, and the first sound of fear is in drawing, not in

expelling the breath; for at that instant to depress and contract the chest would be to relax the muscles of the arms and
enfeeble their exertion.   Or, to put the example in another
form, suppose two men wrestling in the dark, would not
their voices convey to us the violence of their efforts ?   The
short exclamation choked in the act of exertion, the feeble
and stifled sounds of their breathing, would let us know that
they turned, and twisted, and were in mortal strife.   To
an apt observer, two dogs fighting might illustrate the
subject.   Such combinations of the muscular actions are
not left to the direction of our will, but are provided for
in the original constitution of the animal body : they are
instinctive motions.   Yet, the principles of criticism in these
matters have been laid down with surprising confidence by
persons who had no knowledge of anatomy, and whose
curiosity had never been raised, to inquire into the phenomena of their own emotions, or of those they must have
witnessed in others.   I shall transcribe here a passage from
an elegant and ingenious critic, on which I shall freely make
some remarks.

   " In like manner it is not with the agonies of a man, writhing in the pangs of death, that we sympathise, on beholding
the celebrated group of Laocoön and his sons; for such sympathies can only be painful and disgusting : but it is with
the energy and fortitude of mind which those agonies call
into action and display.   For though every feature and every
muscle is convulsed, and every nerve contracted, yet the
breast is expanded and the throat compressed, to show that
he suffers in silence.   I therefore still maintain, in spite of
the blind and indiscriminate admiration, which pedantry
always shews for everything which bears the stamp of high

authority, that Virgil has debased the character, and robbed
it of all its sublimity and grandeur of expression by making
Laocoon *roar like a bull;* and I think that I may safely
affirm, that if any writer of tragedy were to make any one
personage of his drama to roar out in the same manner, on
being mortally wounded, the whole audience would burst
into laughter, how pathetic soever the incidents might be
that accompanied it. Homer has been so sensible of this,
that of the vast number and variety of deaths, which he has
described, he has never made a single Greek cry out on
receiving a mortal wound." *

The criticism here is just, so far as the artist is praised and
the poet blamed ; but the critic has mistaken the ground of
the praise and of the blame. It appears strange that any
one should philosophise on such points, and yet be ignorant
of the most common things in the structure of his own frame,
and of the facts most essential to just criticism in works of
art. What ideas can be conveyed, for example, by "the
convulsion of a feature," and the "contraction of a nerve ? "

The writer has had the impression, which all who look on
the statue must have, that Laocoon suffers in silence, that
there is no outcry. But the aim of the artist is mistaken.
He did not mean to express "energy and fortitude of mind,"
or, by "expanding the breast and compressing the throat, to
shew that he suffers in silence." His design was to represent
corporeal exertion, the attitude and struggles of the body and
of the arms. The throat is inflated, the chest straining, to
give power to the muscles of the arms, while the slightly
parted lips shew that no breath escapes ; or, at most a low

* Mr. Payne Knight on Taste, p. 333.

C C

hollow groan.*   He could not roar like a bull—he had not
the power to push his breath out in the very moment of the
great exertion of his arms to untwist the serpent which is
coiled around him.   It is a mistake to suppose that the suppressed voice, and the consent of the features with the exertion of the frame, proceed from an effort of the mind to
sustain his pain in dignified silence ; for this condition of the
arms, chest, and face, are necessary parts of one action.

The instant that the chest is depressed to vociferate or
bellow, the muscles arising from the ribs and inserted into the
arm-bones must be relaxed, and the exertion of the arms becomes feeble.   Again, in speaking or exclaiming, a consent
runs through all the respiratory muscles ; those of the mouth
and throat combine with those which move the chest.   Had
the sculptor represented Laocoon as if the sound flowed from
his open mouth, there would have been a strange inconsis-
tency with the elevated condition of his breast.   Neither is it
correct to suppose it possible that a man struck down with a
mortal wound, and rolling in the dust, like Homer's ill-fated
heroes, can roar out like a bull.   A mortal wound has an immediate influence on these vital parts and respiratory organs,
and the attempt to cry aloud would end in a feeble wail or
groan.   There is no danger that the tragedian who follows

* " Ille simul manibus tendit divellere nodos,
    Perfusus sanie vittas atroque veneno :
    Clamores simul horrendos ad sidera tollit : .
    Qualis mugitus, fugit quum saucius aram
    Taurus, et incertam excussit cervice securim."
                                    Æneid, Lib. ii. 1. 220.

" Virgilio ci rappresente Laocoonte in smanie e in muggite, come un toro
ferito a morte ; ma Agesendro seppe exprimere tutto il dolore, senza cedere
la bellezza."—*Azara*, p. 53. This is just the criticism of Mr. Payne Knight.

nature should offend the taste of an audience by actual outcry. But these critics think it necessary to refine and go beyond nature, whereas the rule is to learn her ways, and to be cautious of adding the slightest trait of expression, or what we conceive to be such, to the simple, and because simple, the grand character of natural action; instead of making the appeal more strongly to the senses, it is sure to weaken it.

In the statue of David with his sling, there is an attempt at expression which offends good taste, because it is not true to nature. The artist has meant by the biting of the lip to convey the idea of resolution and energy. But that is an action intended to restrain expression, to suppress an angry emotion which is rising in the breast; and if it be permitted, even in caricature, it must be as a sign of some trifling inconvenience, never of heroism. It is not suitable to the vigorous tone which should pervade the whole frame. That vigour cannot be otherwise represented, than by the excitement of the breast, lips, and nostrils, while the posture and the eyes give it a direction and meaning. This is all destroyed by an expression so weak and inconsistent as biting the lip; it is vulgar, not because it is common, but because it is a trick, and not true to nature.

The "Dying Gladiator" is one of those masterpieces of antiquity which exhibits a knowledge of anatomy and of man's nature. He is not resting; he is not falling; but in the position of one wounded in the chest and seeking relief in that anxious and oppressed breathing which attends a mortal wound with loss of blood. He seeks support to his arms, not to rest them or to sustain the body, but to fix them, that their action may be transferred to the chest, and thus assist the labouring respiration. The nature of his sufferings leads to this attitude. In a man expiring from loss of blood, as the vital stream flows, the heart and lungs have the same painful feeling of want, which is produced by obstruction to the breathing. As the blood is draining from him, he pants, and looks wild, and the chest heaves convulsively. And so the ancient artist has placed this statue in the posture of one who suffers the extremity of difficult respiration. The fixed con-

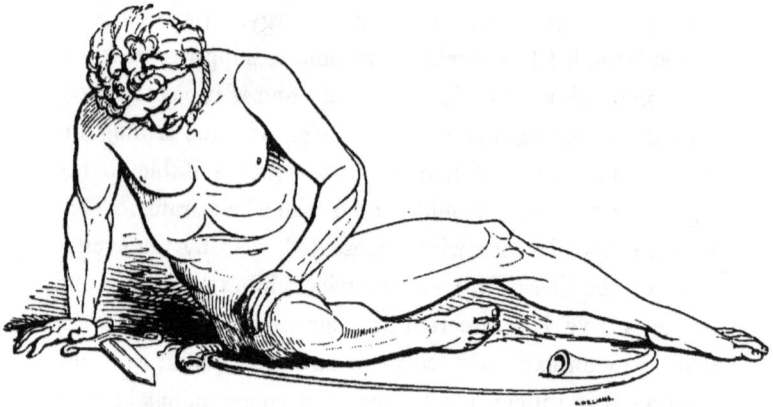

dition of the shoulders, as he sustains his sinking body, shews that the powerful muscles, common to the ribs and arms, have their action concentrated to the struggling chest. In the same way does a man afflicted with asthma rest his hands or his elbows upon a table, stooping forwards, that the shoulders may become fixed points; the muscles of the arm and shoulder then act as muscles of respiration, and aid in the motion of the chest, during the heaving and anxiety which belong to the disease.

When a man is mortally wounded, and still more if he be bleeding to death as the gladiator, he presents the appearance of suffocation ; for the want is felt in the breast, and relief is sought in the heaving of the chest. If he have at that moment the sympathy and aid of a friend, he will cling to him, half raising himself and twisting his chest with the utmost exertion ; and while every muscle of the trunk stands out abrupt and prominent, those of the neck and throat, and nostrils and mouth, will partake the excitement. In this condition he will remain fixed, and then fall exhausted with the exertion ; it is in the moment of the chest sinking, that the voice of suffering may be heard. If he have fallen on the turf, it is not from pain, but from that indescribable agony of want and instinctive struggling, that the grass around the lifeless body is lodged and torn.

So too with the actor. In order to convey to the spectator the idea of human nature agitated by passion or suffering, he must study how the parts of the frame are united and co-operate in expression. Of the success of such an effort we had lately an example on our own stage. It was in witnessing the struggles of a man who had received the mortal thrust, and the representation was horribly correct. The actor having rubbed the paint from his face, presented a hollow cheek, with the countenance haggard and pale ; but it was the heaving of the shoulders attending his deep and painful inspiration,—his difficult utterance,—the gurgling of his voice, as if the blood impeded the breath, which made altogether a most powerfully drawn representation of violent death. Even those who knew nothing of the cause of their being moved felt that it was correct.

But let us take a less appalling instance of the consent of

the frame with the functions of the heart and lungs. It is this connexion between the muscles of the chest and arms which makes a little man oppressed by obesity speak with abrupt gesticulation. His emphatic words are forced out in barking tones, accompanied by jerks and twists of the arms, the reverse of grace; while a tall and ungainly person exhibits an awkwardness of an opposite kind, in a disjointed swing of his arms during the efforts of his elocution.

Are we not now authorised to say, that expression is to passion what language is to thought : that as without words to represent ideas, the reasoning faculties of man could not be fully exercised, so there could be no violence or excess of passion merely in the mind, and independent of the action of the body ?   As our thoughts are embodied and the reasoning powers developed by the instrument of speech, the passions or emotions have also a corresponding organ to give them a determined character and force.   The bodily frame, though secondary and inferior, comes in aid of the mind ; and the faculties owe their development as much to the operation of the instruments of expression as to the impressions of the outward senses.

It is also curious that expression appears to precede the intellectual operations.   The smile that dimples an infant's cheek, which in after-years corresponds with pleasurable and complex emotions, cannot have its origin from such ideas. This expression is not first seen when the infant is awake, but oftener while asleep ; and this first beam of pleasure to a mother's eye is met with the cold observation of the wise old women, that it is caused by some internal convulsion.   They conclude that the child's intellects are not yet matured to correspond with the expression, and attribute the effect to some internal irritation.   The expression is in fact the spontaneous operation and classification of the muscles, which await the development of the faculties to accompany them closely when they do arise, and in some measure to control them during life.   It may be too much to affirm, that without the co-operation of these organs of the frame the mind would remain a blank; but surely the mind must owe something to its connexion with an operation of the features which precedes its own conscious activity, and which is unerring in its exercise from the very commencement.

The expression of pain in an infant is extraordinary in force and caricature; the expression of laughter is pure in the highest possible degree, as indicating unalloyed pleasure, and it will relax by sympathy even the stubborn features of a stranger.   Here the rudiments of expression ought to be studied, for in after-life they cease to have the pure and simple source from which they spring in infancy; the feelings are composed and restrained, the mind is in a state of more compound feeling, and the genuine characteristics ·of passion are to be seen only in unpremeditated bursts of great vehemence.

How much influence the instrument of expression has in first rousing the mind into that state of activity which we call passion or emotion, we may learn from the power of the body to control these affections. "I have often observed," says Burke, "that on mimicking the looks and gestures of angry, or placid, or frightened, or daring men, I have involuntarily found my mind turned to that passion whose appearance I endeavoured to imitate."

Whether it be possible to mould the body, and thus to

steal into another's thoughts, I know not ; but it is of more consequence to recollect that we may in this way ascertain our own. As the actions and expressions of the body betray the emotions of the heart, we may be startled and forewarned, as it were, by the reflection of ourselves, and at the same time learn to control our passions by restraining their expression.

As we hold our breath and throw ourselves into an opposite action to restrain the ludicrous idea which would cause us to break out in rude laughter, so may we moderate other rising impulses, by checking the expression of them ; and by composing the body, we put a rein upon our very thoughts. The powers of language are so great, and minister in so superior a manner to reason and the higher faculties of the mind, that the language of expression, which attends the development of these powers, is in a manner superseded ; good taste and good manners retain it in habitual subordination. We esteem and honour that man most who subdues the passions which directly refer to himself, and cultivates those which have their source in benevolence—who resists his own gratification, and enters warmly by sympathy into what others feel—who despises direct pleasures, and cultivates those enjoyments in which he participates with others. "Whatever is morally just is beautiful in art :" the expression of pain, proceeding from the mere suffering of the body, is repulsive in representation, while the heroic pangs which the artist may raise to the highest degree of expression, in compassion or sympathy with another's sufferings, cannot be too powerfully portrayed, if they be consistent with nature and truth.

In studying expression the artist should attempt all, even that which is disagreeable, so that in higher composition he may avoid deformity and every debasing expression, and this not by chance, but by knowing them and avoiding them ; by this means —and it was followed by the ancients—his power of representation will be improved, and what is dignified and beautiful in form and expression more certainly attained.

ESSAY IX.

OF THE STUDY OF ANATOMY AS NECESSARY TO DESIGN. OF THE
IDEAL, IN THE REPRESENTATION OF THE BODY. OF THE
GENIUS AND STUDIES OF MICHAEL ANGELO BUONAROTTI.

WERE I to attempt a definition of the ideal in the representation of the body, or of the head and face, I should
adopt, as the most harmless to the sculptor or painter, that
which has been given by Cicognara. "The ideal in art,"
says he, "is nothing more than the imitation of an object as
it ought to be in perfect nature, divested of the errors or distortions which secondary causes produce." He takes for
granted that man, like every thing else, has degenerated
from the original design of nature, and "that we ought to
endeavour to present his form as when he rose a newly-
created being, before misery and famine, cold or excess of
heat, had influence upon his frame. To accomplish this, the
artist has to contemplate those acknowledged beauties in the
Venus, in the youthful Apollo, in the vigorous Athletæ, and
in the Hercules. From such sources he must select the perfect forms, which are now to be found no longer in nature,
and recompose them into *a beautiful whole.*"

This is at least intelligible, and, to a certain degree, prac-
ticable. It divests the subject of that mystery which those

throw over it who would persuade the artist that to represent perfection of form, he must avoid what is human, and retain what is divine.

But, when this is attained, and the drawing of the figure is unobjectionable, a higher object still is to be found, in a deeper meditation on human nature. Sentiment and expression may be impressed on the figure, as on the face; but they must be made appropriate to their situation. Some of the most beautiful remains of Grecian art, when deposited in churches, appear out of place; while, in the same situation, the statues of Michael Angelo seem perfectly congenial. The noble forms and grave attitudes of his statues, in the sombre light of the aisles, lead memory back to all that is great in times gone by. Those magnificent designs have the effect of a passage in the historian or the poet, when the reader closes the book to indulge in the associations of ideas which have been awakened. But, were they placed in a gallery or saloon, they might with more propriety be subjected to the flippant criticisms which they have met with.

Individuals, as well as nations, have different manners of representing the same objects,—the human figure, for example. The Egyptians, the Greeks, the people of Hindostan, or of Europe, will raise a monument with more marked peculiarities than are seen even in the designs of Michael Angelo, Correggio, and Raphael; care, therefore, should be taken to give full scope to different dispositions, capacities, or tastes. I cannot help saying, that the method of study in the academies tends to cramp the efforts of genius. In the Academy of Bologna I found the students copying from the plaster-casts, as our youths do at home; and if some means be not afforded to encourage individual genius, tameness and mediocrity must be the result. I think the remedy is to be found in the study of anatomy.

There has been much unnecessary ingenuity exercised on the question, whether the ancients studied anatomy. Undoubtedly they did not study it in our fashion ; yet that they possessed all the knowledge of it which art requires, cannot be denied. The finer specimens of ancient statuary evince a more perfect acquaintance with anatomy, as far as it is shewn in the proportions, general forms, and action of the body, than the productions of those modern sculptors and painters who have pursued this art with the greatest zeal and success,—even than Michael Angelo himself. The only question therefore is, how they acquired this knowledge.

Although in Greece the dead were burned, and no artists dissected the human body, yet they certainly had the means of learning the nature of a bone, muscle, and tendon. No more was necessary ; the rest was before them. Fine as their athletæ were in youth, they were subject to the decay of age. Now, in comparing the frame of a man advanced in years, especially if in early life he had been remarkable for "thews and sinews," with the young and active, every thing essential to the painter and the sculptor may be observed. If the Greeks had before them the most admired forms of youth and manhood, they had also the "time-honoured wrestler," who in old age exhibited, almost as in the dead anatomy, every muscle, origin and insertion, every tendon, and every vein. I know how far this manner of demonstrating the anatomy may be carried. Having in my lectures on surgery taken the living man, the academy model, to illustrate the practice in fractures and dislocations, I was accustomed to introduce a powerful muscular fellow to my class, with

this appeal :—" In the exercise of your profession you have
to judge of the displacement of the limbs, and the joints
disfigured by dislocation, fractures, or tumour; but not one
of you, perhaps, has ever looked on the natural body itself."
In giving these lessons, I became aware how much of the
structure of the muscles and articulations might be demonstrated without actual dissection.

In the heat of the southern countries of Europe, the work-
men, the Galeotti, or men condemned to the public works,
the young people and children, are all accustomed to a state
of nudity; the naked form becomes, therefore, familiar to
the eye.

In the same day I made careful examinations of the
anatomical studies of Michael Angelo, in the collection of
the Grand Duke of Florence, and compared them with his
noble works in the tombs of the Medici. I observed that he
had avoided the error of artists of less genius, who, in shewing their learning, deviate from living nature. I recognised
the utmost accuracy of anatomy in the great artist's studies;
in his pen-and-ink sketches of the knee, for example, every
point of bone, muscle, tendon, and ligament was marked, and
perhaps a little exaggerated. But on surveying the limbs
of those fine statues, this peculiarity was not visible; there
were none of the details of the anatomy, but only the effects
of muscular action, as seen in life, not the muscles. As,
perhaps, this is the most important lesson which can be
given to the artist, I shall venture to transcribe the notes I
made at the time.

"The statue of Lorenzo di Medici, Duca d'Urbino, by
Michael Angelo, is in the Capella di Principi, of the church
of St. Lorenzo. Under the statue are two figures, one of Twi-

light, the other of Daybreak. I observed in the male figure, which is of very grand proportions, the clavicle or collar-bone, the head of the humerus, the deltoid and pectoral muscles developed beyond nature, yet singularly true in the anatomy. Such a shoulder was never seen in man, yet so finely is it imagined, that no one part is unduly exaggerated; but all is magnified with so perfect a knowledge, that it is just as a whole, the bone and the muscle corresponding in their proportions. In the same chapel are the statues of Giuliano di Medici, Duke of Nemours, and brother of Leo X., with the recumbent figures of Day and Night. It is in these finely-conceived figures that we have the proof of Michael Angelo's genius. They may not have the perfect purity and truth that we see in the antique; but there is a magnificence, which belongs to him alone. Here we see the effect of muscular action, without affected display of anatomical knowledge. The back is marvellously fine. The position of the scapula, for example, makes its lower angle throw up the edge of the latissimus dorsi, for the scapula is forced back upon the spine, in consequence of the position of the arm. Michael Angelo must have carefully studied the anatomy in reference to the changes produced in the living body by the action of its members: the shifting of the scapula, with the consequent rising of the mass of muscles, some in action, some merely pushed into masses, are very finely shewn."*

Having just come from observing his sketches of the anatomy of the knee-joint, I was curious in my observation of the manner in which he made his knowledge available

---

* I might make similar remarks on the statue by John of Bologna,— Januarius sitting, shivering under a shower, in a fountain in the Villa-Petraia, near Florence.

in the joints of these fine statues; and they gave rise to the following remarks.

"If an artist, with a knowledge of the structure, look upon the knee in a bent position, he will recognise the different bones and ligaments. But if he look upon it in an extended position of the limb, or during exertion, he will not distinguish the same parts. The contour, the swelling of the integument, and the fulness around the joint, are not produced by the forms of the bones, but by the rising up of the parts displaced by the new position of the bones. The fatty cushions which are within and external to the knee-joint, and which serve the purpose of friction-wheels in the play of the bones upon each other, no longer occupy the same relative places; they are protruded from the depth of the cavity to the surface. How well Michael Angelo knew this these statues of Day and Night evince.

"In these statues, great feeling of art and genius of the highest order have been exhibited; anatomical science, ideal beauty, or rather grandeur, combined. It is often said that Michael Angelo studied the Belvidere Torso, and that he kept it continually in his eye. That fine specimen of ancient art may have been the authority for his grand development of the human muscles; but it did not convey to him the effect which he produced by the throwing out of those magnificent and giant limbs. Here we see the vigour of this sculptor's stroke and the firmness of his touch, as well as his sublime conception of the human figure. We can imagine that he wrought by no measure or mechanical contrivance; that he hewed out the marble as another would cast together his mass of clay in a first sketch. Many of his finest works are left unfinished; it appears that he

found the block of marble in some instances too small, and
left the design incomplete.* For my own part I feel that
the finish and smoothness of the marble is hardly consistent with the vigour of Michael Angelo's conceptions ; and
I should regret to think that such a genius should have
wasted an hour in giving softness or polish to the surface.

"Who is there, modern or ancient, that would thus
voluntarily encounter all the difficulties of the art and
throw the human body into this position, or who could
throw the shoulder into this violent distortion, and yet preserve the relations of the parts, of bone and muscle, with such
scientific exactness ? We have in this great master a proof
of the manner in which genius submits to labour, in order
to attain perfection. He must have undergone the severe
toil of the anatomist, to acquire such a power of design,
which it was hardly to be supposed could be sufficiently
appreciated then or now.

"Without denying the beauty or correctness of the true
Grecian productions of the chisel, they ought not to be contrasted with the works of Michael Angelo to his disadvantage.

* There is one unfinished production of Michael Angelo which discloses
his manner of working ; a statue of St. Matthew, begun on a block of
marble, so small, that it appears to have restrained him. The figure is
distorted, and he seems to have given up the work before it was more than
blocked out of the marble. A contemporary gives an interesting account
of the energy which possessed him while at work. " I have seen Michael
Angelo, when above sixty, and not very robust, make more fragments of
the marble fly off in a quarter of an hour than three vigorous young sculptors
would have done in an hour ; and he worked with so much impetuosity,
and put such strength into his blows, that I feared he would have broken
the whole in pieces, for portions, the size of three or four fingers, were
struck off so near to the contour or outline, that, if he erred by a hair's-
breadth, he would have spoiled all and lost his labour, since the defect
could not have been remedied as in working in clay."—*Blaise de Vigenere.*

He had a noble conception of the august form of man : to my thinking, superior to anything exhibited in ancient sculpture. Visconti* imputes inferiority to Buonarotti ; and to confirm his views, compares the antique statues restored by him, with the limbs and heads which he added. But I can conceive nothing less suited to the genius of the artist than this task of modelling and adjusting a limb in a different position from that which is entire, and yet so as to preserve the proportions and character of the whole. The manner of his working and the urgency of his genius for an unrestrained field of exertion, unfitted him for that kind of labour, while it is a matter of necessity, that a copy shall be inferior to an original.

" What the figures of Night and Morning had to do before the degenerate son of the Medici is another matter. They seem to have been placed there as mere ornaments, and in the luxury of talent, to give the form and posture of the human figure, '*per ornamento e per solo spoggio di giacitura e de' forme.*'

" When in Rome I was impatient until I stood before the statue of Moses, so much had been said of its extraordinary merit,† and also so much of its defects.‡ It is a noble figure, with all the energy of Buonarotti displayed in it. It is not the anatomy alone which constitutes its perfection ; but there is the same mind displayed in the attitude, the habiliment, the beard, and all the accompaniments, as in the vigour of the naked shoulders and arms. It is the realisation of his high conception of the human figure.

* Museo Pio. Clem.
† " Questo e Mosè quando scenda del monte
E gran parte del Nume avea nel volto."
‡ " E una testa da satiro con capelli di porco."

E E

"My brother, in his 'Observations on Italy,' finds fault with the arm, and, perhaps, looking in one direction, it may be imperfect; but this was one of many figures which were intended by the artist to ornament the great monument to Julius II. ; and, consequently, designed to be seen only in a certain aspect.* Besides, we ought rather to teach ourselves to admire what is esteemed excellent than to seek for defects. As to other criticisms on this statue, it should be remembered that it is an ideal figure as much as the Apollo or the Jupiter. From whatever notion derived, Moses is represented with horns rising from his temples; an adjunct which, placed either on the face of the antique or of common nature, would have been truly ridiculous."

To resume the subject of anatomy, we may take the opinion of Vasari :† in addition to the study of the antique he recommends the frequent examination of the naked figure, of the action of the muscles of the back and limbs, and the form and play of the joints; and takes occasion to advise the study of the dissected body, in order to see the true position of the muscles, their classification and insertions; so that by perfect knowledge of the structure the artist may with more security represent the figure in every varying attitude, bestowing, through a knowledge of their action, the proper swelling and contour of the muscles, according to their position and the force exerted; and from this, he truly observes, comes the power of invention, giving natural variety to the figures, as in the representation of a battle or great historical work.

* See the account of this great work in the "Storia della Scultura," by Cicognara.
† In his Preface, "Da che habbia origine il buon disegno."

And here I cannot help expressing a belief that, as it is necessary that the young artist should have an accurate eye to form, the drawing of the bones should be substituted for what is called the "round," that is, the fine indefinite and undulating surface of the antique. By drawing the curious shapes of the thigh-bone or tibia, he will sooner acquire a notion of external form than if set to draw a foot and ankle, or knee, without an idea of what produces the convexities which he is tracing. Drawing from the bones and from the skeleton will give him a desire for learning more, and afford an introduction to the classification and insertions of the muscles, with perfect ease in representing, either from nature or the antique, the slightly defined forms of the joints.

But, as we have seen in the works of the masters, let him avoid exhibiting the anatomy or displaying his knowledge, else he will fall into the caricature of Fuseli, instead of attaining the vigour of Buonarotti. Anatomy is not to be displayed, but its true use is to beget an accurate observation of nature in those slighter characteristics which escape a less learned eye.

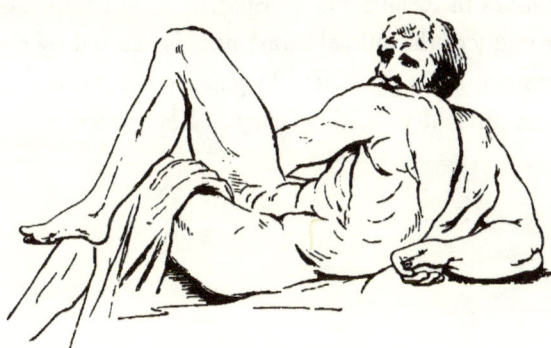

ESSAY X.

—◆—

USES OF ANATOMY TO THE PAINTER—FAULTS INTO WHICH
ARTISTS MAY BE BETRAYED IN STUDYING THE ANTIQUE OR
IN DRAWING FROM THE ACADEMY FIGURE—ANATOMY AS
CONDUCTING TO TRUTH OF EXPRESSION AND OF CHARACTER.

IT is interesting in a very high degree to mark the traits
of emotion, and to compare them with the anatomical structure; and amidst the severer studies of anatomy, as connected with health and disease, I have been able, without
departing too far from professional pursuits and duties, to
pass many pleasant hours in observing and investigating
the anatomy of expression. In the prosecution of anatomy
we never know to what results it may lead. The observations
I have made on the nervous system might be traced to investigations on the present subject. I saw that the whole
frame is affected sympathetically with expression in the countenance; and it was in trying to explain that sympathy,
that I was led to ascertain, that there exists in the body a
distinct system of nerves, the office of which is to influence
the muscles in Respiration, in Speech, and in Expression.

The study of the animal frame, as it is affected by emotion
and passion, is nearly related to philosophy, and is a subject
of great difficulty and delicacy. The question is often

discussed, of what use is anatomy to the painter? The study
of anatomy has been objected to by some persons of pure
taste, and from the belief that it leads to the representation
of the lineaments of death more than of life, or to monstrous
exaggerations of forms. So far this is the case, when an
artist without natural talent, or right feeling, will rather
exhibit the bones or muscles than the fine forms of health
and vigour. But we return to the question, what are the
advantages to be gained from this study by the artist?
As we may define anatomy to be the examination of
that structure by which the mind expresses emotion, and
through which the emotions are controlled and modified, it
introduces us to the knowledge of the relations and mutual
influences which exist between the mind and the body. To
the painter, therefore, the study is necessarily one of great
importance; it does not teach him to use his pencil, but it
teaches him to observe nature, to see forms in their minute
varieties, which but for the principles here elucidated would
pass unnoticed,—to catch expressions so evanescent that
they must escape him, did he not know their sources. It
is this reducing of things to their principles which elevates
his art into a connexion with philosophy, and which gives it
the character of a liberal art.

By anatomy in its relation to the arts of design, I understand not merely the study of the individual and dissected
muscles of the face, or body, or limbs,—but the observation
of all the characteristic varieties which distinguish the frame
of the body or countenance. A knowledge of the peculiarities of infancy, youth, or age; of sickness or robust
health; or of the contrasts between manly and muscular
strength and feminine delicacy; or of the appearances which

pain or death present, belongs to its province as much as the study of the muscles of the face when affected in emotion. Viewed in this comprehensive light, anatomy forms a science, not only of great interest, but one which will be sure to give the artist a true spirit of observation, teach him to distinguish what is essential to just expression, and direct his attention to appearances on which the effect and force, as well as the delicacy of his delineations, will be found to depend.

Among the errors into which a young artist is most likely to be seduced, there are two against which the study of anatomy seems well calculated to guard him. The one is a blind and indiscriminate imitation of the antique; the other, an idea that he will find in the academy figure a sure guide for delineating the natural and true anatomy of the living body. He who makes imitation of the antique the beginning and end of his studies, instead of adopting it as a corrective of his taste, will be apt to fall into a tame and lifeless style; and, in pursuing ideal beauty, will be in danger of renouncing truth of expression and of character. Nay, I suspect that many painters have copied casts of the antique for years, without perfectly understanding what they should imitate, or even perceiving the necessity of previously studying the design of the artist, or the peculiarities of his mode of composition. Into this fault, one who is learned in the science and anatomy of painting can never fall.. But he who has not compared the natural with the antique head, nor understood the characteristic differences, nor studied the principle on which the ancient artists composed, may be betrayed into the grossest misconceptions, by too implicitly following their models. In painting a hero, for example, on whom the Greek artist would have bestowed a character of strength and

grandeur, by bold anatomy and expression, he may be following the ideal form of a deity in which the sculptor had
studiously divested his model of all that might seem to pertain to humanity. As I have before remarked, the ancient
sculptor, in accordance with the mythology of his country
and the spirit of her poetry, studied to shew the attributes
of divinity in the repose of the figure, without any indication
of muscles or veins, and by a face stamped with the mild
serenity of a being superior to human passion ; thus shadow-
ing out a state of existence, in which the will possessed
freedom and activity, without the accompanying exertion of
the bodily frame. But those ideal forms are scarcely ever
to be transferred to the representation of the human body ;
and a modern artist who follows indiscriminately such
models, misapplies the noblest lessons of his art.

Independently of the ideal form of divinity, there are
also some peculiarities in the nature of the ancient sculpture which ought to be well considered by the student in
modern painting.

In the infancy of their art, sculptors did not venture to
give to their figures either animation or character ; they did
not even open their eyelids, or raise the arm from the side.
A stillness and simplicity of composition were thus the
characteristics of ancient sculpture ; and we are told that
Pericles, even in the best period of Grecian art, was anxious
that his pupils should preserve this feature of the early ages
in all their works, as essential to grandeur. The pleasure of
being carried back to old times seems to be a part of our
nature, or, at least, of the cultivated mind. So Pliny speaks
of retaining in everything about a villa its ancient simplicity. It is observed accordingly, that among the excellencies

which distinguish the Greek artists, the first and most admirable is that gravity of style,—that sedate grandeur of expression, and prevailing tranquillity of soul which still appear under the most terrible agitation and passion. Upon this chaste model the taste in sculpture was formed in the better ages of Greece and Rome, and its influence has extended to modern times.

Unfortunately this style of composition has been taken as an additional authority for rejecting powerful expression and character even from the canvass. But, we must never forget the distinction between sculpture and painting. The sculptor, indeed, as well as the painter, has often to represent what is not consistent with beauty; while both must sometimes preserve an indefiniteness, and soften all the harsher, though strictly natural lines of expression. If the statues of Michael Angelo and John of Bologna were as familiar to us as the casts of the antique, they would probably modify the prevailing opinions on this subject. Still there is an essential difference between the principle of composition in painting and in sculpture.

In the works of ancient artists we see a perpetual effort to exalt their productions above the commonness of nature. They studied a grand and general effect, avoiding the representation of minuteness or sharpness of feature, and of convulsions or distortions, however strictly natural; and, indeed, it is scarcely consistent with the character of a statue to represent the transitory effects of violent passion. The sculptor must exercise his genius on the more sublime and permanent feelings, as characterised in the countenance and figure; and much of the difficulty of his art consists in preventing the repose which ought to be preserved in the attitude and expression, from extinguishing all character, and degenerating into tameness and indifference.

It is repose, and not absence of expression, that is to be aimed at. The flashes of passion do not assort with the material, while the languor and the gloom of the features in grief are quite consistent with it. The slaves and mutes on the pedestal of a monumental statue may contribute to the effect; they are mere accessories,—as the frame to the picture. But this principle does not apply to the painter; to transfer to his art the rules of composition which flow from the study of ancient sculpture would endanger all in which it is most excellent. As his materials do not permit a close imitation of the actual forms of nature, a stronger, and more natural character is to be adopted on the canvass, than is proper to a statue. It is true, that he may often maintain much of the same gravity of style as the statuary, and that, in such compositions there may be a certain august majesty; some subjects require this, and others only admit of it, provided the tone and principle of composition be preserved, and the colouring be low and sombre. In general, however, this is neither necessary, nor perhaps suitable to a picture; and it may be at least laid down, that where there is bold light and vivid colouring, there should also be strong expression, and bold characteristic drawing. A painting, with high finishing and bright colouring, demands minute expression, because the same circumstances which display the natural colour, bring out a clear disclosure of the parts, and a sharpness of expression in the features.

Thus the painter must study the traits of human expression. The noblest aim of painting is unquestionably to affect the mind, which can only be done by the representation of

F F

sentiment and passion,—of emotion as indicated by the figure and the countenance. But, if it be contended that an imposing stillness and tranquillity must pervade the higher subjects of painting, I venture to affirm that it is a tranquillity which he can never attain who is not capable of representing all the violence and agitation of passion. It is not such repose as the artist who has despised or neglected natural character may be able to represent, but such as he alone can conceive and execute, who has studied all the variety of expression, and learned the anatomy of the face and limbs in their most violent action. Nay, tranquillity or repose in the strict sense of the words, can only be truly represented by one who can with equal facility give energy to the features and figure; for in rest there must be character, and that character will best be expressed by him who has studied the effect of the action of the muscles. It ought also to be remembered that repose and agitation must ever greatly depend on contrast and opposition. There are few grand subjects in history or mythology, in which the tranquillity and higher beauty of expression in the main figure does not borrow some aid from the contrast of the harsher features, more marked characters, and more passionate gestures of the surrounding groups.

Perhaps I have sufficiently pointed out how dangerous it is for one who aims at excelling as a painter to imitate too closely and indiscriminately the productions of ancient sculpture. But it is natural for the student to believe that the study of the academy figure may serve as a guard against all such danger; and afford him a sure criterion for judging of the anatomy of his figures.

Where is the artist to find the principles of his art when

he desires to express mental suffering under all those influences which form the subjects of design in the higher
departments of art, and especially in historical painting; is
he to grimace at himself in a mirror?—then he falls into
caricature : is he to study the expression of the actor ?—then
he represents what is fantastic and theatrical. For what may
be correct representation on the stage is not correct in
painting, any more than it would be correct for the tragedian
to display on the stage those traits of expression with which
the physician is alone supposed to be familiar.   Powers of
observation, cultivated by good taste, lead us to distinguish
what is appropriate.   The physician in studying symptoms,
the actor in personifying suffering, the painter in representing
it, or the statuary in embodying it in marble, are observers
of nature ; but each sees her differently, and with a feeling
influenced by his pursuit.

The study of the academy figure is, undoubtedly, essential ;
but unless followed with some regard to science, it necessarily
leads to error.   In the first place, it can give no aid in
reference to the countenance.   Here the lessons of anatomy,
associated with the descriptions of the great poets, and the
study of the works of eminent painters and sculptors, afford
the only resource.   But even for attaining a correct knowledge of the body and limbs, the academy figure is far from
being an infallible guide.   The display of muscular action
in the human figure is but momentary, and cannot be retained and fixed for the imitation of the artist.   The effect
produced upon the surface of the body and limbs by the action
of the muscles—the swelling and receding of the fleshy parts,
and that starting out of the sinews or tendons, which accompany exertion or change of posture, cannot be observed with

sufficient accuracy, unless the artist is able to class the muscles engaged in the action ; and he requires some other guide to enable him to recollect these varying forms, than that which is afforded by a transitory view of them.

When the academy figure first strips himself, there is a symmetry and accordance in all the limbs; but when screwed up into a posture, they indicate constraint and want ·of balance. It cannot be supposed that when a man has the support of ropes to preserve him in a position of exertion, the same action of muscles can be displayed as if the limbs were supported by their own efforts ; hence in all academy drawings we may perceive something wrong, from the ropes not being represented along with the figure. In natural action there is a consent and symmetry in every part. When a man clenches his fist in passion, the other arm does not lie in elegant relaxation ; when the face is stern and vindictive, there is energy in the whole frame ; when a man rises from his seat in impassioned gesture, a certain tension and straining pervades every limb and feature. This universal state of the body it is difficult to excite in those who are accustomed to sit to painters ; they watch his eye, and where they see him intent, they exert the muscles. The painter, therefore, cannot trust to the man throwing himself into a natural posture; he must direct him, and be himself able to catch, as it were intuitively, what is natural and reject what is constrained. Besides, those soldiers and mechanics who are employed as academy figures are often awkward and unwieldy; hard labour, or the stiff habits of military training, have impaired the natural and easy motion of their joints.

Until the artist has gained a perfect knowledge of the muscles, and is able to represent them in action without losing the general balance of the figure, he is apt to produce an appearance like spasm or cramp in the limbs, from one part being in action, while the other is in repose. For it is always to be remembered, that whether the body be alive or dead, whether the limbs be in action or relaxed in sleep, an uniform character must pervade the composition. Whether the gently undulating line of relaxed muscle be the prevailing outline, or the parts be large and strong, and the muscles prominent, bold, and turgid, there must be perfect accordance, or there will be no truth of expression.

I think, that in the sketches, and even in the finished paintings of some artists, I have observed the effect of continuing to draw from the model or from the naked figure, without due attention to the regulated action of the muscles. I have seen paintings, where the grouping was excellent and the proportions exact, yet the figures stood in attitudes when they were meant to be in action; they were fixed as statues, and communicated to the spectator no idea of exertion or of motion. This sometimes proceeds, I have no doubt, from a long-continued contemplation of the antique, but more frequently from drawing after the still and spiritless academy figure. The knowledge of anatomy is necessary to correct this; but chiefly, a familiar acquaintance with the classification of the muscles, and the peculiarities and effect of their action.

The true use of the living figure is this;—after the artist has studied the structure of the bones and the groupings of the muscles, he should observe attentively the play of the muscles and tendons when the body is thrown into action and attitudes of violent exertion;—he should especially mark their changes during the striking out of the limbs. By such a course of observation he will soon be able to distinguish between posture and action, and to avoid that tameness which

results from neglecting the effects of the alternate contraction and relaxation of the muscles. And with this view,
after having learned to draw the figure, the painter would do
well to make the model go through the exercise of pitching
the bar, or throwing, or striking. He will then find that it
is chiefly when straining in a fixed posture that there is a
general tension and equal prominence of the muscles ; and
that in the free actions of the limbs, a few muscles only swell
out, while their opponents are relaxed and flattened. He will
not, perhaps, be able at once to catch the character of muscular
expression, and commit it to paper ; but having an accurate
knowledge of the muscles, according to their uses, and the
effect of each action in calling particular sets of them into
activity, knowing to what points his observation should be
applied, and how his preconceived notions are to be corrected
by the actual appearance of the limb, each succeeding exhibition of muscular exertion will advance his progress in the
delineation of the figure. Hence it may well be said, that
anatomy is the true basis of the arts of design ; and it will
infallibly lead those to perfection who, favoured with genius,
can combine truth and simplicity with the higher graces and
charms of the art. It bestows on the painter a minuteness
and readiness of observation, which he cannot otherwise
attain ; and I am persuaded, that while it enables him to give
vigour to the whole form, it teaches him to represent niceties
of expression, which would otherwise pass unnoticed.

Even in drawing from a particular model, the artist versed
in anatomy has a great superiority. When I have seen one
unacquainted with the internal structure, drawing from the
naked figure or from a statue, I have remarked the difficulty
which he experienced in shewing the course of a swelling
muscle or the slight depressions and convexities about a joint;

and this difficulty might be traced to his ignorance of the
relations and actions of the muscles. The same perplexity
he often feels in drawing the knobbed ends of the bones or
the insertions of the tendons, at the articulations : for these
parts being covered over by the integuments, and cushions of
fat of variable thickness, and sheathed in membranes, are but
faintly marked on the surface. The delicate and less definite
indications of the anatomy, though easily traced by one acquainted with the structure of the limb, appear to the unin-
formed only unmeaning variations in the outline ; he has no
means of judging their importance, and he is subject to
continual mistakes in attempting to imitate them.

Suppose that a young artist, not previously grounded in
anatomy, is about to sketch a figure or a limb, his execution
will be feeble, and he will commit many errors if he endeavour merely to copy what is placed before him—to transcribe, as it were, a language which he does not understand.
He sees an undulating surface, with the bones and processes
of the joints faintly marked ; he neglects the peculiar swelling of the muscles, to which he should give force, as implying
motion ; he makes roundings merely ; he is incapable of
representing the elegant curved outline of beauty, with
decision and accuracy, and of preserving at the same time
the characters of living action. Drawing what he does not
understand, he falls into tameness or deviates into caricature.

But with a knowledge of anatomy, if he attempt the same
task, his acquaintance with the skeleton will enable him to
make his first outline of the figure with truth and ease, and
preserve its various proportions ; and the study of the
muscles will enable him to give force to the muscular parts,
and to represent the joints accurately without exaggeration.

It is, however, in composing, much more than in copying,

that this knowledge is truly useful. Without it, all the
original efforts of genius must be checked and repressed.
Every change of posture is accompanied by muscular
action, and in proportion to the painter's ignorance of the
cause of those changes, all his designs will be cramped and
restrained. Leonardo da Vinci gives formally, as a precept,
what is self-evident to an anatomist: "In naked figures,
those members must show their muscles most distinctly and
boldly, upon which the greatest stress is laid; in comparison
with which the rest must appear enervate." "Remember,
further, to make the muscles most visible on that side of any
member which it puts forward to action." Such rules and
precepts are rather the result of anatomical study than useful
to one ignorant of the subject, in pointing out how effect is
to be produced. It is not by following such recommendations
that the end is to be accomplished, but by enriching the
mind with frequent observation of the changes which are
displayed by action, and forming rules for their representation. For example, in vigorous action there is a general
tension of the whole frame; but in order to produce a particular motion, a certain class of muscles is brought into
stronger action than the rest; and the nature of the motion
is expressed by marking the arrangement of the muscles.
If a man be merely pointing upwards, a graceful simplicity
may be all that the painter can attain, or should attempt;
but if he is bringing down a heavy sword to make a blow,
the muscles will start into strong exertion, and the idea of
mighty action will be conveyed by representing those swelling muscles of the chest which pull down the arm and give
the sweep to the whole body. Thus, to compose with truth
and force, it is necessary that the painter should not only
know the place and form of the bones and muscles, but that

he should also have an accurate conception of the classing of the muscles in action.*

Perhaps I may best convey my idea of the advantage to be derived from this study, by contrasting two young artists drawing from a figure; the one trusting to his untutored genius, the other assisted by a knowledge of anatomy. The first is seen copying bit by bit, and measuring from point to point; and the effect, after much labour, is an accurate outline. The other seizes the chief characters of the attitude with facility; because his knowledge of the skeleton has enabled him to balance the trunk upon the limbs, and give the contours boldly. The turn of the limbs, the masses of muscle, and the general forms of the joints, are touched with

* "Socrates one day paid a visit to Clito, the statuary, and in the course of conversation said to him, 'We all know, Clito, that you execute a variety of figures; some in the attitude of the race, and others in the several exercises of wrestling, of pugilism, and of the pancratium; but with regard to the quality which particularly captivates the soul of the spectator,—I ·mean their correct resemblance to the life,—how is this property wrought into your productions?' As Clito hesitated for a reply, Socrates quickly rejoins, 'Is it not by endeavouring to imitate the configuration of the bodies of those who are actually engaged in those exertions of skill and activity that you succeed?' 'Without doubt,' said the artist. 'Well, then,' resumed the philosopher, 'you study, under the various gestures and attitudes of the living body, what parts are drawn up out of their natural situation, or carried in a contrary direction below it. Some which undergo compression, others an unnatural elevation; some which are thrown into a state of extension, others which become relaxed; all this you imitate, and hence you produce that fidelity, that accuracy, which we admire.' The artist acquiesced in the remark. 'And the expression of the passions, again,—how great a pleasure does this produce to the spectator!' 'Surely,' replied Clito. 'Thus those who are in the actual conflict of the battle, are they not to be represented as bearing menaces in their eyes, while satisfaction and joy should sit upon the countenances of the victorious?' 'Unquestionably.' 'It is then equally the business of the statuary to transfuse into his productions the workings and emotions of the mind.'"— Xenophon: *Memorabilia*, Lib. iii. cap. x. p. 6.

a slight but accurate hand, and the spirit and life of the original are recognised at once.   Even in the early stage of his drawing, while his rival is copying parts, he will present the foundation of a correct and spirited sketch ; as he can convey the general idea by a few lines, he also excels in finishing the minute parts.

But this superiority is still better shewn if the model be removed from these two young painters, and they draw the figure from recollection ; or if, keeping the model before them in its original posture, they are required to alter the attitude.   Let us take for example the fighting gladiator. Instead of a young warrior pushing on with great energy, let their task be to represent him receiving the blow of his antagonist, which forces down his shield upon his breast, or brings him with his knee to the ground, as it is beautifully represented on some medals.   Can we doubt for a moment which will excel ?   The one will copy from memory his original drawing, or with great difficulty twist the erect limbs of the statue into a couching posture, while the other will gain by his greater freedom.   Retaining the general air, like one who had understood what he copied, he is aware that a new class of muscles comes into action, while those formerly in exertion are relaxed ; he knows that the bending of the limbs increases their measurements ; he knows how to represent the joints in their new postures ; in short, he gives to his figure energy and effect.

It is a mistake to suppose that, because in many of the finest pictures the anatomy is but faintly indicated, the study may not be necessary to a painter.   Even that which in the finished picture is intended merely to give the idea of muscular exertion, should have its foundation laid in the sketch, by a correct and strong drawing of the full action. It is true, that the sketch is too often a mere indication of the painter's design, intended to be worked up to the truth of representation as he transfers it to the canvass,—that the outlines of the figures are rather shadowy forms, undefined in their minute parts, than studies of anatomical expression, or as guides in the subsequent labour. And, perhaps, it is for this reason that there have been many painters, whose sketches all admire, but whose finished paintings fall short of public expectation. But a sketch that is without vigour, and in which the anatomy has not been defined, is a bad foundation for a good picture ; and even a little exaggeration in this respect is not only agreeable, but highly useful. The anatomy should be strongly marked in the original design; and from the dead colouring to the finishing, its harshness and ruggedness should be gradually softened into the modesty of nature. The character of a sketch is spirit and life ; the finished painting must combine smoothness and accuracy. That which was a harsh outline in the sketch, or the strong marking of a swelling muscle, or the crossing of a vein, will be indicated in the finished composition, perhaps only by a tinge of colour. The anatomy of the finished picture will always be most successful, and even most delicate, where the painter has a clear conception of the course and swelling of each muscle and vein which enters into the delineation of the action.

While artists neglect the study of anatomy, as connected with character and expression in painting, they never can attain the " vantage ground " of their profession. Perhaps it is also to be feared, that while only a few artists are versed in this science, they will be apt to caricature nature ; they are learned above their rivals ; it is their forte, and they are solicitous to display it. But were the study of anatomy more general, the same spirit and love of originality, which tempt them to a style bordering on deformity, would make those very men seek distinction by combining grace, and the other qualities of fine painting, with truth and expression.

It is not enough, however, that the painter should improve himself in the knowledge of anatomy : public attention must also be directed to its importance. For as necessity precedes invention in the origin of the arts, so must general good taste precede or accompany their improvement. The mere conviction in the mind of the painter, that anatomy is essential to the perfection of his art, will seldom be sufficient to insure his application to a very difficult and somewhat repulsive study. The knowledge and opinion of the public must force him to the task, and encourage his labour by the assurance of its merited reward.

APPENDIX.

APPENDIX.

ON

THE NERVOUS SYSTEM.

BY

ALEXANDER SHAW.

IN many parts of this work references are made to an Essay upon the Nervous System; and the last edition contained such an essay. But on examining the copy intended for the present edition, it was found that the author had drawn his pen through the essay, and had not composed another to supply its place. It cannot be doubted that he intended to reconstruct that part of the work; and as some account of his observations on the Nervous System, which bear upon the questions discussed in the volume, may be interesting, I have been requested to give a short review of his opinions. I enter upon the task with much diffidence.

It is stated, in various parts of the essays, that a distinct Class of Nerves is provided, in the human body, for controlling the organ of Respiration; and that it is that class which is principally affected by passion and emotion, so as to give rise to the phenomena of Expression.

In Man, the organ of Breathing is constructed in such a manner, that besides ministering to the oxygenation of the blood, its primary office in the economy, it is the instrument of Voice

and of Expression,—two properties which bear relation to his
Intellectual nature. In order to adapt the organ to these endowments, it is necessary that the mechanism should have a form and
arrangement distinct from that in the lower animals, where it
serves for purifying the blood alone ; and as a correspondence
always exists between the structure of the moving parts of the
frame, and the nervous system, which regulates their actions,
the change in the construction of the organ is accompanied with
a change in the arrangement of the nerves. Accordingly, by
comparing the nervous system in the inferior animals, with its
order and distribution in man, the author found that a distinct
class of nerves is appropriated, in the human frame, to the organ
of Respiration : and to that class he gave the name *Respiratory
Nerves.*

But that conclusion was not arrived at till many other important
observations had been previously made on the functions of the
Nervous System. Medical science has been indebted to the author
of this volume for improvements in our knowledge of the Nerves,
only to be compared, for their extent and value, with those introduced by Harvey, by his discovery of the Circulation of the
Blood. Although no parts of the living body have excited
greater interest, since anatomy was first studied, than the Brain
and the Nerves ; yet when Sir Charles Bell entered upon his
researches into the subject, he found it involved in so much
confusion, and surrounded by so many difficulties apparently in-
surmountable, that physiologists had almost ceased to prosecute
it. Errors on points which bore on the first elements of the
inquiry, had taken deep root. He succeeded in removing these
errors, and in establishing a new principle of investigation. By
adopting that principle as his guide, he was rewarded not only by
making discoveries of the utmost value to medicine, but by communicating a fresh impulse to the labours of other physiologists
in the same field.

The error which formerly prevailed, and had the greatest
effect in retarding improvement, was this :—It was taken for
granted that all parts of the nervous system had certain general
properties belonging to them in common ; so that all were

considered alike in function. The Brain, including the Spinal Marrow, was looked upon as a common store, from which certain powers, such as that of motion, were issued to the body, and into which others, such as sensation, were received, the nerves being regarded as the conductors; and, in conformity with that view, it was further supposed that any part of the brain, or any single nerve, had equal power with all the rest of bestowing the numerous properties commonly assigned to the nervous system. For the sake of illustration, let us take the nerves of the lower extremities; which come off from the spinal marrow. It was conceived that these nerves were all simple in structure; and that, nevertheless, they had the double property of conveying the power of motion and of sensation, to the limbs: and the spinal marrow, being regarded as a prolongation of the Brain, was believed to transmit the powers of motion and of sensation along the nerves, by all its parts promiscuously.

Certain facts probably diverted the minds of physiologists from perceiving the correct views. When we examine the structure of a Nerve, it is found to consist of a number of distinct fibrils, like threads, laid parallel, connected loosely together, and contained in a common sheath; and when the fibrils are inspected narrowly it is impossible to perceive any difference between them; all are exactly alike in size, colour, and consistence. This similarity of structure, it may be supposed, would lead to the inference, that the functions of the fibrils were the same. Then, as to the Brain; although subdivided into several masses of different forms and textures, which give the appearance at first sight of its being composed of separate organs, yet a remarkable uniformity prevails in the general structure of the brain; the distinct substances of which it consists (the medullary and cineritious) are so variously intermingled and diffused, that it seems unavoidable to conclude that its powers are held in common, and are exercised by a combined operation of all its component parts. Again, the phenomena of certain diseases and accidents would probably give strength to the mistaken views. When a person is wounded in the leg, and a principal nerve cut across, the lower part of the limb, isolated from the brain, is

H H

deprived both of motion and sensation. If the spinal marrow be
crushed, or disorganised by disease, so that the communication
between the brain and the nerves beyond the seat of injury,
is destroyed, total paralysis ensues; that is, the limbs lose both
motion and sensation. When a man is struck down by apo-
plexy, owing to sudden effusion of blood into the brain from a
ruptured vessel, he is deprived instantaneously of both motion
and sensation. These occurrences, met with daily, would naturally lead to the belief that sensation and motion were inseparably united in all the different forms of the nervous
system; and when it was imagined that two such distinct functions could belong to the same part, it would not be inconsistent to believe that other powers could be combined with
them.

But Sir Charles Bell had not long commenced his investigations, when it occurred to him that it was contrary to reason to
suppose that two functions so essentially distinct from each other
as motion and sensation, could belong to the same nerve. Let us
consider the direction in which the nervous agency which gives
rise to motion, must necessarily be conveyed along a nerve to
produce muscular contraction. As the volition originates in the
brain, and the force, whatever it is, which acts upon the nerve
must be propagated to the muscle, it is obvious that the force will
proceed *outwardly*, or centrifugally. But when a sensation is felt,
as the effect must be produced by an impression being made upon
the extremity of the nerve expanded on the skin, and by that
being conveyed to the sensorium, it follows that the course of
the nervous agency must be *inwardly*, or centripetally. Hence
the force which causes muscular contraction passes along a nerve
in one direction, and that which causes sensation in a contrary
direction: and it is inconsistent to suppose that the same nerve,
or same portion of the nervous centres, could minister to both
functions at once.

The fundamental principle of the author's discoveries was
originally announced in nearly the following terms:—The nerves
of the body possess distinct and appropriate functions, corresponding with the parts of the brain and spinal marrow with

which they are connected at their *roots;* and when a nerve, which appears simple, is found to bestow more than one endowment, it is a sign that that nerve has more than one origin from the brain, and consists in reality of several nerves joined together.

The mode by which this principle was demonstrated and established to be a law in physiology, was as follows :—

The author first directed attention to the nerves of the Organs of the Senses. These nerves were formerly conceived to be so closely allied to each other, that their functions were regarded rather as modifications of one common property, than as distinct and specific. Thus it was supposed that the nerve of one organ of sense could be the substitute for the nerve of another, if transposed to that organ. For example, it was believed that the optic nerve, on which vision depends, could bestow sensation or pain, like a nerve of the skin; and *vice versâ.* But the author proved these opinions to be incorrect. He showed that each nerve of sense is limited to receiving a distinct and appropriate impression ; that the nerve of vision can only give ideas of light and colour ;* the nerve of hearing, impressions of sound ; the nerve of smelling, the perception of odours ; and so on. He further showed that these special properties depended on each of the nerves of sense having its root in a distinct portion of the brain, provided for receiving its own peculiar impression. This fact could not be easily demonstrated by referring to the human brain alone, where, owing to the organs of sense and the intellectual capacities related to them, having reached their highest point of development, the structure is very complex ; but it could be satisfactorily made out with the assistance of com-

---

* He illustrated that fact in the following manner. Pressure applied to the surface of the eye, between the eyelids, gives rise to pain more acute than that felt in the skin generally, but still of a similar kind ; a sense of touch. But pressure applied to the side of the eye, so as to affect the retina within, produces the appearance of a halo of variously coloured light before the eye, or a totally different kind of sense from touch. In couching for cataract, the needle, when piercing the outer part of the eye, gives rise to pain,—to a sensation like that of pricking the skin ; when it enters more deeply and transfixes the retina, it gives rise to an appearance like that of a spark of fire ; that is, a sense of light and colour, quite different from touch.

parative anatomy. When we examine the inferior classes of animals, it is not found that those lowest in the scale possess the same number of organs of sense which belong to the higher; on the contrary, the organs are bestowed gradually, one after another, in correspondence with the progressive advancement of the creatures in the scale of animal existence. As new organs are added, appropriate nerves appear, which communicate with the central part of the nervous system, analogous to the brain, of the animal. That elementary brain consists, at first, of mere swellings, or accumulations of nervous substance, called "ganglions," collected about the mouth: and it is observed that, according as additional organs of sense, with their nerves, are introduced, new ganglions make their appearance; for the purpose, as it is reasonably concluded, of ministering to the new species of sense conferred on the animal. In proportion as the organization approaches in resemblance to that of man, the ganglions enlarge, coalesce, and become changed in form, so as to be distinguished with difficulty from each other: but they continue, even in the highest animals, to be called after the organs of sense over which they are supposed to preside; hence they get the names of Optic ganglions or lobes, Olfactory lobes, Auditory lobes, &c. That was the first step taken by the author, to show that the nerves possess distinct functions; and that they obtain these from being connected with subdivisions of the brain, which have also distinct endowments.

The next stage in his progress was marked by more striking results. His object was now to explain how the nerves, known to bestow Motor power and Sensation conjointly, are endowed with that double property.

It may here be stated, that by far the greatest number of the nerves which supply the body generally, arise from the Spinal Marrow. Now, the way in which he proceeded to ascertain the source of the double power possessed by the spinal nerves, was this. He took one of them, for example, a nerve of the arm; and tracing it from the arm towards its origin in the spinal marrow, he observed that as it approached that organ, it subdivided into two parts, called its roots—and that one of the roots entered a division of nervous substance, distinct from the other ; one root being further distinguished by having a swelling upon it, termed a ganglion.

That such was the mode of origin of all the spinal nerves, had long been well known to anatomists ; yet no physiological conclusion had been drawn from it. But, following the principle which guided him in his researches, the author was led to suppose that roots, which thus proceeded from distinct portions of the spinal marrow, would possess distinct endowments. He therefore inferred, that one of the roots might be that which gave *motion*, while the other might be that which gave *sensation ;* and, assuming this view to be correct, he further supposed, that the reason why a spinal nerve possessed both motion and sensation was, that the nerve was in reality double, being compounded of fibrils from two distinct roots.

Accordingly, he proceeded to verify his opinion by experiments made directly upon the roots of the spinal nerves, and also by observations and experiments on nerves of the Brain, some of which resemble the spinal nerves in structure, while others differ from them. Following that course of investigation, he proved by indisputable evidence,—that the root which passes to the posterior division of the spinal marrow, and has a ganglion upon it, bestows sensation alone ; and that the root which goes to the anterior division, gives motion alone. Thus he established, for the first time, the important fact, that nerves of Sensation are distinct from those of Motion.

It has just been stated, that the author had recourse to observations and experiments on the nerves of the Brain, to assist him in drawing his conclusions as to the distinct functions of the roots of the spinal nerves : I may therefore describe shortly the results of his inquiries into the distinction between the motor and sensitive nerves of that organ.

With one exception, all the nerves which arise from the Brain, and issue from the skull to supply different parts of the Head, instead of having, like the spinal nerves, double roots, have single roots. A series of these single-rooted nerves arise in a continuous line from a prolongation in the brain, of that division or tract of the spinal marrow, which gives off the anterior or motor roots of the spinal nerves.

The nerve which forms the exception, is the " Fifth " nerve, as it is termed. Previous to the author's investigations, the anatomy of the roots of that nerve, although correctly described in some works, had attracted no particular interest ; and the most import- ant points connected with it, were commonly passed over un- noticed. The author observed that the Fifth is singular among the nerves of the Brain, in having double roots, like the nerves of the Spinal Marrow ; and that while one root arises from the continued tract of the spinal marrow which gives off the motor roots, the other, on which, as in the posterior roots of the spinal nerves, a ganglion is formed, penetrates to a considerable depth, in order to arise from the tract which sends off the posterior, or sensitive roots.

First, in regard to the experiments on nerves which arise by single roots from the brain. The nerve first selected to illustrate the functions of that series, was the one which passes to the Tongue, and is called the Ninth. Arising from the division of the spinal marrow which gives off the anterior roots, just as that division begins to unite with the brain, or at the top of the spinal marrow, the Ninth cerebral nerve may be regarded, in its ana- tomical structure, as an anterior root of a spinal nerve, not joined by any posterior root. The nerve having come off in that manner, passes out immediately, through an appropriate hole in the base of the skull, and without being joined by the fibrils of any other nerve, is distributed to the Tongue. It is remarked that in its passage to the tongue, it avoids going to the surface, endowed with sensibility ; and exhausts all its branches in sup- plying the various muscles which move the organ. When this nerve was cut across in experiment, it was found that the tongue was instantaneously deprived of the power of *motion :* but the sensibility was unimpaired. It was accordingly proved that as the Ninth resembles the anterior roots of the spinal nerves in its mode of origin, it resembles them in function, and is exclusively a Motor nerve.

Next, in regard to the experiments on the Fifth nerve. It will be understood from the Plan, that although this nerve resembles the spinal nerves, in the general structure of its roots, one of

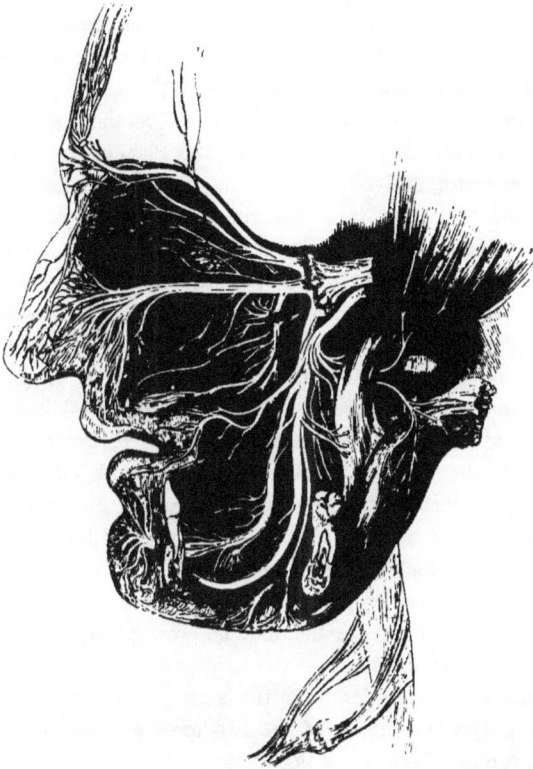

them, the ganglionic, (corresponding with the posterior spinal roots), is greatly larger than the root without a ganglion. It may also be seen, that shortly after its origin, the whole nerve subdivides into three great trunks, which ramify over the entire head ; and that the smaller root joins only one of the trunks, called the third or inferior maxillary, which supplies the lower

part of the face, and the muscles of the jaws. Hence the first
and second great branches are simple in structure, being formed
entirely of fibrils from the larger, or ganglionic, root; while the
third is in part compound, from containing fibrils of the lesser root.

Referring to Plate IV., it may be observed that two large
branches, one above and the other below the orbit, marked respectively I. and II., issue from the bones of the face to go to parts
already abundantly supplied by another nerve, the portio dura:
these are branches, as may be seen in the Plan, of the first two
trunks of the fifth, derived from the ganglionic root alone. Now
it was found that when these branches, called the supra-orbitary
and infra-orbitary nerves, were exposed in a living animal, it
gave the most acute pain to prick or squeeze them; and when
they were cut across, the whole surface of the face to which they
are sent, was deprived instantaneously of sensation; so entirely
was sensation destroyed that the skin could be cut or pinched
without the animal being conscious of the injury—without its
wincing; and yet the motion of the parts was perfectly retained.
Again, when the third or inferior maxillary trunk, composed of
the two roots conjoined, was similarly exposed, and cut across
above the point of union, pain was experienced in the operation,
and the parts to which it is sent were deprived of sensation; but
an additional effect was produced—the muscles of the jaws, to
which the fibrils of the smaller root go, were paralysed. Hence
the conclusion was obvious, that the larger root of the fifth nerve
is endowed with Sensation, and the smaller with Motion; and
that it is only where fibrils of the two roots are combined, that
the nerve can give both properties at once. Hence, also, confirma-
tion was given to the deductions drawn from the experiments on
the roots of the Spinal nerves; the root of the Fifth cerebral
nerve, analogous in structure to the posterior roots of the spinal
nerves, having been shown to bestow Sensation, it was an additional proof that the function of the posterior spinal roots was to
confer Sensation: and the root of the Fifth, analogous to the
anterior roots of the spinal nerves, having been shown to bestow
Motion, it was an additional proof that the function of the anterior spinal roots was to confer Motion.

The author next selected for experiment another nerve, which springs from a different part of the brain from the ninth or fifth,—the Facial nerve, or *Portio Dura*. This nerve arises by a simple root, and, without mixing its fibrils with those of any other, appears externally before the ear, as represented by A in Plate IV. and is distributed to the face. It had been hitherto believed that the portio dura was capable of bestowing both motion and sensation. But the author proved that this nerve was limited to giving motor power. By making a small incision through the skin, not larger than that for bleeding, he exposed the nerve in a monkey,—an animal which he considered better adapted than any other for the experiment, owing to the well-known mobility and activity of its features : when the nerve was laid bare and cut, the motions of the corresponding side of the countenance were at once and entirely extinguished ; but the sensibility was unimpaired. It was even observed, as an additional proof that sensation does not depend upon the portio dura, that the animal manifested no signs of pain during the act of cutting it through, or pinching it.

It will be admitted that the facts and reasoning now brought forward, were sufficient alone to establish the truth of the general proposition—That nerves of Sensation are distinct from nerves of Motion : and that to different parts of the Brain and Spinal Marrow, belong distinct and appropriate endowments. But additional proofs of a still more convincing and interesting kind were soon obtained, by observing the effects of disease in the nervous system of Man himself. Numerous cases early presented themselves where morbid changes in the structure of the Brain, Spinal Marrow, or Roots of the nerves, in man, gave rise to phenomena similar to those which follow experiments on the lower animals.[*]

For example, tumours sometimes grow within the vertebral canal, where the spinal marrow is lodged, and develop themselves in such a manner as to destroy one set of the roots of the spinal nerves, without involving the other : in these cases, only one function of the nerves is lost : if the anterior roots be affected,

[*] The cases referred to were recorded chiefly by the author's zealous assistant in these pursuits, Mr. John Shaw.

I I

242   OF THE NERVES.

there is loss of motion ; if the posterior, there is loss of sensation ;
and the patient is in the singular condition of having feeling in
the limb, although he cannot move it ; or he may be able to move
it, and have no feeling. Cases of a similar kind were met with
more frequently in the face. Owing to the portio dura, and fifth
nerve, which supply the face, arising from parts of the brain
at a distance from each other, and the one taking a circuitous
course apart from the other, disease often affects one nerve and
destroys its function, without reaching the other. In such cases,
where the portio dura is affected, the muscles of the face are
deprived of motion ; the patient can no longer knit his brows,
close his eyelids, inflate his nostril, or hold anything between his
lips ; expression is entirely lost, and, owing to the muscles of the
sound side dragging the paralysed cheek and lip towards them, the
face is distorted ; but there is no diminution of sensibility in the
half of the face, thus completely deprived of motion.* But when
the branches of the fifth nerve, which emerge upon the face, and
arise from the larger root alone, are affected, sensation is entirely
lost, while motion is unimpaired. For example, the surface of the
eye, supplied by superficial branches of the fifth, and a part so
exquisitely sensible that if a fine hair touches it there will be
severe pain and spasm of the eyelids, may, when the nerve is
destroyed, be rudely pressed with the finger, and the patient will
nevertheless be unconscious of pain ; or if the surface be inflamed,†

* And it may be added, that no pain attends the loss of function. Patients
are seldom aware of their face having become paralysed, until told by a friend
or it has been observed by themselves, in the mirror. That is, the nerve, although
formerly conceived to be one of the most exquisitely sensitive parts of the body,
undergoes a process of disorganization sufficient to deprive it of its function, and
yet the patient suffers no pain. This is accounted for by the portio dura being
simply a nerve of motion, and having no power of bestowing sensation, or of giving
pain.

† Loss of sensation in the eye, from disease affecting the ophthalmic branches
of the fifth, is often followed by inflammation, which terminates in the destruction of the organ. This is caused by the eye having been deprived of its important guardian, the sensibility, which induces not only winking, but other efforts,
to protect the tender surface from injury ; dust, and other irritating particles,
lodge beneath the eyelids, and without causing pain, set up inflammatory action.
Cases are sometimes met with, where the surface of the eye has lost sensation,
but where (owing to another nerve, the third, being also affected) the upper

and it be necessary to scarify it with the point of the lancet, in order to withdraw blood, the patient will submit to the operation without pain, and without even winking, although the eyelids retain their power of closing, through the portio dura. It is from a morbid condition of one or other of the branches of the fifth, that the excruciating paroxysms of pain in that dreadful disorder, tic douloureux, are produced. Should the disease which affects the nerve be situated close to its origin, so as to include both roots, then motion will be lost, as well as sensation; besides, all the surfaces of the head which are supplied by the larger, sensitive root, being deprived of sensation, the muscles of the jaws supplied by the lesser root will be paralyzed: so that the patient, in eating, will neither be sensible of the presence of the food in the affected side of his mouth, nor be able to chew it.

From such examples as the above, some idea may be formed of the benefits conferred upon medical science by the discoveries in the nervous system thus shortly described. While it continued to be believed that every nerve, from whatever part it came, had the same kind of functions, and that the different divisions of the brain and spinal marrow were alike, it followed that, when a case occurred of partial loss of sensation or of motion in any part of the body, the physician was led to conclude that disease had commenced in the brain; and his treatment was conducted on that supposition. But when it was proved that the nerves had distinct endowments, it was readily understood that the partial loss, whether of motion or sensation, might depend on an affection of the nerves after they had left the brain, and were external to the skull, and consequently, that instead of the symptoms indicating a serious, or perhaps fatal disease of the brain, they might point to a comparatively harmless disorder. In short, the knowledge now acquired of the nervous system lends, every day, the most valuable aid to the practitioner; it gives him means, not formerly in his power, of exploring disease, and of tracing it along to the precise spot where it is situated.

eyelid has permanently dropped, so as to cover the eye, and defend it from injury: in these cases, inflammation does not occur, and the eye preserves its transparency.

On the Classification of the Nerves into the " Original" and " Respiratory" Systems.

When the author had established the existence of the important distinctions between the nerves of the cerebro-spinal system,[*] just pointed out, it soon became apparent that other questions remained to be solved concerning them. Having been led, in following the principle of his researches, to view the different modes in which the nerves arise from distinct subdivisions of the central organs, as indicating a diversity of function, he was forcibly struck by observing certain distinctions in the origins and mode of distribution of particular groups of nerves. With the object of ascertaining whether these anatomical differences pointed to further differences of function, he proceeded, first, to examine the various parts of the body to which the nerves thus coming from distinct divisions of the brain and spinal marrow, are sent; and, then, to compare the actions and uses of the parts with each other.

When we take a general survey of the nerves of the human body (excluding, for the present, the nerves of the Organs of the Senses, and the Sympathetic system), it is remarked, that there is one extensive series—so large that it embraces nearly all the nerves together—distinguished by the regularity and symmetry with which they are given off and pass to their destinations; while there is another series, arising from a different part of the nervous centres, remarkable for their partial and irregular distribution.

The first class consists principally of the Spinal Nerves. Passing off from the whole length of the Spinal Marrow, at intervals of about an inch from each other, these nerves go in regular succession to the back of the head, the neck, the upper extremities, the whole trunk, and the lower extremities; and as each nerve is composed of two roots, one for motion and the other sensation, they bestow these double properties wherever they are sent. To this extensive

---

[*] The *cerebro-spinal* nerves include all those which arise from the Brain and Spinal Marrow. They are so called in contradistinction to the "Sympathetic" system, which consists of a series of nerves and ganglions distributed to the viscera of the chest and abdomen, and in many important points differing from them.

series must be added the Fifth cerebral nerve, which both in structure and function, as it has been already shown, is a spinal nerve; by its larger root it confers sensation on all parts of the head not supplied by the superior spinal nerves; and by its lesser root it gives the power of motion to a limited set of muscles, viz. those by which *mastication* is performed.

As to the second class, they arise near the point of union of the brain and spinal marrow, from a comparatively circumscribed portion of cerebral structure; the tract or division of nervous substance from which they originate, is distinct from either of those which give off the roots of the spinal nerves and fifth cerebral nerve; and in passing out to the body, they course in a radiating manner to parts of the head, neck, and chest, where nerves of the former class are already plentifully distributed. When we examine the structures thus supplied, we perceive that they enter into the formation of the organ of Respiration.

Consequently, a question was here presented for solution— What is the particular character of the organs superintended by the first class, which distinguishes them from the organ of Breathing supplied by a different class; or that will account for the former organs being supplied by a series of nerves so regular in their origins and distribution, and so widely extended, as the spinal nerves and fifth cerebral nerve; while the respiratory organ is provided with an appropriate set of nerves, comparatively few in number, and differing in several anatomical features from the others?

To solve that problem, the author found it necessary to call in the aid of comparative anatomy, and to take a general survey of the nervous system as it is presented in the whole animal kingdom. First: it is known that in all living animals, from the lowest to the highest, an analogy exists in the structure of their bodies; so that Man, and all animals below him, have certain organs in common. That being the case, the author expected to find that in the nervous system, which controls those organs, there would be a corresponding commonness of character visible in the whole animal kingdom. But again, as, in the various organs composing the body, a gradual process of development takes place, so that the organization of each rises in perfection in proportion as animals ascend in the scale; and as, in some particular parts, the mechanism undergoes material changes, giving rise to quite a new arrangement of the structures, he thought it reasonable to expect that corresponding modifications would be introduced into the nervous system, to adapt it to the new construction of such parts.

Proceeding on that view, he was led to observe that the numerous members of the body which are supplied by the spinal nerves and fifth cerebral nerve, form together a system, which, as regards the uses they serve in the economy, presents a remarkable uniformity through the whole animal kingdom ; while in the organ of Respiration supplied by the other set of nerves, a striking difference in that respect exists ; the apparatus of Breathing, in the lowest animals, is applied exclusively to oxygenating the Blood ; its mechanism is adapted to no other office : but in the higher animals, although it continues to execute that necessary function of purifying the blood, it has a new and distinct office superadded to it ; the mechanism is altered and arranged in such a manner as to adapt it to be the organ of Voice ; and in Man it is besides the essential part of the organ of Speech and Expression.

Hence, the author was led to conclude :—First, That the class of spinal nerves and fifth cerebral nerve represents in Man a system which exists, under different phases, in every animal, and he called it the " Original " class : Secondly, That the nerves of the organ of Respiration are a new system, introduced in correspondence with changes which take place in the structure of that organ, in the course of its development, to adapt it to Man's intellectual nature, and he called them the " Superadded," or " Respiratory " class.

To give a full exposition of the grounds on which the above classification is founded, would occupy more space than my limits allow. But I may point out briefly some of the leading facts on which it is based.

First, as to the statement, That the spinal nerves and fifth cerebral nerve, called the " Original " class, superintend organs common to the lowest animals and Man,—it is necessary, in order to judge of its correctness, to inquire, What organs are possessed alike by Man and all the inferior animals ?

To give the most comprehensive answer to that question, the best mode is to consider—Which are the organs that distinguish a member of the Animal kingdom from a member of the Vegetable kingdom ? By thus going to the bottom of the scale of living beings, and observing what instruments are essential for the existence of the animal of simplest structure, as well as of Man, and then taking into view the nerves required for controlling such parts, we shall arrive at a knowledge of the nervous system in its " Original," or least developed condition; and by tracing both the organs and the nerves upwards to Man, we shall be able to judge of the persistence of the class, through the whole animal kingdom.

Now, when we compare Animals and Vegetables together, we find that they are not so distantly related to each other as might at first be thought. Indeed, some animals, living on the confines between the two kingdoms, bear such a close resemblance to plants, and plants to animals, that zoologists often meet with difficulties in deciding whose subjects they are. But if we take a general principle for our guidance, and disregard these approximations, (for in the works of Nature there are no sudden, trenchant divisions,—she never arranges the objects of creation in squares, circles, or parallelograms ; but proceeds, even in her progress from the inorganic to the organic world, by slow, uniform gradations,) we shall find that the Animal possesses organs essentially distinct from the Vegetable.

The organs *common* to the vegetable and animal, are those connected with the nourishment, growth, and reproduction of the structures. Thus, a plant imbibes nutritious matters from the earth ; circulates that matter, as sap, along the branches and leaves ; the sap is subject to a process of purification similar to that effected upon the blood of animals, by the lungs; it has, besides, organs, like secreting glands, for eliminating various substances from the sap. All those organs are analogous to the parts in the animal frame which serve for digestion, assimilation, oxygenation of the blood, secretion, excretion, &c. It is not, therefore, among them, that we look for distinctive characters between Vegetables and Animals.

The difference will be found when we consider, that a plant is *motionless*—is a fixture to the part of the earth where it was originally sown, and obtains its nourishment by the very roots which fix it to the soil; while an animal, on the contrary, is *locomotive*, and must shift from spot to spot, in quest of nutriment.

Here, then, is the great and prominent distinction between a member of the vegetable and of the animal kingdom. The one is stationary; the other endowed with spontaneous motion. To ascertain, therefore, what are the characteristic, distinctive parts of an Animal body we have to inquire—What organs must be supplied to adapt it to move from place to place in search of food, and to enable it when it has reached its food, to seize and appropriate it?

The First set of organs which an animal will require, will be, organs of *Locomotion* or progression; in other words, parts analogous to our limbs; if the creature be aquatic, they may be fins, or paddles; if it move in the air, they may be wings; if it inhabit dry land, they may be extremities and feet. The Second will be instruments which the animal may put forth, as we do our hands, to seize and secure the objects of nourishment; and they may be presented under various forms, as tentacles, paws armed with claws, projecting muzzles with teeth of peculiar shape: these are the *Prehensile* organs. The Third will be a *Mouth*, provided with appendages more or less resembling teeth, for dividing and triturating the food, and preparing it for passing along the gullet to the stomach. The Fourth will be organs capable of regulating the combined machinery of the body; that is, parts endowed with the power of initiating motion, and senses to guide the movements of the animal; that is, a *Nervous System*, consisting of nerves of motion, nerves of sense, and a sensorium analogous to the brain.

If we take a general survey of the animal kingdom, we shall find that every living being, whatever may be its place in the scale, possesses a representative, of one kind or other, of all the organs just enumerated. It is true that their structure, in the lowest, is greatly varied; in many, the signs of affinity to vegetables obscure their proper character; in others, the organs serving for distinct purposes are more or less fused into each other, so as to be distinguished with difficulty; again, we meet with infinitely varied modifications in the mechanism of the same organs, to accommodate them to the innumerably different modes by which animals obtain their food : yet from the lowest animal inhabiting a stagnant pool, up to Man, a single type or plan of formation is adhered to.

We may now perceive how the author came to believe, that the spinal nerves and fifth cerebral nerve, in Man, is a class common to all grades of the animal kingdom. Let me recapitulate the organs to which the nerves of that class are sent. 1st, the spinal nerves supply the Lower Extremities—the organs of progression in man, corresponding with those members by which other animals move from place to place in search of food : 2dly, they are sent to the Upper Extremities, the arm and hand—the instruments of prehension in man, analogous to those organs by which the inferior animals seize and secure objects of nourishment; 3dly, the branches of the motor root of the fifth cerebral nerve are distributed to the muscles of the Jaws—the manducatory organ— corresponding with the oral aperture of the lower animals, where food is delayed and submitted to trituration, previous to being swallowed and passed into the stomach. Finally, this system supplies nerves to the two organs of sense which are most essential for guiding the movements of an animal in search of nourishment : it gives the nerves of Touch, and of Taste.[*]

Secondly : as to the "Respiratory" class of nerves, and their being a superadded system, introduced in the higher animals in correspondence with changes of structure which the organ of breathing undergoes, in its course of development through the

---

[*] As it is by the sense of Taste, combined with touch, that animals distinguish their food, we can understand why the nerve of taste—the Gustatory branch of the fifth cerebral nerve—should be included in a system, common to all members of the animal kingdom, found in the earliest period of animal development, as in the latest. It has been stated before (p. 236), that the other senses, viz. seeing, hearing, and smelling, are bestowed upon animals, one after the other, according as they rise in the scale, and their organization becomes adapted to the possession of such additional senses. That may explain why the optic, auditory, and olfactory nerves should have distinct origins from the brain.

K K

animal kingdom, to adapt it to Voice, in Man—the correctness of
that theory will be best perceived by taking a general survey of
the apparatus for respiration, as presented in the lowest and the
highest animals.

To follow the short description I am about to give, it may be
of advantage to consider, at the outset,—What are the conditions
required in the organ of respiration, to accommodate it to produce
Voice, besides carrying on its primary and ordinary function of
oxygenating the blood?

The first thing is, that the air, with which the blood to be
purified is brought in contact, shall be collected within a partially
closed cavity; and that the walls of that cavity shall be capable
of contracting on the volume of air, so as to expel it with an
impetus sufficiently strong to produce vibrations, and thus give
rise to sound. The second essential thing is, that a tube, or windpipe, shall communicate between the cavity and the external air;
and that, connected with that tube, there shall be an appropriate
apparatus for varying and modulating the sounds produced by the
expulsion of air through the tube. That is the simplest view of
an organ of Voice, such as belongs to man.

But in the lowest animals, we find no vestige of a structure
like what has been described. The air which oxygenates the
blood, instead of being drawn into the interior of the body,
exercises its influence on the blood from without—that is, by
coming in contact with the exterior surface of the animal;
and there is no provision at all, connected with the organ of
breathing, for producing sound. In the whole extent of comparative anatomy, so fertile in subjects calculated to inspire
admiration, there is nothing which raises that feeling more,
than observing the series of simple changes which gradually
take place in different animals, as they ascend in the animal
scale, to conduct the air, applied, at first, to parts situated
externally, into the interior of the body, there to be partially
closed in, and made available for producing Voice and Articulate
Language, besides purifying the blood.

In the inferior animals which are only a grade above Vegetables,
no distinct respiratory organ exists. That deficiency corresponds

with the absence of a system of vessels for circulating the blood in these creatures. The fluids obtained by assimilation of the food, and representing blood, are diffused through the cellular structure of the animal's body; and it is simply by the air being brought in contact with the integument, that a process of oxygenation, analogous to what takes place in the lungs of the higher animals, is effected: so that the mode of purification of the fluids in animals at the bottom of the scale, differs but little from that in vegetables. As soon as distinct tubes are formed for circulating the nutrient fluids (scarcely to be called blood at that early period) through the body, traces are perceived of a respiratory organ. A congeries of vessels directing their course to a particular spot, indicates that the apparatus for respiration is situated at that part: but we find nothing as yet approximating in appearance to Lungs. The animals referred to live in the water: and all that can be seen to represent a respiratory organ, is a set of loose fringes, or tufts, formed by duplications, or prolongations, of the integuments. By floating freely in the water, these tufts expose the blood circulating in them to the action of the air with which the water is charged, in a more effectual manner than can be done by the integument generally. As the circulating system becomes more distinct, the fringes are exchanged for small sacs within the animal, formed by the integument folded inwards upon itself, and open for the ingress and egress of water. These pouches are, at first, mere shallow cavities; but as the organization advances, their lining membranes, on which the blood-vessels are spread, are disposed into numerous folds, so as to increase the extent of surface with which the water and its contained air come in contact. The apparatus for respiration in Insects, is a modification of the latter kind of structure; ranged along the sides of their bodies, at regular intervals, there is a succession of holes, which are the openings of a series of infinitely small tubes, extending in all directions through their interior; these openings and tubes conduct the air into their bodies, where it has the effect of purifying the blood. A higher form of respiratory organ is presented in branchiæ or gills. These are possessed by such animals only as have the circulating system so

far developed, that the elements of a heart, and a distinct set of
vessels for conveying the blood to be oxygenated, appear for the
first time ; and they therefore indicate a greater concentration both
of the respiratory organ and of the circulating system. But even
gills pass through many gradations before they acquire that high
degree of development with which we are most familiar in
Fishes.

What we have chiefly to remark in all the modes of respiration
hitherto mentioned is; first, that until we arrive at the order
Fishes, the lowest of the Vertebrata, the Mouth has no connexion
with the organ of breathing ;—in all the Invertebrata, that aperture serves exclusively for taking in the food and manducation.
Secondly, that it is in fishes, that we have the earliest example
of an internal skeleton, in which is blocked out, as it were, the
first rude form of a chest, for containing lungs, and for drawing
in and expelling the air through a single tube, the trachea, or
windpipe, communicating with the Mouth.

It may be new to many of the readers of this work to be told
that the Air-Bladder, which serves in most fishes to accommodate their specific gravity to the various degrees of density of
the water in which they swim, is, in reality, an elementary Lung.
Yet that is proved to be the case by many facts in comparative
anatomy. It is sufficient to state, that a set of fishes exist called
Sauroid (from their resemblance to the inferior kinds of Reptiles),
in which the air-bladder communicates with the mouth by a tube
(termed ductus pneumaticus), which resembles, in all respects, a
windpipe ; and these fishes, when left on dry land, can respire
by this apparatus, independently of their gills. The same structure passes through various gradations in other animals intermediate between fishes and reptiles, till the gills at length
disappear, and the air-bladder becomes a more perfectly organized lung.

If we trace the progressive changes by which the sac, thus
introduced for the first time, into the interior of the body in
communication with the mouth, becomes at length surrounded
by an apparatus of ribs and muscles, capable, by alternate expansion and contraction, of drawing in and expelling air, we shall

find that the mechanism makes important advances towards a perfect form of that kind of respiration, in the order Reptiles. In the lowest of the order, viz. those reptiles immediately above fishes—Frogs and Tortoises—the development of ribs is so imperfect, that instead of the sac, or lung, being filled with air by an expansive motion of the thorax, it is gradually distended by successive actions of the Mouth, like swallowing: and Nostrils, through which the air is thus sucked, are now perceived. In the higher reptiles, as the Crocodiles, the membraneous sac becomes more compact, and like the proper substance of lung: it is permeated by numerous branches of the windpipe, which subdivide and terminate in air-cells: and the lungs are now for the first time surrounded by the Ribs, and Sternum, provided with muscles to expand and contract the cavity. Although, in consequence of the weak, flexible structure of the bones of the chest (corresponding with the tortuous movements of the reptile in creeping), the process of alternate expansion and contraction is carried on imperfectly, the quantity of air received and discharged, small as it is, is sufficient for animals which are cold-blooded, and have a torpid circulation like theirs.

But however near an approximation is thus made, in reptiles, by the introduction of Nostrils, a Windpipe, and Lungs encased in a Thorax, to the apparatus of respiration as it exists in Man, a great change remains to be effected, before the resemblance is complete. Not only in reptiles, but in Birds, which is the order of vertebrata next above reptiles, the lungs occupy a part of the body common to them and the viscera generally: the thorax and abdomen form a single large cavity. It is not till we ascend to the Mammalia, the order above birds, and next to Man,—those vertebrate animals which have Lips, and can suck the teat—that a subdivision of the trunk into two distinct chambers, is found. That separation is accomplished by means of the Diaphragm, a muscular partition, which stretches across from the lower border of the ribs on one side to that on the other. When that muscle is added, the lungs are closed in on all sides by moveable walls, capable of expansion and contraction ; so that by enlarging th cavity, or inspiring, air is received freely into the chest ; and it

can then be expelled, by respiration, with whatever degree of
force is desired. In short, when the diaphragm is introduced, the
organ of breathing attains its highest condition of concentration in
the animal kingdom : and it is not only adapted in an admirable
manner for oxygenating the blood, but for propelling the air along
the windpipe, with such regulated force as is necessary to produce
Vocal sounds.

When the chest has acquired the compact form just described,
several modifications in the structure of different parts of the
frame, which do not at first appear directly related to breathing,
take place. New sensibilities, intended to guard the apparatus,
and which have the power of animating numerous distinct muscles,
to co-operate rapidly in producing appropriate defensive actions,
are also introduced, in correspondence with the change of mechanism. It is necessary, in order to understand properly the
uses of the nerves distributed to the organ, to bear those arrangements in view ; and I may therefore direct attention to a few of
them.

The first example will be from the act of Swallowing. We are so
familiar with deglutition as an action performed in the same passage
by which we receive our breath, that it does not seem remarkable,
that food for nourishment, and air for respiration, should both be
safely admitted by one entrance : and yet in about nine-tenths of
the animal kingdom, namely, all the invertebrata, the mouth is
appropriated exclusively to taking in food, and has nothing to do
with respiration. But let us suppose a morsel in the mouth, and
trace its progress to the stomach. I only allude, in passing, to the
arrangements by which, when the mouth is full, and no air passes
into the lungs by that inlet, it is provided that the breathing shall
proceed uninterruptedly, by the Nostrils, which open into the throat
behind, directly over the proper orifice of the windpipe. When the
morsel has been chewed, and is ready for swallowing, it is propelled
into the back of the mouth : and here it comes in contact with
a part of the throat, which is endowed with a remarkable sensibility,—a sensibility of such a nature that, when excited, there
is an irresistible desire to swallow ; and the consequence is, that
whenever the sensible spot is touched by the morsel, a large class of

muscles, consisting not only of those immediately adjoining, but of others situated at a distance, are brought into combined action, to grasp and propel the food rapidly into the gullet. Here a great variety of movements takes place consentaneously. The windpipe is closed by its valve, the epiglottis, falling over it; the posterior nostrils are shut, by the folding upwards of the curtain, called the soft palate; certain strong muscles surrounding the upper part of the gullet compress the morsel, and urge it quickly past the opening of the windpipe into that canal; but, before the food can reach the stomach, it must pass through muscular fibres of the diaphragm, encircling the gullet; these fibres consequently relax, and there is a momentary interruption of the regular action of the diaphragm. Now all these actions, which show so remarkable a consent between the muscles of deglutition and of respiration, are excited and regulated by the peculiar sensibility seated at the back part of the throat. If, however, there should be any disturbance in the act of swallowing, and a small portion of the food should pass the wrong way, a different set of actions will occur, under the influence of another kind of sensibility; for example, if a crumb of bread should lodge in the throat, near the opening of the windpipe, a sensibility distinct from that which gives rise to swallowing, will be excited; and will rouse the muscles to produce a set of movements altogether different from the former: the same muscles which are at one time engaged in deglutition, will now be combined in such a way as to cause a succession of violent extirpations or fits of coughing, which will continue till the irritating particle is expelled from the top of the windpipe, and the danger of choking removed. So there are various other sensibilities seated in distinct parts of the passages, which differ in kind as well as degree, from those just mentioned; and, when these are excited, similar concatenated actions of the muscles are produced, modified according to the structure which requires to be cleared or defended.

I shall take the next example from the Circulating System. Comparative anatomy shows that, according as the apparatus of respiration becomes more perfectly organized, the heart and blood-vessels begin to be subdivided into two distinct systems; the one

for sending the blood to the lungs, and returning it when purified :
and the other for distributing the purified blood to the body, and
returning it for renewed oxygenation. That is the origin of the
distinction drawn by anatomists, between the *pulmonic* circle,
which includes the part of the heart and blood-vessels that belong
to the lungs ; and the *systemic* circle, or part of the heart and
blood-vessels which send the blood over the body, and return it to
the heart. This separation takes place in the animal kingdom,
slowly and gradually, and is only complete in the warm-blooded
animals. Thus, in man, the division of the circulating system
appropriated to the lungs consists of cavities of the heart and
of blood-vessels, quite distinct from those provided for propelling
the blood over the body. Yet these two divisions act in perfect
concert with each other ; a concert mechanically secured by the
peculiar structure of the heart ; for the two sets of muscular
cavities constituting the heart, are joined together, to form a single
organ, and they contract in unison. Thus, so close a sympathy
is established between the heart and the organ of respiration,
that any interruption to the breathing will not only affect the
action of the division of the heart which belongs to the lungs, but
it will disturb the action of that part, joined to it in structure,
by which the purified blood is conveyed through the body. Again,
agitation of the heart, by disturbing the regular flow of blood to
and from the lungs, will in like manner disturb the actions of
respiration.

Another point, still connected with the Circulating system,
deserves to be noticed, as throwing light on some of the questions
treated in the work. The blood which returns to the heart by the
veins, flows towards the chest in a slow and easily interrupted
stream ; the force which propelled it when issuing from the heart
by the arteries, being exhausted before it enters the veins. From
this weakness of the current, it follows that the blood collected in
the great veins close to the entrance of the chest—as the jugular
veins, for example—may be stopped by a slight cause ; when
congestion of the minute branches will be the consequence, and
serious injury may be occasioned to the more delicate organs
from which the blood returns. Now there are certain conditions

of the chest in breathing, during which the venous blood is thus interrupted. As we draw in the breath, the blood flows along the veins with perfect facility, because the superior opening of the chest is then enlarged, and the suction, which draws air into the windpipe, has also the effect of increasing the force of the current of returning blood. But when we expel the air, and thereby diminish the area of the chest, an obstruction takes place in the flow of blood in the veins, and if the act of expiration be strong, regurgitation may be produced. This interruption, and retrograde motion of the blood in the large veins of the neck, gorges the smaller vessels ; the effect of which may be seen in a person seized with a fit of coughing or of sneezing : for his face then becomes suffused with red, and the superficial veins turgid with blood. It is therefore obvious, that if the veins of the surface of the head become congested, in such violent conditions of breathing, the deeper veins, returning the blood from the Brain and the Eye, will also be over distended from the same cause. Consequently, the delicate textures of these important organs will be in danger of suffering serious injury from the loaded and turgid condition of the veins. But both organs are defended from such dangers by a beautiful arrangement of the muscles of the neck, which cover and protect the venous trunks. These muscles act in sympathy with the movements of respiration ; so as to compress the large veins when the chest is contracted, and there is a tendency to regurgitation of the blood ; and to take pressure off them, when the chest is expanded, and the channel to the heart is free. It is further to be noticed, that the flat web of muscular fibres which covers the eye—the orbicularis muscle, by which we wink, and shut the eyes—is a part of the same provision. It acts in compressing the eye-ball whenever the chest is violently contracted, as in coughing, &c.; by that means it closes the veins at the back of the orbit, and prevents engorgement of the fine branches which ramify on the delicate coats within the eye-ball.*

* The orbicularis muscle is wanting in animals which have not the same con-centrated apparatus for breathing as man. I have shewn elsewhere that in man and mammalia another provision exists besides that mentioned in the text, for guarding the eye against the irregularities of the venous circulation. The small

L L

Hence it may be perceived by what close ties of sympathy the Circulating System and the Respiratory Organ are held together, when both are in the concentrated condition presented in Man. The heart acts upon the organ of breathing: and it, in its turn, is acted upon by the lungs. It is in this manner that the troubled motions within the breast, which sensibly accompany intense Emotion or Passion, exhibit themselves outwardly. Sudden changes of colour in the countenance denote disturbances in the heart's action ; laboured, irregular movements of the chest, extending to the neck and face, mark interruptions to the action of the respiratory organ : and both give rise to the varieties of Expression. If in this agitated condition of the organ of breathing, Voice is exercised, it partakes the disturbance, and the words uttered carry an effect as if they came directly from the heart. Language then exerts its highest influence over the feelings of others.

It was from studying the human body with these views, that the author concluded :—that the nerves which arise from a part of the brain distinct from that which gives off the nerves generally, and which are distributed to the organ of respiration, are bestowed in correspondence with the changes of mechanism which take place in that organ, and the new relations which are established between it and other parts, during its course of development in the animal kingdom. He believed that the main design of those progressive changes was to afford to Man an instrument suited to the superior endowments conferred on him :—to supply him with an organ for the communication of thought, and for thus exercising and evolving the powers of his Mind—the great attribute by which he holds his exalted

veins which ramify in the interior of the organ between the delicate membranes that support the retina, join the larger trunks, before these pass out from the eye-ball, in a peculiar manner ; each branch makes a circular sweep, so as to describe nearly a complete circle, previous to entering its principal vein, and being arranged in concentric circles, they produce an appearance whence the name *vasa vorticosa* has been applied to them. Nothing can be more admirably adapted than this structure for breaking the force of a retrograde current of blood, and gradually diffusing it over the membranes. A similar vorticose arrangement, though not so distinct, is observed in the superficial veins of the brain, and is obviously designed for a similar object.

position in Creation. But as for intercourse with his fellow-men, Man does not depend upon articulate language alone; there is the language of Expression; a mode of communication understood equally by mankind all over the globe;—not conventional, or confined to nations,- but used by the infant before speech, by untutored savage visited by civilized European—he thought that the apparatus which was introduced for Voice and Language, was the same by which passion and emotion address themselves to us. Accordingly, he concluded, that the nerves of Respiration are at the same time the nerves of Expression.

Of these nerves, the "Nervus Vagus," from its extensive distribution, and the importance of the organs which it supplies, must be accounted the most considerable. As its name implies, it takes a long, wandering course. Arising from the same part of the brain as the other respiratory nerves, it first gives branches to the back of the throat and posterior orifices of the Nostrils; descending a little in the neck, it sends a nerve to the upper part of the larynx, the organ of Voice; having passed further down, and entered the chest, a branch is reflected upwards, which goes, like the last, to the Larynx, but supplies its lower part; branches are next transmitted along the principal blood-vessels, to the Heart; while others, following the course of the bronchial tubes, enter the Lungs : the nerve having now expended nearly all its fibrils, descends along the gullet, and terminates in branches to that tube and the orifice of the stomach, where they are encircled by muscular fibres of the Diaphragm. The use of the nerve appears to be, to unite the various structures which have been enumerated, in sympathy; so that although situated at remote distances, and for the most part intrinsically distinct in function, they may act in concert with the organ of respiration generally; and harmony may be established in the many complicated actions which they are associated together in performing. The "Spinal Accessory" nerve passes obliquely down the side of the neck, to supply muscles attached to the upper part of the chest and the shoulder-blades; and as these muscles co-operate with others in expanding the chest, and assist also in preventing irregularities in the venous circulation during the excited conditions of breathing, it is concluded that the function of the nerve is to associate the muscles to which it goes, with the organ of respiration. The name of the next nerve in order, the "Glosso-pharyngeal," indicates the parts to which it is distributed, the Tongue, and the Pharynx, or funnel-like expansion at the back part of the throat, which forms the common opening of both the windpipe and the gullet: as it is here that the numerous complicated and finely arranged actions by which the entrance into the air-tube is protected during deglutition are performed, the glosso-pharyngeal nerve seems provided to regulate those actions, and connect them with the operations of the organ of breathing generally. The last nerve to be specially mentioned, is the "Portio-dura :" coming out from the place of common origin of the respiratory nerves, before the ear, it sends branches first upon the side of the neck, to supply muscles which overlay and compress the veins in that part ; it next gives nerves to the lips ; afterwards to the nostrils ; then to the orbicular muscle of the eye-lids ; lastly, to the muscles of the brows ; and, in order to reach the parts of the face, to which it is destined, the nerve has to travel across the large masseter muscle, and the equally large temporal muscle, to neither of which (being muscles of mastication, and supplied by the Fifth nerve) does it give even the smallest branch : the chief use of the portio-dura is to associate the muscles of the Lips and of the Nostrils, the two external orifices of the air-tube, with the rest of the organ of respiration ; but it fulfils other duties at the same time ; its branches which descend upon the neck, and those which go to the orbicular muscles of the eye-lids, control movements connected with disturbances in the venous circulation, produced in certain excited states of the respiration ; while the whole nerve, in virtue of its commanding the motions of all the features of the countenance, is the great source of Expression in the Face.

Having shewn the gradual process by which the organ of breathing is newly modelled, to adapt it to voice and expression, it is not out of place to point out how those other organs of the body, which have been described as superintended by the "Original" class of nerves,—viz., the spinal nerves and fifth cerebral nerve—accommodate themselves to the new mechanism. It will be seen that, in the early stages of development of animals, owing to the defective organization of the Locomotive and Prehensile instruments, the Mouth is embarrassed by having to perform offices, connected with obtaining food, which preclude its being used as an orifice for breathing; it has consequently no connexion with the organ of respiration. But by degrees those subsidiary organs improve, free the Mouth from performing more duties than those of manducation, and it is converted, at last, into an opening which serves not only for receiving food, but for respiration, voice, and speech. As it is the adaptation of the size of the jaws, and of the cavity of the Mouth to Speech, which, according to the principles of the author,* impart the characters of nobleness and beauty to the permanent form of the human head, which distinguish it from the brute, I may briefly trace the steps in the development by which that is effected.

It was intimated before, that animals placed at the bottom of the scale of living beings, have an organization in many points resembling vegetables; nevertheless, those creatures possess an organ corresponding to the Mouth. But at that pristine stage of animal life, there are no distinct prehensile or locomotive organs to minister to the mouth; the "oral aperture" is little more than one of the spongioles in the root of a vegetable, by which nutritious fluids are attracted from the soil. Take the example of the Sponges : fixed to a rock in the sea, the sponge cannot transport itself from place to place in search of food : it has no feelers or arms to procure nourishment; it is, in short, like a plant † in every respect but this, that instead of imbibing its food from the spot from which it grows, its numerous pores or mouths placed on the free surface of its body, receive the nutritious substances floating or dissolved in the water around it; the currents and undulations of the sea sweeping its pendulous body from side to side, and to and fro, compensate in some degree for the deficiency of locomotive and prehensile organs. Advancing

---

* Page 32.
† Whence the name, "Zoophytes."

higher in the scale, animals are met with still fixed to a rock, and wanting in locomotive organs; but the mouth is now provided with instruments corresponding to prehensile organs. Thus certain species of Polypes, attached to corals, exist, which have their open mouths surrounded by rows of tentacles or ciliary processes,* the principal use of which is to cause circles or eddies in the water near them, so that the nourishing matter in their neighbourhood may be attracted to their mouths, caught, and swallowed. In ascending a little higher, we find animals in general structure like those just described, having a mouth provided with tentacles capable of directing nourishing matter into it; but instead of these animals being fixed by moorings to a rock, they are let loose to float in the ocean; and we perceive, for the first time, indications of locomotive organs, combined with mouth and prehensile organs. The creatures to which I refer, are such as the "Sea-nettle." That animal consists of a mass of buoyant soft substance; by alternate contractions and expansions of its body, it has a slight power of directing its movements; but it trusts chiefly for its changes of feeding-ground to the effects of the tides and currents of the sea: like a boat without oars or rudder, it is drifted from sand-bank to sand-bank, and floating along passively, a prey to stronger creatures, and defended only by its stings, it picks up the food which casually falls within its reach; in short, its organs of progression are in the lowest stage of development. And here it may be remarked, that it is in the ocean, lakes, or rivers, where we must look for creatures such as those described, which have their organs of prehension and of locomotion, and mouths, least advanced in organization: not only does the density of the water assist in buoying up their bodies and make them independent of solidly constructed members to rest or move upon; but the fluid divides or dissolves the nutritious matters, so as to be more easily received into their mouths of simple structure. Accordingly, when we ascend higher in the animal series, and arrive at those animals which possess the earliest distinct representations of legs, such as belong to the

---

* Like petals of flowers, whence the name, "sea-flowers."

highest, we perceive that the numbers of creatures capable of living on dry land begin to increase. I allude to animals which have an internal skeleton, that is, a skeleton composed of bones, found for the first time in the class Vertebrata. But amongst these the parts corresponding to legs and arms are, at the commencement, so imperfectly formed, that the animals to which they belong partly inhabit the water, and partly the land; and when they do visit the dry land, they crawl upon their bellies, that is, they assist their weak and slender extremities by the tortuous motions along the earth of their trunks and tails; as we see in the crocodile or lizard. Gradually, as the development proceeds, and the bones acquire increased solidity of structure, the body is well lifted up from the ground, the legs are longer levers, more powerful and more active, as we see in the condition of Quadrupeds.

Next, let us observe the progressive advancement from the state of quadrupeds to that of Man. As the four-footed animals ascend in the scale, a contrast becomes evident between the power and dimensions of their *fore* and their *hind* legs. Originally, both these sets of members participated equally in sustaining the weight of the trunk and head, and moving the body; but, by degrees, the hind legs increase in size and strength disproportionately to the fore-legs; and the latter become possessed of freer and more diversified motion. In short, in the strong hind-quarters of the horse, deer, &c., we see a preparation for the parts corresponding to the lower extremities of Man, becoming the exclusive organs of progression; and in the light, agile forms of the fore-legs, a preparation for those corresponding to the upper extremities, taking on the part of arms, to act exclusively as instruments of prehension. But it is only in Man that this distinct appropriation of each member to its own peculiar function is found complete. The monkey, Man's nearest relation in the family of animals, can rest upon the hind legs; but it is feebly and imperfectly; he can skilfully grasp a cocoa-nut with parts resembling human hands; but his so-called hands are still instruments of progression; they enable him to warp himself with agility along the branches of trees, his proper habitation. Man is distinguished above all other animals

by his lower extremities having solidity and power sufficient to
sustain his body without the aid of other members, and so as
to be his sole organs of progression : hence his erect position.
Again, as man's upper extremities are emancipated from the duty
of assisting in locomotion, they are free to execute whatever rapid
and varied movements may be called for, either for self-defence or
for procuring nourishment. And, in correspondence with that
freedom of action, a *Hand* is added, which, for the perfection of
its endowments and mechanism, has been, in all ages, a constant
theme of admiration.

Now let us ask, what influence have the improvements thus
shown in the construction of the organs of locomotion and
of prehension, upon the structure of the Mouth ? The chief
use of the prehensile organs being to seize food for the supply of
the mouth, it may be expected that, as they become more highly
organized, the mouth will undergo a change in its form. Let us
inquire, then, what effect has the improved organization of the
prehensile organ, as seen in the hand of man, in allowing the mouth
to be adapted for a vocal organ—an organ of Articulate Language ?

It has been stated that in all the vertebrate animals below
man, the member analogous to the arm and hand, is an instrument of progression as well as of prehension. Whether we take
the fin of the fish, the anterior extremity of the reptile, the wing
of the bird, the paddle of the dolphin, or the fore leg of the horse
or dog, the principal, if not the only use of the member is to assist
in locomotion ; only a few quadrupeds, like the squirrel, the feline
animals, &c., besides using their paws for running, climbing, burrow-
ing, &c., employ them to carry food to the mouth. Now the consequence of using the organ intended to convey the food to the
mouth as one for progression, will be, that the office of appropri-
ating the food will be thrown upon the mouth itself. Accordingly,
in all animals below Man, the mouth is a prehensile, as well as a
manducatory organ. If the animal be graminivorous, it must crop
the herbage with its teeth before chewing and triturating it ; if it
be carnivorous, it must be provided with large, sharp fangs or
tusks, to fight, seize, and tear its prey, before it can reduce its
food to a fit state for swallowing. In short, the mouth, with its

delicate sense of touch, its hairs or whiskers projecting from it as feelers, and its jaws armed with large teeth, is to be looked upon, in conjunction with the long, flexible neck commonly belonging to brutes, as combining the functions of the human arm and hand, with that of an organ of mastication.

But it is obvious that a mouth of the large capacity and irregular shape of an animal like the horse, ox, dog, or lion, could never be adapted to produce articulate sounds. In a cavity such as the mouth of the horse, we can understand how neighing may be produced ; but we cannot suppose that, by any adjustment of the tongue or lips, the air, even if it were properly vocalised in the larynx, could be confined, and then be let suddenly free to give rise to explosive sounds ; or be impinged against the palate, to cause guttural sounds ; or be directed into the back of the nostrils, to produce nasal sounds. In short, none of those numerous, finely-varied changes in the shape of the interior of the mouth, produced by the combined action of the tongue, palate, cheeks, and lips, which give rise to the infinite modifications of sound in speech, could take place in such gross structures. For the vibrating air expelled from the larynx to be divided and modulated so as to produce words with proper tone and accent, it is necessary that the cavity of the mouth should be small, its boundaries regular and uninterrupted, and the communication between it and the nostrils free.

Now that is the very character of the mouth in Man. Provided with an arm and hand, free to execute all the objects of his will, man is under no necessity to use his mouth as the brute does. Being limited to manducation, the jaw-bones may be of small size and light construction, while the teeth may likewise be small, be set erect, and ranged in uniform, regular rows, so important for distinct articulation. On the whole, from the mouth being ab-solved, by the perfection of the *hand*, from performing more offices than those of mastication simply, the cavity admits of being diminished in size, the jaws and teeth of being reduced to moderate dimensions, and the whole form is suited in the most admirable manner for an organ of articulate language.

On looking to the skulls of different races of mankind, it

will be seen that nature, in fashioning the mouth of man to be a speaking organ, has not departed from her usual course of carrying on the process of development by slow and gradual steps. Observe what a contrast exists between the skull of the Negro and that of the European, caused by the inordinately large size of the jaws and projection of the teeth in the former. The well-formed skull of the European is distinguished by having the jaws and teeth of comparatively diminutive size; while the cavities formed in the interstices between the bones of the face, at the brows and cheeks, and which communicate with the nostrils, to allow a free circulation of air around the chambers where sound is produced, being parts of the organ of Voice, are full and prominent.

Thus we perceive how the genius of the sculptors and painters of antiquity led them to discover a principle of beauty, in designing the human head, founded on a profound view of the relation existing between Man's physical structure and his mental constitution—the principle expounded in the first essay of this work. Regarding his supremacy over all created beings to be in virtue of his possessing a Mind, they looked for the signs of his superior organization, to those structures which minister most directly to the mind. The cranium was represented capacious and full, it being the part where the Brain, the seat of intellect, is lodged. But they studied, at the same time, the organ by which the operations of the intellect are embodied in Speech, and intercourse is established between the minds of man and man. The lower part of the face, including the jaws and teeth, which in brutes have such a preponderating size to enable them to seize and rend their prey, was made small and delicate; while the upper, composed of passages and chambers permeated by the air, and accessory to the organ of Speech, were expanded and elevated into due dimensions, so as to give them characteristic prominence.

Thus, in whatever view we study the development of the animal frame, new proofs present themselves of the final aim of all the modifications which we successively trace, being to confer upon man an instrument adapted to his intellectual nature—an organ of Speech. It is the fine adjustment of the various members of his body for that object, that renders his organization the most perfect in the animal kingdom. Additional strength is, therefore, given to the author's opinions, that our conceptions of human beauty, both as regards the form of the head, and the moveable features, have a direct relation to the fitness of the structures for Speech, Voice, and Expression.

Such is a brief account of the leading parts of the discoveries made by the author of the volume, in that important part of the anatomy of the body—the Nervous System. He first established that the nerves of Motion are distinct from those of Sensation ;— and that the nerves generally, possess different endowments, according to the divisions of the brain or spinal marrow from which they arise. He then arranged the nerves of the whole body into three distinct systems, corresponding with the organs which they respectively control. The First class is that composed of the Spinal Nerves and Fifth Nerve of the brain ; this class, he proved, bestows both motion and sensation on all the parts to which it is distributed ; and these parts, he further shewed, are organs which belong to man in common with the lowest creatures, their united function being to supply food, the first necessary want of all animals : he termed this set of nerves the "Original" class, and included in it the nerves of the various organs of the senses. The Second class comprises a series of nerves distinct from the former, both in their origin and mode of distribution ; they pass off from a circumscribed central portion of the nervous system, the medulla oblongata, and diverge to different parts of the head, neck, throat, and chest, already supplied by the original class : he shewed that these structures form together a mechanism for respiration, not found in the lowest animals, but gradually introduced by a slow process of development into the animal kingdom, in order that, besides oxygenating the blood, it may be, in Man, the organ of Voice and Expression : to this set of nerves he applied the name, " Respiratory " class. In these two classes are combined all the nerves together which arise either from the Brain or Spinal Marrow. The Third class consists of a series of nerves which have their centre in large ganglions, scattered principally among the viscera of the abdomen ; this forms the system called ganglionic or "Sympathetic :" and their use has been generally supposed to be, to unite in sympathy those organs by which the various organic functions are performed : such as secretion, absorption, assimilation of the food, the growth and decay of the body, &c. When the nerves belonging to these different classes are viewed, as by the anatomist, in their combined condition, crossing, joining, and interlacing, in the different parts of the body, nothing can exceed their apparent confusion ; but when examined by the aid of the principle, and the arrangement, introduced by Sir Charles Bell, order and design are found to pervade every part.

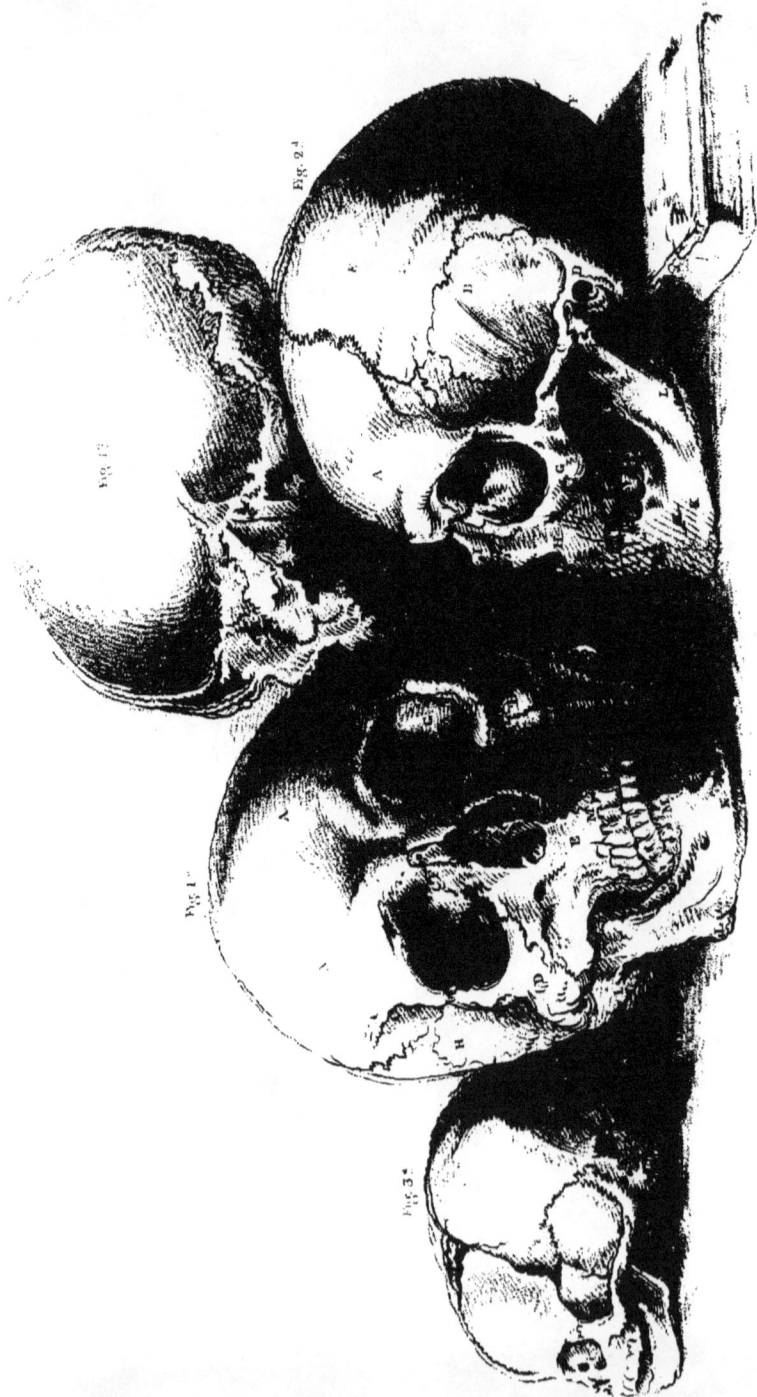

Fig. 1ᵃ

Fig. 2ᵃ

Fig. 3ᵃ

EXPLANATION OF THE PLATES.

PLATE I.

Fig. 1. The Skull of a Man fully grown, presented in a front view.

A. The Frontal Bone (os frontis).

B. The Protuberances formed by the Frontal Sinuses.

C. The Temporal Ridge of the frontal bone; on which the form of the temple depends.

D. The Cheek-Bone (os malæ).

E E. The Upper Maxillary Bones.

F. The Nasal Bones.

G G. The Orbits or Sockets for the Eye-balls. The circle of their margin is seen to be formed by the frontal bones, the cheek-bones, and the superior maxillary bones.

H H. The Temporal Bones. These hollows are filled with a strong muscle, which arising upon the side of the skull, passes down, through the arch, to be inserted into the lower jaw-bone.

I I. The Mastoid or Mamillary Processes of the Temporal Bone. These are the points into which the strong mastoid muscles, which give form to the neck, are inserted.

K. The Lower Jaw.

L. The Angle of the Lower Jaw.

M. The Processes of the jaws which form the sockets for receiving the roots of the teeth.

Fig. 2 is the Skull of an Adult seen in profile, in which we have to remark these parts:—

A. The Frontal Bone.

B. The Temporal Bone.

c. The Zygomatic Process of the temporal bone, which, with the process of the cheek-bone, forms an arch, under which the tendon of the temporal muscle passes, to be inserted into the lower jaw.

D. The opening of the tube of the Ear; a little below this is the mastoid process of the temporal bone.

E. The Parietal Bone; so called because it forms the greater part, as it were, of the wall of the skull.

F. The Occipital Bone.

These bones are united by sutures, in which the processes of one bone seem to indent themselves, as they grow, into those of the opposite bone, without there being an absolute union between them. That which unites the frontal and parietal bones is called the coronal suture; that which unites the parietal and temporal bones is called the squamous or temporal suture; the line between the occipital and parietal bones is the lambdoidal suture: and the line between the parietal bones is called the saggital suture, because it is laid between the lambdoid and coronal sutures, like the arrow between the bow and the string.

There are many lesser sutures which unite the smaller bones of the face; but they need not be mentioned here.

G. The Cheek Bone (os malæ).

H. The Upper Jaw-bone (maxilla superior).

I. The Bones of the Nose (ossa nasi).

K. The Lower Jaw (maxilla inferior).

L. The Angle of the Jaw.

M. The Process of the Jaw which moves in the socket in the temporal bone.

N. The Coronoid Process of the Jaw, into which the temporal muscle is fixed, to move the jaw in conjunction with other muscles.

Fig. 3 represents the Skull of an Infant, in which the sutures are not yet formed, the bones of the cranium being loose, and attached by their membranes only; while the spaces may be observed, left unprotected, from the imperfect ossification of the bones. The individual parts require no references; they will be understood from their correspondence with fig. 2.

Fig. 4 is the Section of a Cranium, in which the only thing meant to be particularly remarked, is the cavity which is seen in the frontal bone, viz. the frontal sinuses.

PLATE II.

OF THE MUSCLES OF THE FACE.

This Plate represents the Muscles of the Face as they appear in a front view.

There are muscles attached to the eyebrow which produce its various motions.

A A. The Frontal Muscle. A thin muscle, expanded over the forehead, and inserted into the skin under the eyebrow. We do not see here the whole of the muscle, but only a part of what is properly called Occipito-frontalis.

It arises in a web of fibres, from the back of the skull (from a ridge of the temporal and occipital bones): becoming tendinous, it covers all the upper part of the skull with a membrane or sheet of tendon, and terminates in the anterior muscle, which is seen in this view.

B B. The Corrugator Supercilii arises from the lower part of the frontal bone near the nose, and is inserted into the integument under the eyebrow. It lies nearly transversely, and its office is to knit and draw the eyebrows together.

C C. The Circular Muscle of the Eyelids (the orbicularis palpebrarum). There is a little tendon at the inner angle of the eye, which is a fixed point for this muscle, attaching it to the maxillary bone, and being both origin and insertion.

The descending slip of the Occipito-frontalis, or pyramidalis nasi, is a fasciculus of fibres which descends from the frontal muscle to be attached to the side of the nose: it has a distinct operation, and may be considered as a separate muscle. It draws the inner extremity of the eyebrow downwards.

These four muscles move the eyebrow, and give it all its various inflexions. If the orbicularis palpebrarum and the descending slip of the frontalis act together, there is a heavy and lowering expression. If they yield to the influence of the frontal muscle, the eyebrow is arched, and there is a cheerful or an alert and inquiring expression. If the corrugator supercilii acts, there is more or less expression of mental anguish, or of painful exercise of thought.

Muscles moving the nostrils :—

D. Levator Labii Superioris Alæque Nasi. It arises from the upper jaw, and is inserted into the upper lip and nostril, which it raises.

E. Compressor Nasi. A set of fibres which compress the nostril.

L. The Depressor Alæ Nasi lies under the orbicularis oris. It arises near the incisor teeth, and is inserted into the moveable cartilage, which forms the wing of the nostril.

These three muscles serve to expand and contract the nostril. They move in concert with the muscles of respiration.

Muscles of the Lips :—

F. Levator Labii Proprius. It arises from the upper jaw-bone, near the orbit, and is inserted into the upper lip, which it raises.

G. Levator Anguli Oris. This muscle, lying under the last, is, of course, shorter : it raises the angle of the mouth.

H. Zygomatic Muscle. So called, because its origin is from the zygomatic process of the cheek-bone. It is inserted into the angle of the mouth.

K. Orbicular Muscle of the Lips.

M. Nasalis Labii Superioris. Draws down the septum of the nose.

N. Triangularis Oris, or Depressor Labiorum. A strong muscle arising from the base of the lower jaw, and inserted into the angle of the mouth.

O. Quadratus Menti, or Depressor of the Lower Lip.

P. Levatores Menti. Small, but strong, muscles. They arise from the lower jaw near the alveolar processes of the incisor teeth, descend, and are inserted into the integument of the chin. By their action they throw up the chin and project the lower lip.

Q. The Buccinator forms the fleshy part of the cheeks. It acts principally in turning the morsel in the mouth. Its fibres are inserted into the angles of the mouth.

R. Fibres of the Platysma Myoides, which ascend from the neck upon the side of the cheek.

PLATE III.

⌐ MUSCLES OF A DOG'S FACE. •

AA. Circular Fibres, which surround the eye-lids.'

B F D. Accessory Muscles, which I' name Scintillantes. They draw back the eye-lids from the eye-ball.

G H. Muscles of the Ear. '

I K. A Mass of Muscular Fibres, always the strongest in this class of animals, and which, with those concealed under them, I call Ringentes. They raise the upper lip and expose the teeth.

L. Muscles which move the nostril in smelling.

M. Circular Fibres of the Mouth, which yet do not make a perfect orbicular muscle.

N. A Muscle which answers to the Zygomaticus in man, and which has great power in this animal : it reaches from the ear to the angle of the mouth. It opens the mouth, retracts the lips, and disengages them from the teeth, as in seizing their prey.

O. The Cutaneous Muscle. It sends up a web of fibres from the neck on the side of the face : they are stronger here than in man.

PLATE IV.

NERVES OF THE FACE AND NECK.

I. Frontal or supra-orbitary branch of the fifth nerve of the brain; the terminating branch of the first or ophthalmic division: arising simply from the larger or ganglionic root of the fifth nerve, it bestows sensation alone.

II. Superior maxillary, or infra-orbitary branch of the fifth nerve, the terminating branch of the second division : arising simply, like the last, from the sensitive root, it bestows sensation alone.

III. Mental, or inferior maxillary branch of the fifth nerve : it arises from the third division : by referring to the wood engraving (p. 239)-it will be seen that this branch comes simply from the sensitive root ; and it gives sensation alone.

IV. Temporal branches of the fifth nerve : they arise in common with the preceding branch, and bestow sensation alone.

V. This nerve is the only branch of the fifth, arising from the smaller or motor root, which appears superficially : it is called buccalis-labialis, from supplying the buccinator muscle, and muscles at the angle of the mouth ; and it associates these parts with the muscles of the jaws in mastication.

The branches of the motor root of the fifth, which go to the more powerful muscles of the jaws, are situated deeply, and are not represented in the plate. Their distribution may be understood by looking to the wood engraving (p. 239).

VI, VII, VIII, IX. These are spinal nerves ; the first of the series which come out, between the vertebræ, in the whole length of the spine, to supply the body generally with motion and sensation.

    A. Portio Dura, or Facial Nerve : the motor nerve of the features. Arising from the medulla oblongata, close to the origins of the Nervus Vagus, the Glosso-Pharyngeal, and Spinal Accessory nerves, included in the respiratory class, it appears superficially before the ear. In front of the ear, and while lying upon the two principal muscles of mastication, viz., the masseter and temporal muscles, it forms a web or plexus ; but it gives no branch to any of the muscles of the jaws. Its branches pass off as follows :—

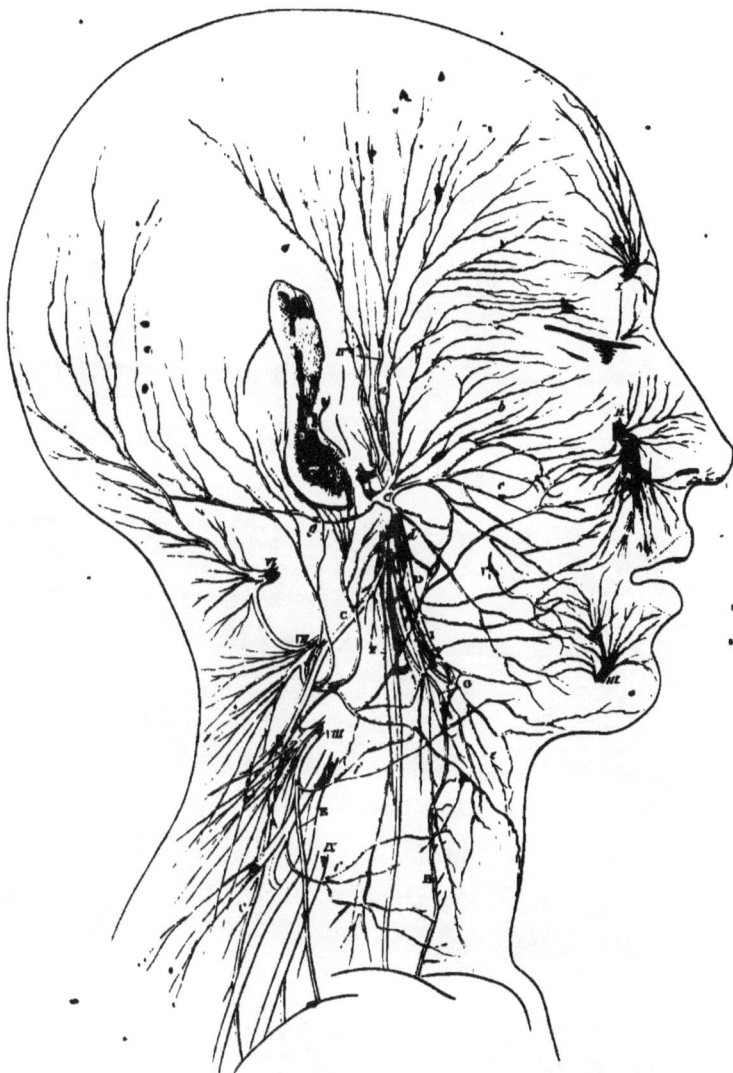

a. Frontal branches to the muscles of the forehead and eye-brow.

b. Branches to the eye-lids.

c. Branches to the muscles which move the nostrils and upper lip.

d. Branches to the lower lip.

e. Branches going down upon the side of the neck.

f. Connections with the Cervical Spinal Nerves.

g. A Nerve to the Occipital portion of the Occipito-frontalis muscle, and to muscles of the ear.

B. The Nervus Vagus, or grand respiratory nerve.

C. The Spinal Accessory Nerve.

D. The Ninth Nerve ; motor nerve of the tongue.

E. Diaphragmatic Nerve.

F. Branch of the Sympathetic Nerve.

G. Superior Laryngeal Nerve, a branch of the Nervus Vagus.

H. Inferior or Recurrent Laryngeal Nerve, a branch of the Nervus Vagus.

I. Glosso-Pharyngeal Nerve.

THE END.

R. CLAY, SON, AND TAYLOR, PRINTERS, BREAD STREET HILL.

www.ingramcontent.com/pod-product-compliance
Lightning Source LLC
Chambersburg PA
CBHW020509270326
41926CB00008B/800